Exploring Colorado with Kids

HELP US KEEP THIS GUIDE UP TO DATE

Every effort has been made by the author and editors to make this guide as accurate and useful as possible. However, many things can change after a guide is published—trails are rerouted, regulations change, facilities come under new management, and so forth.

We would love to hear from you concerning your experiences with this guide and how you feel it could be improved and kept up to date. While we may not be able to respond to all comments and suggestions, we'll take them to heart, and we'll also make certain to share them with the authors. Please send your comments and suggestions to the following address:

Falcon Guides
Reader Response/Editorial Department
Falconeditorial@rowman.com

Thanks for your input, and happy trails!

Exploring Colorado with Kids

71 Field Trips + 142 Nature-Inspired Activities

Jamie Siebrase and Debbie Mock

ESSEX, CONNECTICUT

For all moms everywhere, especially Sally and Joyce
—Jamie and Debbie

FALCONGUIDES®

An imprint of Globe Pequot, the trade division of
The Rowman & Littlefield Publishing Group, Inc.
4501 Forbes Blvd., Ste. 200
Lanham, MD 20706
www.rowman.com

Falcon and FalconGuides are registered trademarks and Make Adventure Your Story is a trademark of The Rowman & Littlefield Publishing Group, Inc.

Distributed by NATIONAL BOOK NETWORK

British Library Cataloguing in Publication Information available

Library of Congress Cataloging-in-Publication Data available
ISBN 978-1-4930-7995-7 (paperback)
ISBN 978-1-4930-7996-4 (e-book)

∞™ The paper used in this publication meets the minimum requirements of American National Standard for Information Sciences—Permanence of Paper for Printed Library Materials, ANSI/NISO Z39.48-1992.

Contents

The Activities

Acknowledgments

A heartfelt thank-you, first and foremost, to you, our reader, for picking up this book and trusting us to guide you through some of our favorite Front Range destinations for families. We had the best time writing this one-of-a-kind guide, and we hope you have fun exploring and learning with your children.

We'd like to thank our FalconGuides editor, Mason Gadd, who has been so fun to work with on this project. You've helped us take this book from concept to bookshelf, and for that we are truly grateful. Thanks to the Dorst family, too, for being our cover models. This book wouldn't look nearly as good without you.

We're thankful for the sources who helped us fact-check the information in the pages ahead. From park rangers and nature center employees to local artists, passionate gardeners, museum curators, and history buffs, many people have provided their time and invaluable information. Can we also express our profound gratitude to the many folks who work to protect and nurture Colorado's precious natural spaces, and those educating the next generation of outdoors enthusiasts? Your legacy of crystal waters, thriving creatures, and grassy spots to sit and watch the clouds will be felt for generations.

I, Jamie, couldn't get anything done without ongoing support from my husband. Thank you, Ben, for putting up with me and supporting my writing career. Thanks to my kids, who are always pushing me to get out of the house and try new things. Jon, Brian, and Louise, you keep me on my toes, and your senses of adventure are contagious. A final note of gratitude goes to my parents, Sally and Brian, who always provide love, support, and free childcare.

I, Debbie, am grateful to my parents, David Mock and Joyce Hansen, who have always encouraged my sense of adventure and insatiable curiosity. Thank you for providing the roots and wings this introverted kid needed to become a passionate journalist. I'm eternally grateful to my husband, Michael, for all the love, support, and frequent midnight reminders to get some sleep. To Kathy, Marla, and Kandi, everyone needs adventure buddies like you. Thanks to Diane and Nikki, the best cheerleaders around. Thanks to my two furry kids, Suki and Cali, who were at my side, literally, throughout the writing of this book.

Content from several of the chapters in this book first appeared in *Colorado Parent* magazine, the go-to parenting guide for local families. Thanks to all of the past editors and publishers who helped hash out the initial ideas that eventually morphed into this book.

Meet Your Guides

Jamie Siebrase is a journalist, children's book author, and trained community naturalist. She is also a Leave No Trace certified trainer. Her other nonfiction titles are *Hiking with Kids Colorado: 52 Great Hikes for Families* and *Mythbusting the Great Outdoors: What's True and What's Not?* Jamie's picture book, *Tonight! A Bedtime Book*, celebrates two important things: (1) a mom's tireless love, and (2) nature. When she isn't writing about the outdoors and parenting, Jamie's usually on an adventure with her family of five. Her home base is in Littleton, Colorado.

Debbie Mock is an editor, journalist, and travel enthusiast who goes through untold pairs of athletic shoes each year. She is the former editor in chief of *Colorado Parent* magazine, *Memory Makers* magazine, and *Rocky Mountain Dog* magazine. This is her debut guidebook. When she's not writing, Debbie is in her garden, walking with her husband and dog, or honing her packing skills for a dream walk across England's Lake District. She lives in Centennial, Colorado.

Introduction

In our opinions, few things beat sneaky, hands-on education. You've probably heard the term *experiential learning*, which is the idea that real-world, tactile experiences are way more meaningful to students than textbooks and lectures. When we educators venture outside the classroom and let children and adolescents wander around the historical buildings at the Centennial Village Museum or touch a cloud inside the National Center for Atmospheric Research, that's when a spark is ignited and the best kind of learning happens.

"Wait a minute!" you might be mumbling to yourself right now. "*We* educators? But I don't have a background in teaching."

You don't have to have any special training to be your child's best teacher. As a parent, grandparent, caregiver, or guardian, you're not only an educator, you're arguably your child's most important instructor. Classroom teachers will come and go, but you're in it for the long haul. You know your child as nobody else can or will, and so really, you're in a unique position to give your kiddo a personalized education, one nobody else can come close to replicating.

After homeschooling my own children for a few years, I, Jamie, realized that one of the real joys of running the classroom was the freedom to explore Colorado with my kids. I had a chance to bring textbooks to life by taking my kids into the world to see, feel, and experience what we were studying. I'm not homeschooling anymore, and yet the realization that I'm my children's teacher has stuck with me. I'm constantly searching for ways to engage my adolescent boys and sweet preschooler outside of their classrooms.

We really hope this book can lend a hand to hardworking homeschool parents who'd like some fodder for unforgettable educational outings with their students. If you homeschool your children, we applaud the effort you put in on a daily basis, and we're here to make your job just a little bit easier.

But you hardly have to be a full-time homeschooler to enhance your child's primary education in a big way. Whether you're a busy mom or dad in need of some activities to fill that long stretch from Memorial Day to Labor Day, or a grandparent looking for interesting ways to connect with grandkids, or an aunt or uncle vying for the title of coolest in-law . . . this book is for you!

In writing, the old adage is, "Show, don't tell." We think the rule works equally well for education. With this book in hand, it'll be easy to take advantage of the multitude of hands-on learning opportunities you'll encounter while exploring Colorado with children. In a nutshell, that's what *Exploring Colorado with Kids* is all about.

There are so many ways you could use this guide. Start at chapter 1, if you'd like, and work your way down our alphabetical list of Front Range destinations, seeing how far you can get in a single summer or calendar year. If your child has a specific interest, let them geek out. Highlight all of the chapters pertaining to their favorite topic, and hit those destinations first.

Another option is to use the chapters that follow to boost classroom lessons. There's nothing like an impromptu field trip to enhance what your child read in a textbook. Ask your kids and their teachers what they're studying in school, then flip through this guidebook to determine which sites best align with the current curriculum. You'll discover plenty of destinations that can supplement units on everything from biology and botany to city planning, ecology, engineering, and state history, for starters. Get ready to discover nature centers you didn't know existed, urban farms, outdoor history museums, history hikes, art walks, hidden wildlife-viewing spots, and so much more.

Don't forget to read through the Learn sidebar at the end of every chapter. This is where you'll really get a sense of what sorts of educational extensions a specific site has to offer. We've tried to include ideas for incorporating all of the core subjects—math, language arts, science, and social studies—and we've also added in plenty of notes on STEAM offerings, too.

Whatever you do, please don't let our notes and ideas be a ceiling. If anything, we like to think of this book as a jumping-off point that will inspire parents to add their own creative flair to family activities for years to come.

We're about to have a lot of fun together, but before we dive into specific destinations, there are a few items we need to cover.

Outdoors enthusiasts are responsible for protecting the environment, for the sake of the wildlife inhabiting it and for future human generations who wish to experience it. The following section will help you and your kids better understand how to preserve delicate ecosystems while still making the most of every adventure. Anyone can spend time recreating in the great outdoors, but doing it well is an art. This might be the most important lesson you impart on your children.

Trail Etiquette

Some destinations in this guide are trails and/or natural, outdoor areas. When recreating outdoors, it's important to practice good trail etiquette by using Leave No Trace principles.

Zero impact. Always leave an area exactly as you found it, if not better than you found it. Pack out all trash and extra food. No exceptions, no excuses. This is the golden rule of hiking.

If your child needs to pee during a hike, walk at least 200 feet away from the trail and any water sources. If your daughter is shy about squatting, you can hold up a jacket for privacy. On a slope, always pee facing downhill so the urine flows away from you.

Stuff happens, especially when you're recreating with kids. Never leave human waste or toilet paper on the ground. It might not seem like a big deal "just this one time," but imagine what Colorado's beautiful trails would look like if everyone thought that way. The easiest option for feces is to bring along a dog bag, and pack out your child's excrement. If this is too gross, carry a small shovel. Generally, human waste should be buried at least 100 feet from water sources under 6 to 8 inches of topsoil. Families who don't camp should go online to learn about the proper technique for burying feces.

Stay on the trail. There's nothing an inquisitive child loves more than wandering off a trail. Teach your child that paths serve an important purpose by limiting impact on natural areas. Straying from a designated trail might seem innocent, but it can cause damage to sensitive areas that may take years to recover, if they recover at all. Even simple shortcuts can be destructive.

Leave no weeds. Noxious weeds tend to overtake other plants, which in turn impacts animals and birds that depend on them for food. To minimize the spread of noxious weeds, hikers should regularly clean their shoes and hiking poles of mud and seeds. Brush your dog to remove any weed seeds before heading into a new area.

Keep your dog under control. Speaking of dogs, if a four-legged family member is tagging along, always obey leash laws, and be sure to pack your dog's waste out in sealable plastic bags. Check beforehand to make sure the area you're visiting allows pets. They're not permitted in all parks and preserves—we've learned this lesson the hard way.

Respect other trail users. With the rise in popularity of multiuse trails, you'll often encounter mountain bikers and equestrians using the same trail. A little common sense and courtesy goes a long way. If you hear activity ahead, step off the trail, just to be safe. You won't always hear a mountain biker coming, so be prepared and know ahead of time whether you share the trail with them. Cyclists should always yield to hikers, but smart hikers are aware of their surroundings. When approaching horses or pack animals on the trail, step quietly off the trail, preferably on the downhill side, and let them pass. If you're wearing a large backpack, it's a good idea to sit down. To some animals, a hiker wearing a large backpack might appear threatening.

Preparedness

Even on a short outdoor excursion, parents should be prepared by having the following bases covered.

Water. Invest in stainless-steel bottles; brands such as EcoVessel and Klean Kanteen make excellent insulated products. Colorado's dry climate causes sweat to evaporate quickly, so you may not realize how much water your body is losing on a hot summer day. Even on a cold day, water is critical. As a general rule, pack 2 cups of water—per person—for every hour you'll be on the trail. Then pack some extra water, just to be safe. Don't expect to find water in the woods; and unless you know exactly how to treat it, do not rely on natural water sources.

Food. The last thing you want when recreating with kids is to be short on snacks. Try to avoid foods that are high in empty calories. Instead of candy bars and potato chips, fuel your adventures with healthy snacks, including Gorp trail mix, dehydrated fruit, applesauce squeeze packs, and energy bars (try Kate's Real Food bars and bites). When it's cold, carry high-energy snacks that won't freeze, such as nuts, chocolate, and cheese.

First aid. It's always a good idea to carry a first-aid kit. Many companies make lightweight and compact options, and big-box stores like Target carry inexpensive, prepackaged kits containing some of the following recommended items:

- Adhesive bandages
- Moleskin or duct tape
- Various sizes of sterile gauze and dressings
- White surgical tape
- Ace bandages
- An antihistamine
- Aspirin
- Betadine solution
- Tweezers
- Antibacterial wipes
- Triple-antibiotic ointment
- Sterile cotton-tip applicators

The wilderness can seem like a scary place if you don't know how to prevent and treat potential ailments. Here's a quick rundown. Yes, there's a lot that could go wrong. But most of the time, it won't. So don't get panicky on us. Instead, let the knowledge you're about to gain empower you to hike confidently with your kids.

Sunburn. At higher elevations, the sun's radiation is intense. Use sunblock, sun-protective clothing, and sunglasses. A wide-brimmed hat is a good idea. If somebody gets burned, treat the area with aloe vera gel and protect it from further exposure.

Blisters. These hike-spoilers can be quickly treated mid-trail with moleskin (a lightly padded adhesive), gauze and tape, or bandages. An effective way to apply moleskin is to cut out a circle of moleskin, remove the center like a doughnut, and place it over the blistered area.

Insect bites and stings. Treat most insect bites and stings by applying hydrocortisone 1% cream topically and administering a pain medication such as acetaminophen or ibuprofen (ibuprofen also helps to reduce swelling). If you forgot to pack these items, a cold compress or a paste of mud and ashes can sometimes relieve the itching and discomfort. Remove any stingers by using tweezers or scraping the area with your fingernail. Don't pinch the area—that will spread the venom.

Poison ivy, oak, and sumac. These skin irritants grow across Colorado and come in the form of a bush or a vine, having leaflets in groups of three, five, seven, or nine. The oil they secrete can cause an allergic reaction (usually blisters) about 12 hours after exposure. Prevent contact with poisonous plants by wearing clothing that covers the arms, legs, and torso. If you think you or your children were exposed, take a hot shower with soap when you're back home. This will help remove any lingering oil. If a rash appears, use an antihistamine to reduce itching.

Dehydration. Symptoms of dehydration include fatigue, headache, and decreased coordination and judgment. When you're hiking, your body's rate of fluid loss depends on the outside temperature, humidity, altitude, and your activity level. It's important to always carry plenty of water and to stop often and drink fluids regularly. If keeping your children hydrated is a struggle, try adding electrolyte-rich Nuun tablets to their water bottles. On cold days, fill steel canteens with warm herbal tea from Celestial Seasonings, made locally in Boulder.

Heat exhaustion. Drinking plenty of electrolyte-rich fluids can prevent heat exhaustion. Avoid hiking during the hottest parts of the day, between 10 a.m. and 2 p.m., and wear breathable clothing. Common symptoms of heat exhaustion include cramping, exhaustion, fatigue, light-headedness, and nausea. You can treat heat exhaustion by getting out of the sun and drinking an electrolyte solution made with 1 teaspoon of salt and 1 tablespoon of sugar dissolved in 1 liter of water.

Hypothermia. This may sound strange, but hypothermia is one of the biggest dangers for day hikers in the summer. You start a hike in the mountains on a sunny morning in shorts and a T-shirt. It starts to rain, the wind picks up, and before you know it, you're wet and shivering—the perfect recipe for hypothermia. More-advanced signs include decreased coordination, slurred speech, and blurred vision. Avoid hypothermia by packing a windproof/rainproof shell and a fleece jacket.

Altitude sickness/acute mountain sickness (AMS). Altitude sickness is your body's reaction to insufficient oxygen in the blood due to decreased barometric pressure. While some hikers may feel light-headed, nauseous, and experience shortness of breath at 7,000 feet, others may not experience these symptoms until they reach 10,000 feet or higher. Slow your ascent to give your body a chance to acclimatize. If you live at sea level and are planning a weeklong vacation to Colorado, start by staying below 7,000 feet for one night, and avoid strenuous exertion. Even those living in Denver can succumb to AMS while exploring higher elevations. It's important to eat light food and drink plenty of water. The treatment for AMS is simple: Stop heading uphill. Descend to a lower elevation and you'll feel better.

Natural Hazards

Besides tripping over a rock or tree root, there are some legit hazards to be aware of.

Lightning. Thunderstorms build over the mountains almost every day during the summer, and lightning can strike without warning, even several miles from the nearest overhead cloud. Lightning takes the path of least resistance. If you're the high point, it might choose you! Leave exposed peaks, ridges, and canyon rims by noon, at the latest, and always keep an eye on cloud formation. If you're caught in a thunderstorm, don't duck under a rock overhang. Dash below tree line, if possible, and avoid standing under the only tree or the tallest tree. If you're caught above tree line, stay away from anything metal. Move down off the ridge to a low, treeless point, and squat until the storm passes. Avoid having both your hands and feet touching the ground at once, and never lie flat. If you hear a buzzing sound or feel your hair standing on end, move quickly: An electrical charge is building up.

Flash floods. The spooky thing about flash floods, especially in western canyons, is that they can appear out of nowhere from a storm many miles away. While hiking or driving in canyons, keep an eye on the weather. Always climb to safety if danger threatens. Flash floods usually subside quickly, so be patient, and don't try to cross a swollen stream.

Bears. Colorado does not have a grizzly bear population, although rumors exist of sightings where there should be none. Black bears, however, are plentiful. There are several things you and your family can do to avoid startling a black bear:

- Watch for bear tracks (five toes) and droppings (sizable, with leaves, partly digested berries, seeds, and/or animal fur).
- Talk or sing, and be especially careful in spring to avoid getting between a mother and her cubs.
- If you do encounter a bear, move away slowly while facing the bear, talk softly, and don't make eye contact. Give the bear room to escape. Since bears are curious, they might stand upright to get a better whiff. Stay calm.
- If a black bear attacks, fight back.

Mountain lions. Attacks are rare, but encounters are possible in both day-use areas and the backcountry. The best thing is to avoid mountain lions altogether by taking a few precautions: Don't hike at dawn or dusk. Stay on established trails. As you walk, make noise and look for signs of mountain lions, including scat, claw marks, and scratch piles. If you see a cougar and it doesn't see you, alter your route. If there's a confrontation, remain calm. Give the lion a chance to escape. Back away slowly while facing it, and talk firmly. If you run, you'll look like prey, which—duh!—is bad. Instead, make yourself appear large and formidable by opening a jacket or waving hiking poles. Without turning away from the lion, pick up small children. If the lion behaves aggressively, throw stones, sticks, a water bottle, or whatever you can. If a lion attacks, always fight back.

Moose. Because they have very few natural predators, moose don't fear humans like other animals do. You might find moose in sagebrush and wetter areas of willow, aspen, and pine, or in beaver habitats. Mothers with calves, as well as bulls during mating season, can be particularly aggressive. If a moose threatens you, back away slowly while talking calmly to it.

Other considerations. Hunting is a popular sport in Colorado, especially during rifle season in October and November. Learn when the different hunting seasons start and end in the area in which you'll be recreating. During this time frame, be sure to wear at least a blaze-orange hat, and possibly put an orange vest over your pack. If you would feel more comfortable without hunters around, stick to national parks and monuments and/or state and local parks where hunting is prohibited.

Gear

The outdoor market is flooded with products, but the truth is you won't need much gear to enjoy the activities listed in this guide with your kids. Keep it simple. When you're trying to get out the door with children, the last thing you want is a bunch of stuff weighing you down. Sturdy athletic shoes and water are the two most important things. Here are a few more items to keep you and your family safe and comfortable.

Whistle. Kids should carry safety whistles. If your child isn't old enough to keep a whistle around their neck, buy a small backpack with a whistle built into a strap buckle. Teach children to use the whistle to call for help if they get lost.

Clothes. Since a good outdoorsperson is prepared for anything, get into the habit of packing rain protection and an extra layer. Eddie Bauer's kids Rainfoil jacket is a great item to stash in a backpack, since it can be used as a raincoat or windbreaker. Shop the company's website in off-seasons for steep discounts.

Summer: Carry sunscreen, wide-brimmed hats, and sunglasses. Roshambo makes flexible, durable shades for kids. Brands such as Eddie Bauer, Lands' End, and Coolibar sell sun-protective clothing for kids. If your children are sensitive to the sensation of grass on their legs, check out Eddie Bauer's quick-dry convertible pants, which transform into shorts by zipping off the legs.

Winter: It's all about layering. Start with a wicking layer, preferably long underwear made from synthetic fibers. Reima's bamboo viscose base layer is sized for toddlers, kids, and adolescents. Build on your wicking layer by adding a breathable insulating layer (fleece), followed by a waterproof/windproof shell with a hood that fits over a hat. Repeat after me: Cotton kills! Avoid this fabric entirely. Don't forget to protect your hands and face. In chilly, windy, or rainy weather, wear or pack hats made of wool or fleece, plus insulated, waterproof gloves.

Opt for affordable clothing. Some Gore-Tex jackets cost as much as $500, but there are less expensive fabrics that work just as well. Keep an eye out for sales at REI. Sierra Trading Post carries off-price merchandise for outdoor recreation, and local shops such as the Wilderness Exchange and Feral sell used and discounted gear. If you're visiting one of Colorado's mountain towns in the summer, look for shops selling last season's gear at discounts.

Footwear. Children don't need hiking boots. An athletic sneaker should do the trick for everyone in your group. If you want to shell out the money for something fancier, go with lightweight boots or a trail running shoe. Brands such as Keen and Merrell make excellent waterproof shoes with traction.

Traction. Between November and April, stash spikes or micro-spikes in the trunk of your car so you'll be prepared for snowy/icy trail conditions. Yaktrax are a lightweight and affordable traction device for older kids, and brands such as Milaloko and Freahap make traction cleats specifically for young children. Employees at REI can help you find the right sizes for your kids.

Hiking poles. Similar to technical footwear, poles are a discretionary item. They can be useful for balance on steep, rugged trails, and for us parents, poles take pressure off the knees. If you meet a mountain lion or unfriendly dog, poles can make you look a whole lot bigger. But before you buy them, think about your child's age and disposition. Will you be carrying several sets of poles by the end of the hike? If so, don't bother.

Backpacks. No matter what type of outdoor adventuring you plan to do, you'll need a pack to carry basic essentials. Buy a good-quality backpack, and set it aside as your family's designated outdoor pack. Fill your pack with first-aid supplies, several medium-size plastic bags for trash, extra Smartwool socks (hello, puddles!), stuffable rain gear, and a few spare diapers if applicable. Toss in healthy granola bars, an unopened bag of dried fruit, and other shelf-stable snacks. Store the backpack in a safe place, and replenish supplies as needed. There! Now you can head out the door with minimal fuss.

There are a variety of backpacks on the market. For the activities in this guide, you'll need a daypack with external pockets to carry water and other items such as keys, a knife, and a wallet. Brands such as Topo Designs, Mountainsmith, and Osprey make excellent daypacks for hikers. Backpacks can be a big-ticket item—remember to shop clearance sales online and at local retailers.

For very short excursions, some parents might prefer to use a fanny pack to store food, a compass, a map, and other small essentials. Many fanny packs have pockets for two water bottles. Since kids love having their own gear, one option is to outfit an adult with the family's main pack and allow children to carry extra items in a fanny pack.

How to Use This Guide

Aside from a pair of sturdy shoes—and this book—you really don't need any special skills or equipment to get outside with your kids. There are a few things, though, that are useful to know before hitting the trail.

The activities in this book are listed in alphabetical order. While most can be enjoyed any season, whenever the mood strikes, we've focused our writing on the summer months, when the days are longer, schools are closed, and more families will find time to participate in the great outdoors.

Every section begins with a brief introduction listing basic information on the particular site, including hours of operation, address, accessibility, and the availability of bathrooms. Most of these categories are self-explanatory.

The drive times are from the Colorado State Capitol, which, by the way, has an excellent free guided tour for families looking to learn more about civics and our local government. If you don't live in or near downtown Denver, then you'll have to adjust your drive times accordingly.

There's nothing worse than being stuck in the car with kids for hours, so we tried our best to hone in on Front Range destinations that would be well within reach for families living along the I-25 corridor, between Fort Collins and Colorado Springs, and out to Boulder.

It was exciting to discover how many of these destinations are free or low cost. Great news for parents trying to keep kids entertained on a budget! For locations with an admission fee, we tallied the cost for a family of four, including two adults and two young children. Admission fees change frequently, so rather than actual amounts, you'll see the price for each destination represented with dollar signs. Here's how we broke it down:

Price for a Family of Four

$ Low cost ($24 or less)

$$ Budget friendly ($25 to $49)

$$$ Splurge ($50 or more)

We've also included information about accessibility. Destinations are making strides to offer features that create better access to nature, like Terrain Hopper chairs to navigate trails, auditory devices that read interpretive signs, designated quiet spaces or low sensory events, bilingual signs, and more. When accessibility features for a destination were too numerous to include in our allotted space, we've referenced where to find a destination's list of features.

As you dig into the chapters, look for the Learn sidebar in each. We developed the book to guide you as you explore with your kids, and along with that, we wanted to offer educational activities to keep the learning buzz alive. Some of the activities can be done on the spot and some are easier to do once you get home. They're all fun!

You'll notice the occasional mention of a nature journal. This is a place for kids to draw, color, write, or record something about each excursion. Maybe they saw a beaver dam or found an interesting flower. Encourage them to take time on each adventure to add at least one thing to their nature journal. There's no need to invest in a pricey journal—an inexpensive school notebook or small blank book will do just fine—and it won't add extra weight to the backpack. Don't forget colored pencils for a no-mess, no-melt coloring option. Watch as the journal's pages fill up and become a sort of scrapbook of your adventures together.

1 Barr Lake State Park and Nature Center

Take an adventure through Colorado's something-for-everyone state park.

Cost: Daily vehicle pass required to enter Colorado state parks, or purchase a Colorado Parks & Wildlife annual parks pass.
Hours: Park open 5 a.m. to 10 p.m.; nature center open Mon–Fri 9 a.m. to 4 p.m., Sat–Sun 9 a.m. to 5 p.m.
Location: 13401 Picadilly Rd.
Nearest Town: Brighton
Denver Drive Time: 30 minutes via I-76 East
Accessibility: Accessible nature center and ADA-compliant fishing pier. Terrain Hopper all-terrain mobility vehicles available to borrow. Niedrach Nature Trail is a short loop trail with a mix of gravel, dirt, and boardwalk. The boardwalk includes a railing and accessible viewing scope.
Bathrooms: Full restrooms with sink, changing table, and water bottle refill station inside the nature center; restroom with flush toilet and sink near boat dock; pit toilet by the archery range
Gear Suggestions: Walking shoes, hat, sunscreen, binoculars, nature journal, water gear, change of dry clothes for water activities like kayaking or paddleboarding (swimming and wading are not allowed)
Insider Tip: The archery range at Barr Lake State Park offers 12 lanes with targets from 10 to 100 yards away. Anyone who has taken an archery safety course is welcome to use the range for free. Archery equipment is available to check out from the nature center.

Explore

Whether your family loves paddleboarding, nature hikes, or troll hunting, Barr Lake State Park is one of those great "something-for-everyone" places . . . wait, troll hunting? Yep, more on that later. Located south of Brighton, the park's recreation history goes back to the 1880s when it was an exclusive destination for wealthy sportsmen from Denver. Today, the sprawling 2,715-acre park invites everyone to explore a peaceful lake, thriving wildlife refuge, and miles of trails, as well as an engaging nature center.

Those wealthy sportsmen from the 1880s weren't the only folks who made this a recreation haven. A couple decades later, the area became well-known among bird-watchers. More than 350 species of birds have been identified at the park, including numerous waterfowl and raptors. Your kids are almost guaranteed to add a couple species to their birdng life list. And if they haven't started one of these lists of all the bird species they've seen in their (short) lives, this is an ideal spot to start one. A hawk hunting its prey landed right outside the nature center door as we chatted with a naturalist. Pelicans, great blue herons, cormorants, and owls all regularly appear at the park, and bald eagles have been seen at Barr Lake every year since 1986.

Begin your visit at the Barr Lake Nature Center to chat up the park rangers and naturalists. They are happy to share trail and activity suggestions. You'll have plenty of time to talk, because the kids will likely dig into the many hands-on displays. A collection of bird specimens, nests, and a buffalo are just for viewing, but there is a table full of "please touch" items, like a turtle shell, ram skull, antlers, and bones, in the center of the room. Everywhere you turn, there's a learning experience. Really! An 8-foot curtain rod in the birding alcove holds, yes, curtains, but also a label explaining that the rod is the same width as an eagle's nest found in the park.

When you're ready to hit the trails, start with the easy Niedrach Nature Trail for a short loop through prairie grasses, along the lakeshore, and out to viewing boardwalks on the water. To reach this trail, cross the bridge outside of the nature center, then turn left onto Lake Loop. This 8.8-mile main perimeter trail circles the lake and is frequented by hikers, runners, and even horses. It also leads to a variety of shorter trails and viewing boardwalks. Niedrach Nature Trail is just a few steps away from the bridge.

This mini adventure begins with a walk past shady cottonwood trees and down a boardwalk to a quiet spot on the lake. Along the trail, you'll encounter interpretive signs about wildlife viewing and ways to use your senses in nature. If parents need a quiet moment, this is the place. Signs encourage trail users to walk quietly and listen, for the best chance at finding wildlife. Ask little ones to be as quiet as a mouse; then ask what sounds they are able to hear around them. As you wind back to the main trail, follow the path through a grassy field where an explosion of leaping grasshoppers punctuates your every step.

Have some extra time and energy? Turn right when you reach Lake Loop. About 1 mile down the trail is the Gazebo Boardwalk, where kids can use the binoculars to view birds nesting around the rookery.

OK, back to the trolls. If your family has jumped on the trend of finding troll sculptures like the ones created by Danish artist Thomas Dambo, Barr Lake has two of their own creations—these were done by Barr Lake volunteer Wayne Girten. Although it's not an official park activity, the trolls, made of carved tree trunks and branches, are absolutely worth finding, if only for a delightful selfie to end the day.

LEARN

From sunny blue waters to red berries and gray-brown bark, Barr Lake is full of artistic inspiration. Try these activities to hone your child's nature observation skills and artistic eye.

- **Create a Nature Color Wheel: What colors can you find in nature? It's easy to find green and blue, but can you find yellow? How about violet? Draw or print a color wheel. Then as kids find various colors in nature, snap a photo or, if allowed, bring the item home. Match the natural item to its corresponding color and attach it to the wheel. Keep looking until you've filled every color. It's also fun to reflect on the names given to colors. How many have names derived from nature? Grass green, sky blue, sunny yellow. Ask kids to imagine names of their own based on things they see around the park. How about pelican white or ranger hat green?**
- **Build a Troll: It's inspiring to see how people can turn broken branches or withered flowers into art. Use the Barr Lake trolls, or even the homes that birds, insects, and animals craft from elements in nature, as inspiration to craft your own nature art. Use elements found around the backyard or neighborhood.**

2 Bear Creek Nature Center

Discover four foothills habitats in one location.

Cost: Free
Hours: Nature center open Tues–Sat 9 a.m. to 4 p.m. Nature trails open daily from dawn to dusk.
Location: 245 Bear Creek Road
Nearest Town: Colorado Springs
Denver Drive Time: 1 hour and 15 minutes via I-25 South
Accessibility: Wheelchair-accessible nature center; sensory bags available to check out at the information desk; Terrain Hopper off-road mobility vehicles available for reservation late spring through early fall. Songbird Trail (0.1-mile loop starting from the nature center) is wheelchair accessible and includes the VIP (Visually Impaired Persons) Trail with a braided guide rope leading to interpretive signs. Folks with visual impairments may request a Pen Friend audio device inside the nature center: Touch the pen to raised buttons on the interpretive signs and it will read aloud the text on the sign.
Bathrooms: Full bathrooms inside the nature center
Gear Suggestions: Walking or hiking shoes, sunscreen, hats, insect repellent
Insider Tip: Purchase a Junior Naturalist Field Journal for a couple dollars inside the nature center. Complete the activities in the booklet to earn a Junior Naturalist badge.

Explore

Tucked in a canyon on the west side of Colorado Springs, Bear Creek Nature Center is close enough to the city for a morning or afternoon of play, yet far enough away to feel like you've stepped into a secret garden. This location between the mountains and the plains is home to four distinct and thriving habitats—riparian, shrubland, conifer forest, and mountain meadow—and plenty of short, accessible trails that guide visitors in a discovery of plant and animal life.

You could begin on one of the trails, but we recommend starting your visit in the nationally recognized nature center. The bright, engaging building, opened in 2002, is on the site of Colorado's first nature center—Solar Trails, which was built in 1976 and burned down in an arson fire in 2001. Rising from the ashes is Bear Creek Nature Center, filled with hands-on activities to teach curious kids and grown-ups about the surrounding areas.

Inside, active little ones can cross a footbridge, nuzzle in a giant tree trunk with a book, compare their wingspan with that of bald eagles and wild turkeys, or watch the inner workings of a live, buzzing bee colony. Informative displays and interactive exhibits introduce the plants and animals that live in the habitats around the nature center. Look closely on the corners of the habitat displays and you'll find a list of activities to do in each area (in the riparian habitat, for instance, listen for different birdcalls). Did you know Colorado has a state fish? Seek out the large fish tank for an up-close view of the greenback cutthroat trout, covered in playful spots and sporting

reddish color around their gills. This symbol of Colorado is listed as threatened on the endangered species list, but a genetically pure strain of the fish calls a stretch of Bear Creek home.

After learning about Bear Creek's habitats, it's time to head out to one of the four trails that start right at the nature center. The shortest trail, Songbird Trail, is an easy 0.1-mile loop with a mix of pavement and boardwalk surfaces, and interpretive signs. The other trails are 0.5 mile, 0.8 mile, and 1.2 miles, the perfect lengths for short legs or short attention spans. For a longer hike, pick up the Regional Trail in the northwest corner of the parking lot or connect with it at the end of Songbird Trail or along Coyote Gulch Loop. Not sure which trail to hike? Just ask the friendly folks at the nature center's front desk for suggestions.

Before you head home, sit down for an end-of-the-trail snack or lunch at the picnic tables, on the deck behind the nature center. This quiet area offers a happy setting with a view of active birds visiting the gardens and feeders.

LEARN

With multiple habitats supporting oodles of organisms, this nature center serves as a valuable study zone for young naturalists.

- **Identify Habitats: You'll hear the word *habitat* frequently as you visit nature centers. But what is a habitat? It's an area where particular species of plants, animals, and insects make their home. Bear Creek Nature Center is surrounded by four habitats: conifer forest, shrubland, riparian, and mountain meadow. Each habitat needs to provide four elements for the organisms that live there: food, water, shelter, and space. Collect information as you explore the indoor exhibits and outdoor trails to help you identify distinct characteristics of each habitat. Who lives there? What do they eat? What do their homes look like?**
- **Bark Up the Trees: Don't forget, plants need the four basics as well! Different habitats are home to different types of trees. Look closely at the bark on the trees around the nature center. Are they rough or smooth? Are they dark or light? Who might live in each tree? Use this as a way to launch a deeper study of trees.**

3 Benson Sculpture Garden

Colorado's Sweetheart City adores the arts.

Cost: Free
Hours: Open daily from sunrise to sunset
Location: 1125 West 29th Street
Nearest Town: Loveland
Denver Drive Time: 65 minutes via I-25 North
Accessibility: Accessible sidewalks work for wheelchairs and strollers, and braille signs are available for guests with vision impairments. Weekends can get crowded; for a low-sensory experience, visit on a Monday or Tuesday morning, when foot traffic is sparse.
Bathrooms: Public restrooms with flush toilets located near the parking lot off Aspen Drive
Gear Suggestions: Comfortable walking shoes, sunscreen, a hat, sunglasses, water, snacks to enjoy at one of the many park benches, a Frisbee or ball to use at green spaces, simple art supplies
Insider Tip: For an amped-up art walk, visit Benson Sculpture Garden during the second weekend in August, when the Loveland High Plains Arts Council hosts its "Sculpture in the Park" event. The exhibition is the largest outdoor juried sculpture show in the country, featuring thousands of three-dimensional designs created by hundreds of national and international artists.

Explore

There's a lot to love about Loveland. Situated at the base of the Front Range, Colorado's so-called "Sweetheart City" is a place where Valentine's Day lasts all season long. But the 35.56-square-mile town also maintains a year-round love affair with sculptural arts, boasting four sculpture gardens, two bronze foundries, and a finishing house, as well as 380-plus public works of art. A visit to Benson Sculpture Gardens is one of the best ways for families to get acquainted with the local art scene.

It's no wonder the 10-acre sculpture garden has been named one of the country's top twenty must-see contemporary art sites. A flat, paved trail anchors the site, weaving guests around a series of ponds feeding Lake Loveland. During your walk you'll pass a massive collection of permanent sculptures interspersed throughout a natural landscape punctuated with Japanese lilacs, chokecherries, and crabapple trees towering over a wide variety of colorful, flowering plants.

In 2015 the garden expanded across 29th Street with the installation of three new pieces. (Since then, many additional sculptures have been added to the south portion of the park.) If spots are available, it's easiest to park in the lot off Aspen Drive, then begin a clockwise loop around the garden. While it's fine to walk in either direction, this option allows families to tour the majority of the park's installations before ending at North Lake Park (2750 North Taft Avenue), featuring two large play structures overlooking the water, along with sports courts, fields, and a shaded picnic area.

The sculpture garden was made to be interactive, and kids can definitely touch the art. Look for the saddle as you walk—that's meant to be sat on. While younger

children will get a lot out of play-based exploration, older kids might enjoy learning about some of the artists who created the sculptures. If that's the case, make a pit stop at the Loveland Visitors Center, located right off I-25, at McWhinney-Hahn Sculpture Park. Here you'll find a brochure with additional information about artwork in the garden plus a longer Benson Sculpture guide.

If you're digging the town's public art scene, then take Loveland's self-guided public art tour. After downloading the free Otocast app, available through Apple and Google app stores, you'll have access to a virtual art tour featuring twenty of Loveland's most notable downtown sculptures, including art at the Civic Center, Foundry, and on East Fourth Street. In addition to learning about each sculpture's location, families can listen to artist interviews and view photos of the pieces.

Up for even more art? You can always swing by Chapungu Sculpture Park at Centerra, at 5971 Sky Pond Drive, for a one-of-a-kind outdoor exhibit featuring eighty-two monumental stone sculptures from Zimbabwean artisans displayed across 26 acres of natural and landscaped gardens.

LEARN

Art is the fourth component of STEAM education, and Benson Sculpture Garden offers plenty of lessons in three-dimensional art, art history, and even city planning when you take into account the role public art installations can play in beautifying a town.

- **Get Inspired: Why not pack a few simple art supplies for this trip, so your children can create their own masterpieces? With Wikki Stix or a portable kit of air-dry modeling clay, budding artists can work on sculptures, en plein air, while parents enjoy the views from on-site picnic tables.**
- **Dive Deeper: If you'd like to learn more about the artists behind the sculptures, visit the Loveland High Plains Art Council's website, sculptureinthepark.org, where you can download a map of Benson Sculpture Garden and view the organization's Artist Cross Reference Guide. Back home, enhance the experience by asking your child to research the artist behind their favorite sculpture.**

4 Bison Herd Overlook

Glimpse Denver's herd of bison at Genesee Mountain Park.

Cost: Free
Hours: One hour before sunrise to 1 hour after sunset
Location: Genesee Mountain Park claims 2 bison-watching areas, both conveniently located off I-70, at exits 254 and 253.
Nearest Town: Genesee
Denver Drive Time: 25 minutes via 6th Avenue to I-70
Accessibility: While the overlook itself is wheelchair accessible, Genesee's dirt hiking trails are too rugged for standard wheelchairs and strollers. Hikers with visual impairments will discover the Braille Trail branching off from Beaver Brook Trailhead, at exit 253.
Bathrooms: Pit toilets at the Beaver Brook Trailhead
Gear Suggestions: Binoculars, nature journaling supplies, a coat or windbreaker, comfortable walking shoes, sunscreen, a hat, sunglasses, plenty of water, snacks
Insider Tip: For a no-fuss family campout, check out Chief Hosa Campground, situated off exit 254. This 58-acre campground has two dozen tent sites plus RV sites with water and electric hookups. Campground facilities are open annually, from May 1 through the fourth week of September, and reservations are required. Take note: Campground reservations typically open in February; book early to secure a spot.

Explore

From camping, hiking, and picnicking to stellar wildlife viewing, there's a lot to love about Genesee Mountain Park. And while many elements come together like Voltron to make Genesee special, the park truly stands out for being Denver's first—and largest—mountain park.

Denver Mountain Parks has been around since 1912, making it four years older than the National Park Service. When Genesee was created in 1914, it was originally developed as a drive-through wildlife park with bison, elk, and bighorn sheep.

Technically, you can still spot Genesee's wildlife from your car. The first thing you need to know is that I-70 bisects the site, cutting it into two distinct sections. South of the highway, families gain access to spectacular 360-degree views by hiking to Genesee Summit Trail's 8,284-foot crest. At 7,988 feet, Bald Mountain is a prominent viewpoint on the north side of the park, where the historic Beaver Brook Trail stretches through the backcountry, all the way to Clear Creek Canyon in Golden.

Wildlife viewing is one of Genesee's top offerings, and the park offers a wide walking trail plus two overlooks where families can observe the first buffalo herds reestablished in Colorado over one hundred years ago. Bison neared extinction by 1914, with less than 1,000 in existence. With conservation in mind, the City of Denver partnered with Denver Zoo to acquire animals from City Park and also the Bison Range, formerly the National Bison Range, a nature reserve on the Flathead Indian Reservation in western Montana. Mountain Parks staff have cared for the ungulates

ever since, maintaining them as a conservation herd managed at about forty bison, though it varies by year. The Genesee program was so successful that, in 1939, a new bison herd was established at Daniels Park in Douglas County.

To keep its herd at a healthy, manageable level, the City of Denver initially auctioned off surplus bison. In 2021, though, the city began transferring bison to the Northern Arapaho Tribe, Cheyenne and Arapaho Tribes, and Tall Bull Memorial Council, to reintroduce wild bison and support conservation efforts on tribal lands. There's more to learn about this bison conservation program online at denvergov.org.

Since Denver's bison are descendants of some of the last wild bison in the world, modern-day parkgoers get a glimmer of the past while watching a herd of living, breathing relics roam pastures along I-70. Technically Genesee Mountain Park maintains two bison-watching areas, both located off I-70, at exits 254 and 253. But the overlook at exit 253 is more scenic, with better interpretive signage, so we recommend using this location as a starting point for adventure.

The overlook is easy to reach. From I-70, take exit 253, and drive north to Stapleton and Moss Rock Roads. Turn right onto Stapleton Road; follow it for about 0.5 mile, until you reach a parking lot and the overlook.

Read about Denver's bison herd, and learn the difference between buffalo and bison, while perusing a series of panels at the exit 253 overlook. (You won't find interpretive signs related to the animals at exit 254.) People frequently confuse bison and buffalo, but there are a few key differences between these two large, ox-like animals. For starters, bison are wildlife, and they've never been domesticated. They're considered a keystone species, too, making them a critical part of the ecosystem.

When the animals were removed from Denver's landscape, it created a collapse, so bringing them back has been regenerative, to say the least.

Your kids can distinguish bison from buffalo by focusing on the three Hs: home, hump, and horns. Britannica.com has a great video that elaborates on the topic. Be sure to bring snacks and plenty of patience; wildlife viewing is a little like fishing: It takes time. If you really want to up your odds of seeing the herd, visit just after dawn or before dusk, when all wildlife tend to be more active. Remember to avoid hiking past dark, though, especially with children.

LEARN

For budding zoologists, and any children studying animals, mammals, undulates, ecosystems, or conservation, the Buffalo Herd Overlook is an awe-inspiring pit stop for real-life learning.

- **Creativity Calls: Back home, young children can add a little beauty to their adventure by making handprint buffalo. First, dip a hand into brown paint and make a print on thick paper. Your child's four fingers make up the buffalo's legs, and the thumb serves as a tail. From there, use a paintbrush and brown paint to add the bison's hump and head. Draw horns and eyes, and some scenery, too.**
- **Social Studies Extension: At the nearby Buffalo Bill Museum and Grave, located on Lookout Mountain at 987 1/2 Lookout Mountain Road, families can learn about William F. "Buffalo Bill" Cody, the legendary frontiersman, showman, and bison hunter. From exit 254, the popular tourist attraction is only a few minutes up the road. Follow the signs toward Lookout Mountain Nature Center, then continue on to Buffalo Bill's grave and the adjacent museum. The museum, which charges an entry fee, is a little corny, yes, but it's also brimming with historical artifacts and displays packed with information. It's definitely worth visiting once with kids.**

5 Bluff Lake Nature Center

Visit this revitalized airport crash zone that now gives wildlife, plants, and humans a peaceful layover spot.

Cost: Free
Hours: Daily sunrise to sunset
Location: 11255 East Martin Luther King Jr. Blvd.
Nearest Town: Denver
Denver Drive Time: 25 minutes via East 17th Avenue and East Montview Boulevard
Accessibility: ADA-compliant parking spots. Wide trails consist of crusher fine mixed with some areas of larger gravel; there is also a sloping ramp of crusher fine and road base gravel leading down into the lake zone. A flat boardwalk goes out to a lake-viewing deck. Visit the website for details and site conditions.
Bathrooms: Three portable toilets with hand-washing stations. Accessible portable toilets near the parking lot and the amphitheater.
Gear Suggestions: Sturdy shoes, water bottles, hats, sunscreen, binoculars
Insider Tip: Visit blufflake.org for links to maps, self-guided tours, games, and activities to use during a visit.

Explore

Many things have grown out of the relocation of Denver's airport in the 1990s, including a number of areas for families to recreate and nature to thrive. Bluff Lake Nature Center, once in the "crash zone" for Stapleton Airport, is one of those spots. In the time since the airport moved, the open space has become a protected home for diverse species of wildlife and plants, as well as a unique nature center.

Bluff Lake Nature Center is split between two levels: a parking lot and entry area situated on a bluff and the main nature preserve and trails—with prairie, riparian, and wetland habitats—below. What makes this nature center unique? There are no indoor displays. Don't worry, there are still plenty of hands-on features and interpretive signs, but here they are all scattered on the trails outside.

To get started, take in a view of mountains, city, prairie, and wetland from the pergola on the bluff. Before heading down to the Lake Loop Trail, follow a winding path behind the storage area to wander through a thriving prairie habitat. Bluff Trail zigs and zags among rabbit brush and other native shrubs. Kids with a good eye can identify the blue grama, Colorado's state grass. In the depth of summer, even the "short" grasses here can grow tall enough to make the Bluff Trail feel like a magical maze for kids. Let the trail wind you through the habitat past hidden picnic tables and scenic overlooks. You'll also see insects fluttering between wildflowers and, if you're very quiet, you may spy a rabbit resting in the shade. It's the perfect trail for young kids or short visits.

On the northwestern corner of the Bluff Trail, look for a short gate. This entrance connects to a set of stairs that will meet up at the bottom with Lake Loop, the 1-mile

main trail around the nature center. If you need to use the ramp instead, go back through the pergola and look for a gated entrance on the south side. Follow the trail past the enormous elevated eagle's nest to meet up with the ramp, which ends in the same spot as the stairs.

Starting at the bottom of the stairs, Lake Loop travels through three habitats, beginning in the riparian forest. Turn right for a brief extension of the trail that follows the base of the bluff to one of the first "Nature Play Stations." Another unique element of this nature center, the five play stations, spread out along the trails, encourage kids to get active outside. One station asks kids to explore shelters made of logs, another to climb into a giant eagle's nest to scan the area, and another to crawl through burrows like a prairie dog.

At the first fork in the trail (look for marker post E), the brief 0.4-mile Creek Loop takes a pretty detour along the Sand Creek. A loud chorus of chirping cicadas and tumbling water from the creek will serenade you, along with just a bit of street traffic from Martin Luther King Jr. Boulevard. Once you reconnect with Lake Loop, be sure to backtrack a few yards; you don't want to miss the cattail-lined boardwalk that leads out to a viewing deck on the lake. Back on Lake Loop, follow the gnarled tree stumps along the shady shore to a bird blind on the western end of the lake. Bluff Lake is a popular place for bird-watching, so take advantage of this hidden spot to scan the water and trees for busy birds.

Continue on Lake Loop into a prairie habitat and past the prairie dog colony. As you reach Storm Water Outfalls, look for the bat house—hundreds of bats call this home—and wrap up the loop back at the base of the stairs or ramp.

The wide, quiet trails at Bluff Lake—no bicycles, horses, or dogs allowed—make it an ideal spot to meander with kids and stop to watch wildlife.

LEARN

Pick one of the Nature Play Stations in this all-outdoor nature center to inspire at-home activities.

- Become a Bird-Watcher: The pandemic spurred a bird-watching craze, and the hobby is just as exciting for kids as it is for retirees. Avid bird-watchers know how to identify the different species of our winged pals. Research identifying characteristics of birds such as field marks, their homes, and their call or song. Grab a pair of binoculars and a field guide and get out there. Keep a family journal or sketchbook of all the different types of birds you find and identify.
- Build a Shelter: One of Bluff Lake's Nature Play Stations takes you into a shaded forest clearing to learn about a vital element of every habitat: shelter. As you follow the trails, look for the many shelters—either natural or man-made—around the nature center. Do you see nests? Clumps of cattails? A bat house? At home, look around your yard or neighborhood to find shelters used by wildlife.

6 Broadmoor Manitou and Pikes Peak Cog Railway

Chug-a-choo your way to the top of Colorado's most famous mountain.

Cost: $$$ Select reserved seating when you make your reservation to ensure that the family sits together. Standard seating is auto-assigned, so there is no guarantee that your seats will be together. Fee for parking.
Hours: Train schedule varies by season. Visit the website to select a date and time.
Location: 515 Ruxton Avenue
Nearest Town: Manitou Springs
Denver Drive Time: 1 hour 30 minutes, via I-25 South
Accessibility: Call ahead to reserve ADA seating and storage space for wheelchairs and walkers on the train. ADA-compliant interpretive walkway at the summit. Be aware: Strollers are not allowed on the train.
Bathrooms: Full restrooms at the depot and in the Summit Visitor Center at the top. No restrooms on the train.
Gear Suggestions: Walking shoes and water bottles. Also check the forecast and bring any additional warm clothing. The temperature at the summit is usually 30 degrees cooler than at the base.
Insider Tip: Weather at the top of Pikes Peak can be unpredictable, even in the early summer. If snow blocks the tracks or lightning is a threat, rides may not travel all the way to the summit. In this case, the railway usually offers visitors a chance to reschedule. Manage the kids' expectations.

Explore

Kids of any age get caught up in the giddy excitement of summiting a breathtaking Colorado mountain, and Pikes Peak is one of the most well-known peaks around. The historic Pikes Peak Cog Railway gives kids the opportunity to do something the peak's namesake never actually did himself: Reach the top. The best part is, there's a fun train ride to get you there.

Many historic railways were once hardworking lines that hauled freight or transported gold and silver ores from mines, but the route to the top of Pikes Peak has always been for the pure joy of tourism and carrying folks up, up, up for the spectacular views. Before the tracks were built, the only way to the top was an arduous two-day trip by mule. In the late 1880s, Zalmon Simmons, inventor and founder of the Simmons Beautyrest Mattress Company, took the mule excursion himself. He thought there had to be a better way for visitors to access the inspiring views at Pikes Peak's summit. So, he developed the idea of a train ride to the top.

Fast-forward 130 years and visitors today have a number of options for reaching the top of Pikes Peak, including hiking, bicycling, driving, and railway. The train is perhaps the easiest and most relaxing way for families to reach the summit. Everyone—even the parent who usually gets stuck behind the wheel while the rest of the family oohs and aahs at the scenery—has a chance to admire the view along the way.

Purchase your tickets for the train online to ensure your preferred day and time. Definitely plan to arrive in Manitou Springs 30 minutes before your ride. This will leave enough time for parking, getting to the depot, and making a restroom stop (or two) before getting on the train. Then settle in for the 1-hour ride to the summit in comfy, spacious seats surrounded by large viewing windows. Those windows are key in watching the stunning natural scenery as the train travels through the bristlecone pines of Pike National Forest, along the tumbling waterfalls of Ruxton Creek, and past stacked boulder formations. Watch for the moment the train reaches the tree line near 11,700 feet. The forest surroundings disappear into a rocky alpine ecosystem. Your conductor will likely mention it as they share other historical and natural points of interest throughout the trip. If you are lucky, the conductor may break out singing "America the Beautiful." Kids who have studied Pikes Peak in school will know that a trip to the summit inspired professor and author Katharine Lee Bates to write the iconic song.

As the train reaches the top of the mountain, you'll see similarly inspiring views, as well as the City of Colorado Springs–owned Summit Visitor Center, which was updated and reopened in 2021. Use your time at the top to explore the interpretive exhibits inside the visitor center and follow the outdoor walkway, guided by the downloadable and informative Summit app.

Before jumping back on the train for the return trip to the depot, grab one of the Pikes Peak donuts—the only ones made above 14,000 feet—and snap a family selfie by the summit sign. There are numerous opportunities to learn about science and nature at Pikes Peak, right down to the high-altitude recipe developed to make the donuts stay fluffy at 14,115 feet above sea level.

LEARN

Riding to the top of this majestic mountain, kids will experience inspiring vistas as well as natural wonders. Pair this adventure with activities that reflect both art and science.

- Use Your Inspiration: Listening to the story of how Katharine Lee Bates wrote "America the Beautiful" after visiting Pikes Peak helps kids tap into creative inspiration. When you reach the summit, discuss how the sweeping views and heights inspire each of you. Do they make you feel like drawing or singing, or maybe learning more about the science of mountain formation? Act on that inspiration when you get home.
- Trace the Manitou Mineral Springs Trail: Manitou Springs, home to the Pikes Peak Cog Railway, is the location of eight naturally carbonated mineral springs. Water from each one has a distinct taste due to the different minerals present in the spring. Pick up a map to the eight springs at the Manitou Springs Chamber of Commerce & Visitors Bureau on Manitou Avenue. They also provide a chart showing the minerals present in each spring. Walk the trail, note the minerals, and talk about how each one tastes.

7 Butterfly Pavilion

Look into the realm of the often-misunderstood heroes of our ecosystem.

Cost: $$$ Children under age 2 free
Hours: Daily 9 a.m. to 5 p.m.
Location: 6252 West 104th Avenue
Nearest Town: Broomfield
Denver Drive Time: 20 minutes via I-25 North and US-36 West
Accessibility: Wheelchair accessible. Sensory Friendly Afternoons allow families with specific sensory needs to experience the exhibits with limited admission, natural lighting, and quiet tones. The quiet corner in the back of the Colorado Backyard exhibit has comfy chairs and books to read. A downloadable social story is available at butterflies.org, near Sensory Friendly Afternoon information. All exhibit signage is in both English and Spanish.
Bathrooms: Full bathrooms are available inside the museum. A lactation room is located in Tykes Peak inside the Colorado Backyard play area.
Gear Suggestions: Comfortable walking shoes, reusable water bottles, outdoor gear for exploring the Discovery gardens
Insider Tip: Free-flying butterflies in the Wings of the Tropics exhibit are most active during the brighter hours of the day. Plan to visit this area in the morning or early afternoon.

Explore

Invertebrates (animals without a spine) make up a staggering 97% of all animal species on Earth. These busy creatures really keep our planet thriving. In fact, you may hear the folks at Butterfly Pavilion say, with a wink, that these spineless animals are the *backbone* of our ecosystem. When Butterfly Pavilion opened in 1995, there was nothing else like it. It was the first freestanding butterfly house and invertebrate zoo in the United States. Today it's the only Association of Zoos and Aquariums–accredited stand-alone nonprofit invertebrate zoo and aquarium in the world. But kids will love it just for the bugs.

Begin your visit in the Survival exhibit to observe live arthropods and learn how they have adapted to the challenges of life as a crawly, creepy, or winged creature. View the thriving beehive, where the bees are free to come and go through a tube connected to the outside world. Lean in close to a posted speaker. You'll hear what it sounds like inside the busy hive. This exhibit is also home to Butterfly Pavilion's mascot Rosie, a Chilean rose-hair tarantula. Anyone above the age of 3 is welcome to hold Rosie, with the help of a staff member. Kids earn bragging rights for letting her crawl across their hands, and they'll get an "I Held Rosie" sticker awarded to them after the experience.

Next, move on to the marine realm of Water's Edge, where you'll find shallow water and deep ocean invertebrates. Here, kids have an opportunity to touch a sea star and a spider crab and look for the friendly octopus. You'll notice butterfly stickers on some of the tanks. These indicate each animal's level of endangerment.

The star of Butterfly Pavilion is the spectacular Wings of the Tropics exhibit, a 7,200-square-foot tropical rainforest setting where around 2,000 butterflies flutter freely and mingle with visitors. On any given day there are approximately eighty different species of butterflies busily exploring the space, along with one vertebrate, a seed-eating dove named Larry. Don't miss the case by the doors filled with a collection of butterfly chrysalises. This provides a look at the various stages of a butterfly's development. If you're lucky, you may even see a butterfly emerging from a chrysalis. Twice each day there is a butterfly release, where you might witness the release of newly emerged butterflies. Take your time strolling the lush indoor tropical rainforest landscape.

The final indoor exhibit, Colorado Backyard, is an education and play zone where kids can expend some energy on a play structure, attend story time, and learn about invertebrate habitats in Colorado's ecosystems.

On a nice day, wrap up the visit in the outdoor Discovery Gardens to stroll through native plants and flowers as kids look for local invertebrates and pollinators in their natural habitat.

Butterfly Pavilion is compact in size, but they plan to break ground on a new 81,000-square-foot facility in Broomfield, Colorado, in 2025. The new facility will include immersive, state-of-the-art learning opportunities for visitors, as well as research and lab space for the world of invertebrates.

LEARN

Observation is a valuable practice of scientists. Watching the planet's hardworking insects gives kids a chance to hone their science skills.

- Observe Invertebrates: One way to learn more about invertebrates–insects specifically–is to invite one for a visit. Ask the kids to look around the backyard for an interesting insect. Once you've gently collected the creature, do a little research to identify the species, learn about its ideal home, what it eats, and what it needs to survive. Set up a healthy habitat where it can live for a couple of days. Take the opportunity to observe this visitor at different times of day. Does it sleep? When does it eat? Then happily release it back into its natural habitat.
- Build for Bugs: If the kids are into engineering, search the internet for simple plans to create a "bug hotel" or "bug house" for the backyard. This will encourage more close encounters with invertebrates.

8 Carson Nature Center

Nature programming awaits along the South Platte River.

Cost: Free
Hours: Noon to 4:30 p.m. Tues–Fri and on weekends from 9:30 a.m. to 4:30 p.m. The nature center is closed Mon and holidays. South Platte Park surrounds the nature center and is open daily from sunrise to sunset.
Location: 3000 West Carson Drive, near the intersection of Mineral Avenue and Santa Fe Drive
Nearest Town: Littleton
Denver Drive Time: 25 minutes via Santa Fe Drive
Accessibility: The nature center is ADA compliant, and the paved regional trail that runs alongside the South Platte River (the Mary Carter Greenway) is wheelchair and stroller accessible. An accessible fishing pier is located at Blackrock Lake (near CO 470), at the park's south entrance. While the nature center doesn't host designated low-sensory hours, the experience is typically quiet and foot traffic tends to be light.
Bathrooms: Flush toilets inside the nature center and at Reynolds Landing Park; vault toilets at the parking lot serving Blackrock Lake (near CO 470).
Gear Suggestions: Binoculars, nature-journaling supplies, comfortable walking shoes, sunscreen, a hat, sunglasses, plenty of water, snacks
Insider Tip: Led by park rangers and naturalists, Carson Nature Center's year-round classes are perfect for families looking to learn more about local flora and fauna. Family classes are typically held nights and weekends, and homeschool classes are scheduled on weekdays. Whether you're into stargazing, birding, or animal tracking, there's something for just about everyone. Register through the South Suburban Parks & Recreation web portal at ssprd.org.

Explore

Measuring in at 880 acres, stretching from Breckenridge Brewery in Littleton to the lake abutting CO 470, South Platte Park is the kind of place where families can easily idle away an entire day. While there are several points of access to the park, one of the best places to park is the lot servicing Carson Nature Center (behind Aspen Grove Shopping Center).

Carson Nature Center is a beautiful, eco-friendly building with three sunlit rooms containing a range of nature-themed information. My kids always start at the interactive river table, tucked away in the back of the building. Here, budding engineers can construct a town with homes, motorhomes, and bridges, and then re-create the area's infamous flood!

In June of 1965, a wall of water a mile wide and 20 feet high surged through the South Platte River Basin, leveling houses and washing away fourteen bridges. It was one of the worst natural disasters in Denver's history. The flood prompted the Army Corps of Engineers to build the Chatfield Dam and Reservoir. South Platte Park, though, was a deviation from the original hazard plan. The natural area preserves the

floodplain, and even today its primary purpose is to absorb water, though outdoor recreation is certainly a nice bonus.

After visiting the river table, retreat to the nature center's main rooms to view dioramas showing local animals such as bobcats, beavers, and a great blue heron in their habitats. The nature center is also home to warm- and cold-water fish plus native reptiles, amphibians, and crayfish. The expansive wooden deck behind the building overlooks a variety of bird feeders drawing in goldfinches, hummingbirds, red-winged blackbirds, and white-crowned sparrows, among many other species. Enjoy a snack on the deck, then meander to the river, where you can always find signs of local wildlife, including deer, coyotes, and beavers. In addition to mallards, the nearby river is home to twenty-three different kinds of ducks.

The Mary Carter Greenway is popular among bikers, but hikers and runners also use the paved trail. To reach it, follow the gravel path extending from Carson Nature Center toward the river. Look left to discover a metal flood sculpture that shows how high the water rose in 1965. Past the sculpture, you'll come to a long bridge. To escape bike traffic, bear left onto the dirt trail preceding the bridge, and walk downhill toward a dirt singletrack trail meandering past several river access points.

LEARN

Carson Nature Center is a natural destination for anyone studying wildlife biology, mammals, birds, habitats, and/or ecosystems. The river table can enhance units on civil engineering and city planning.

- **Watch Wildlife: South Platte Park is one of the best places in Colorado to view wildlife because the riparian habitat is located in a transition zone, making it extremely biodiverse. Over 300 animal species visit annually. Early mornings and late afternoons are always the best times to look for wildlife. Pack a science notebook and field guide, and encourage budding biologists to identify and record any animals they discover. While younger children should focus on species, older kids can learn more about animal classification by including information on domain, kingdom, phylum, class, order, family, and genus. If you don't own a field guide, free wildlife lists are available inside Carson Nature Center.**
- **Do Your Homework: Back home, you and your children can learn more about the South Platte Flood of 1965. Colorado Encyclopedia is a great online resource, and several books are available at public libraries in the Denver area.**

9 Castlewood Canyon State Park

Learn about civil engineering while you hike through history.

Cost: Daily vehicle pass required to enter Colorado state parks, or purchase a Colorado Parks & Wildlife annual parks pass
Hours: Open daily from sunrise to sunset; park gates locked promptly at sunset
Location: 2989 South Highway 83
Nearest Town: Franktown
Denver Drive Time: 50 minutes via I-25 to East State Highway 86
Accessibility: The park's paved Canyon View Nature Trail (near the visitor center) is wheelchair and stroller accessible, and the Castlewood Canyon Visitor Center is ADA compliant. While the site doesn't host specific low-sensory hours/days, the park is usually very quiet on weekdays and in the early morning.
Bathrooms: Flush toilets available inside the visitor center; vault toilets near the Lake Gulch Trailhead. During the summer there are flush toilets at Canyon Point; in the winter, vault toilets are available.
Gear Suggestions: Comfortable waterproof hiking shoes, sunscreen, sunglasses, a hat, windbreakers, binoculars, plenty of water, snacks
Insider Tip: Before or after your hike, be sure to swing by the Castlewood Canyon Visitor Center, situated off the parking lot just past the park's main (east) entrance. The building houses a small museum with exhibits and a video recreating the dramatic flood of August 3, 1933.

Explore

Remember the time Denver was submerged by 4 feet of standing water? (Neither did we!) The second-worst flood in the city's history started in 1933, at Castlewood Dam. Families can hike to the ruins of the massive dam when visiting Castlewood Canyon State Park, a 2,636-acre space preserving an ecologically unique area known as the Black Forest. In addition to its unusual history, Castlewood Canyon contains several hiking trails that wind past a waterfall, homesteading ruins, and spectacular geological formations.

First things first: There are two entrances into Castlewood Canyon. Both have trails leading to the dam ruins, but we prefer to enter via the park's main (east) entrance, where facilities include a visitor center, flush toilets, and picnic areas.

Because it's hidden in the plains—away from Colorado's mountains—outdoors enthusiasts often overlook Castlewood Canyon. As a result, families who do venture out to Franktown are greeted with a quiet network of easy-to-moderate hiking trails. To circle past the ruins with your children, start at the Lake Gulch Trailhead bulletin board, and combine the Lake Gulch and Inner Canyon Trails to make a 2.2-mile lollipop. Lake Gulch Trail is easy to follow, but it's a good idea to grab a trail map at the visitor center before heading out.

As you follow the flat trail, stop to read interpretive signs about the land's geological history. After squeezing through two boulders and crossing Cherry Creek, follow

the sandy singletrack uphill to a three-way trail intersection. You'll turn left here to visit the dam ruins.

Castlewood Dam was built in 1890 to provide irrigation for the agricultural development of Douglas County. Its foundation was poor, though, and in August of 1933, the dam collapsed, sending a massive 15-foot-high wall of water through Denver. The disaster ultimately led to the construction of the Cherry Creek Dam and Reservoir.

Take your time exploring the dam ruins and surrounding area. Slightly north of the dam, you'll discover a waterfall. But don't build this up too much for your kids: It really only runs when there's been substantial rain.

Families craving a bigger adventure can combine the Creek Bottom and Rim Rock Trails to create another loop, adding an additional 4.2 miles of difficult hiking to the Lake Gulch and Inner Canyon route described above. Or when you're finished at the dam, simply backtrack to the three-way trail intersection near Cherry Creek, and this time continue straight through the juncture to take Inner Canyon Trail back to the place where you started. Over the next half mile, you'll cross several wooden bridges, climb stairs, and pass some very interesting rock formations. When the dirt trail becomes a sidewalk, you're on the Canyon View Nature Trail, a stroller-friendly and wheelchair-accessible path leading to the very scenic Bridge Canyon Overlook.

LEARN

If you hiked to the Castlewood Dam and read the interpretive signs, then you already got a good dose of history. Why not spend some time studying dams with your young engineers?

- **If You Build It: Back home, watch the PBS *Science Trek* episode on dams, then ask your kids to create their own backyard dams using a garden hose, water containers (buckets, bottles, cups, et cetera), digging tools, sticks, rocks, bricks, and whatever else is available to block running water. If you get a chance to visit the Mordecai Children's Garden at Denver Botanic Gardens York Street (see chapter 20), your children can continue their exploration while damming up Springmelt Stream.**
- **Water Footprint: When constructing dams, civil engineers need to know exactly how much water demand their design must meet. Round out your dam curriculum by learning more about Denver's per capita water usage at History Colorado Center, 1200 Broadway in Denver, where a fascinating exhibit with a Water Footprint Calculator helps put modern-day water usage into perspective. Feeling inspired? National Geographic's website has tons of water conservation facts and tips for families.**

10 Centennial Center Park

Uncover interesting facts about Colorado as you play in this must-visit park.

Cost: Free
Hours: May 1 through Oct 31 daily 5 a.m. to 10 p.m.; Water Play hours Memorial Day through Labor Day 10 a.m. to 8 p.m. Park hours Nov 1 through Apr 30 6 a.m. to 8 p.m.
Location: 13050 E. Peakview Avenue
Nearest Town: Centennial
Denver Drive Time: 25 minutes via I-25 South
Accessibility: ADA-compliant paved trail and restrooms
Bathrooms: Flush toilets and sinks throughout
Gear Suggestions: Sturdy walking-playing shoes, swimsuit and a change of dry clothes, picnic blanket or beach towels
Insider Tip: Search for "Centennial Center Park Event Documents" on the website, at centennialco.gov, and look for the Park Activity Book. Download this booklet for coloring and connect-the-dots pages and a list of trivia questions to enhance your visit to the park.

Explore

If you happen to find yourself in the area near I-25 and Arapahoe Road with the kids, take the exit and head east about 10 minutes to South Vaughn Way. You'll know you've arrived when you see the Centennial Civic Center on your left. Take that left turn. Just behind and to the west of the building—though you won't see much of it from the street—is one of the metro area's most cleverly designed parks.

Spanning 11 acres, Centennial Center Park encompasses an 8,000-square-foot sunken playground complex where kids can do all the things kids love to do: Climb, swing, dig in the sand, and cool off in a splash pad. The splash pad was named fifth best in the nation in *USA Today*'s 10 Best Reader's Choice 2023. While the kiddos play in the water, busy parents get a chance to do what they *need* to do: Roll out a blanket on a shaded stretch of artificial turf and rest. It will (almost) feel like a beach day.

Even if the kids are playing outside of the water, there are plenty of shaded benches and picnic tables throughout the park where parents can sit and still keep a close eye on

the kids. And, because the designers of the park thought of everything, you can also tap into free Wi-Fi from the picnic pavilions.

But this park has more than play features. Fun, interactive activities spread throughout the park engage kids in lessons about the history and character of Colorado. You may not realize it at first, but if you look high and low at nearly every aspect of this park, it will reveal something about the Centennial State.

When you arrive, park in the large lot on the east side of the park—there are plenty of spaces—and enter through the stone-pillar gateway. This park is full of cleverly incorporated surprises, starting with the shadows made by metal overhangs on top of the pillars. When the sun passes over the overhangs, a nature scene appears on the sidewalk below. And that's just the beginning. As you stand and survey the kids-on-the-loose–style playground complex, the first element of the "Viewfinder Walk" is at the top of the stairs. The park was designed with a number of educational features, including three blue viewfinders that challenge kids with Colorado trivia questions. Read the question, look through the viewfinder, and go in search of the answer hidden somewhere in the park. Clues to help you find the answer—and the next stop on the walk—reveal themselves as you read.

Next, follow the "Colorado Statehood Walk" by searching for imposing vertical boulders imprinted with the word "Colorado." Search around the stones to uncover

Colorado's iconic state symbols. Travel the trail to find them all, and don't forget to search the playground complex and amphitheater.

At this point, the kids may have already disappeared into the balance ropes or headed down the 22-foot slide that dips into the play area. The playground features a multilevel fort, climbing web, swings, and three climbing walls, including a 15-foot-tall scalable relief map of Colorado. Go down the stairs and follow the path to find the play area for kids 2 to 5 years old, the splash pad, main plaza, and bathrooms. A short trail on the south side of the park winds past three quieter play zones, away from the noise and activity of the playground.

To wind down the day, follow the paved trails around the park for blooming gardens full of flowering Colorado plants, a xeriscape garden, and the grassy amphitheater. The tree-shaded trail around the amphitheater follows another educational path, this one dedicated to the four periods of human history in Colorado.

Phew! Everywhere you turn in this park there is something to play with and something to learn. To wrap up your visit, head back to the main plaza and look for the gravel path and steps that lead to the top of a butte. It's a simple climb up to a sweeping view of the park, the Lone Tree Creek, and the mountains.

LEARN

Yes, play like crazy at Centennial Center Park! But also delve into the creative ways it incorporates discovery and learning.

- **Pick Your Own Signature Symbols: Centennial Center Park highlights many of Colorado's official symbols throughout its Colorado Statehood Walk: state flower, state mineral, state fish. Ask kids to think about what symbols they would use to represent themselves (for very little kids, ask them about their "favorites"). What is Mason's official song or Helen's official food? What about an official color, animal, flower, or sport? Kids could even create their own personal flag; what colors and symbols would they incorporate? Ask kids to draw and color their signature items on a poster or use a variety of arts-and-crafts supplies to create a display. Talk about why they chose their symbols.**
- **Craft a Discovery Walk: It's easy to elevate a neighborhood walk with clues that lead you along the way. First pick a fun final destination—a favorite park or interesting tree—then lay out a mystery route with a number of identifiable landmarks. To guide children along the walk, write clues to unravel that will take them to each landmark and the final destination.**

11 Centennial Village Museum

Step back in time at Greeley's living history museum.

Cost: $ Discounted rates available for families and SNAP and EBT cardholders
Hours: Open Fri–Sat only, 10 a.m. to 4 p.m., typically from Memorial Day through Labor Day. For annual operating hours, visit the museum's website, greeleymuseums.com/locations/centennial-village/.
Location: 1475 A Street
Nearest Town: Greeley
Denver Drive Time: 75 minutes via I-25 to US 34
Accessibility: The site accommodates strollers and is largely accessible, with ADA-compliant bathrooms and ramps to most buildings, though some historic buildings are a little cramped with a wheelchair. A dial-in audio tour is available for those with visual impairments.
Bathrooms: Flush toilets located throughout the site
Gear Suggestions: Comfortable walking shoes, sunscreen, a hat and sunglasses, plenty of water, snacks (but note that eating and drinking are not permitted inside historic buildings)
Insider Tip: In the spring, prior to the summer season, keep an eye out for Baby Animal Days, when 4-H youth bring in newborn animals for museumgoers to see. Animal lovers can return in early August for the museum's annual Pets 'n' Popsicles event, when kids are invited to visit with the site's furry personnel.

Explore

Sorry, but we're suckers for living history experiences. There's something fascinating, nostalgic, and totally magical about stepping back in time and seeing how previous generations lived. That's exactly what awaits families on the south side of Island Grove Regional Park (don't miss the park's giant new playground) at Centennial Village Museum. The charming, 8-acre village transports visitors to Weld County, Colorado, circa the turn of the century, when settlers were busy staking claims on western land and building homes and businesses on the high plains.

Groups of ten or more can schedule a guided tour of the village, but with kids in tow, self-paced exploration might be more enjoyable. That's easy to do thanks to interpretive panels scattered throughout the site plus a dial-in audio tour (dial in from your cell phone upon arrival; English and Spanish available).

Start your journey at Selma's Store, where you can check in, grab a map, and inquire about the day's demonstrations and activities, ranging from printmaking at the High Plains Post to blacksmithing and chuck wagon cooking. Activities aren't listed online in advance, so you'll just have to show up and see what's happening on the day of your visit. The element of surprise is all part of the fun.

One thing you can count on: Volunteer docents and professional staff interpreters will be decked out in full period attire, giving children the unique experience of interacting with historical figures as they go about their "daily lives," doing tasks such

as shucking corn or cutting timber. Have your camera handy: There are tons of great photo opportunities throughout the village.

Wide sidewalks connect several dozen historic structures, and you'll walk a little more than a mile while visiting some of Weld County's oldest, most distinct buildings, including the original Weld County courthouse (a log cabin built in 1861) and the 1917 Weld Centennial Church. The village's eastern area celebrates Weld County's diverse immigrant stories, with a Swedish American *stuga* (cottage), German Russian shanty, and Spanish colony house, showing that people came from all over the world to live and work in northeastern Colorado.

Don't miss Rattlesnake Kate's house; it's a real crowd-pleaser, complete with a replica of her famous snakeskin dress. Psst: You can see Kate's real dress at Greeley History Museum, 714 8th Street, along with her rattlesnake shoes and accessories.

Farm animals appear throughout the Centennial Village Museum, and guests can interact with ducks, chicks, pigs, rabbits, and goats. Other kid-approved highlights include the fire station, with its 1921 American LaFrance chain-driven fire engine, and an on-site, nonoperational trolley. On a warm summer day, there's something so satisfying about slowing down to watch your children make corn-husk dolls and laugh as they attempt to do laundry on a scrub board.

LEARN

This is the place to learn about Colorado state history, westward expansion, and immigration. Here are a few ways to enhance your academic adventure.

- **Family Roots: Centennial Village Museum celebrates all of the people who called northeast Colorado home at the turn of the century. Were any of your distant relatives indigenous Americans or immigrants from Sweden, Spain, Germany, or eastern Europe? If you have a personal connection, why not spend time learning more about immigration? A librarian at your local public library can help find books about your heritage, and History Colorado Center in downtown Denver has a fantastic exhibit on the immigrant experience in Colorado. To take this further, work with your kids to create a family tree.**
- **Home on the Range: Back home, extend the experience by partaking in some bygone homesteading tasks. Bake a loaf of bread with your kids, and while the dough's rising, try churning butter. You could also do a load of laundry the old-fashioned way, washing clothes by hand in a bucket, then hanging them to dry in the sun. At the very least, your children will walk away with a better appreciation for modern conveniences.**

12 Chamberlin Observatory

Gaze at the stars from this urban observatory.

Cost: $ For Public Night and Open House events
Hours: Only open to the public during Denver Astronomical Society events. Visit the DAS website at www.denverastro.org for event dates and details.
Location: Observatory Park, 2930 East Warren Avenue
Nearest Town: Denver
Denver Drive Time: 15 minutes via I-25
Accessibility: The historic observatory tour is not accessible for wheelchairs, but paved sidewalks lead to the front of the observatory where the south lawn viewing party is held during Open House events.
Bathrooms: Use the park restrooms (ADA compliant) near the corner of the playground, at South Fillmore Street and East Warren Avenue. Restroom inside the observatory open during Open Houses and Public Nights, but it is not wheelchair accessible.
Gear Suggestions: Dress for the weather during events. If you have a telescope, bring it to open houses.
Insider Tip: The quiet, historic park around the observatory, appropriately called Observatory Park, makes a pleasant place for a picnic under the shady trees while kids play on the playground equipment.

Explore

A distinguished 130+-year-old red sandstone building resting in a quiet University of Denver neighborhood hardly seems like an attraction for the kids, but it's what's inside this building—and what happens around it once a month—that makes it an interesting family spot.

Beneath the silvery dome of the Chamberlin Observatory is a historic 26-foot-long telescope with a 20-inch diameter doublet lens aimed at the night sky. It's primed to give visitors a window into space. Though the observatory, which is owned by the University of Denver, is not generally open to the public, special events hosted by the Denver Astronomical Society (DAS) give families a chance to step inside. Public Nights on Tuesday and Thursday invite the general public to view a multimedia presentation, glimpse Victorian details throughout the building, and look through the telescope. The only restriction is that children must be at least 42 inches tall to stand on the platform—accessed by a ladder—and look through the historic telescope. Public Night events require a reservation—and can sell out months in advance—so keep an eye on the DAS calendar of events at denverastro.org for open dates.

Once a month, on the Saturday closest to the first-quarter Moon, DAS hosts an open house at Chamberlin with a chance for visitors to tour the observatory and look through the telescope. The very first group of visitors looked through "Denver's Great Telescope" in August of 1894, when there was little more in the area than the observatory itself. As you walk around the main floor of the observatory, look for

the small photo of the University of Denver campus from 1894. You'll glimpse the neighborhood at the turn of the century.

Perhaps the most exciting part of the monthly Open House event is the viewing party that assembles on the south lawn of the observatory. Members of the DAS set up their telescopes and invite the public to have a look at the night sky. Take the opportunity to chat them up about their equipment and passion for astronomy. Families are encouraged to bring the kids for a chance to ask questions. If you have a telescope of your own, or one that is new to you, come early and DAS members will surely help you use it. Setup for this event starts before dusk, but the stars of the show (usually included in the name of each month's event) are visible later in the evening, so dress for the evening weather and make this an up-past-bedtime treat. Early birds will still get a glimpse of the moon and often one or more of the brighter planets, such as Jupiter, through member telescopes, at dusk. Another note about weather: Looking through the telescopes (and actually seeing anything) is weather dependent. Mostly clear nights are best.

The Denver Astronomical Society also lists star party events for Standley Lake Stargazing, which hosts their own Summer Stargazing Series each Friday night in outdoor locations around Arvada.

LEARN

Wide-eyed from a close-up glimpse of the moon's surface or a distant planet, kids are revved up to dig deeper into space. Don't miss the opportunity to turn their wonder into learning moments with these stellar activities.

- **Keep a Moon Journal: Even very young children may notice how the moon changes throughout the month. To learn more about the phases of this harbinger of bedtime, ask the children to draw the shape of the moon throughout the month. Add notes about its brightness and locations in the sky. Write the date next to each drawing, then watch how the shape changes as the month passes by. Search online for NASA's lunar phases to learn the difference between your waxing crescent and waning gibbous.**
- **Visit a Dark Sky Location: Colorado is home to a number of International Dark Sky Parks and Communities; find lists of all the locations at darksky.org. These places have minimal artificial light polluting the sky, which allows humans to see more stars with just the naked eye. Seek out one of Colorado's Dark Sky Places for a visit—Florissant Fossil Beds National Monument (see chapter 28) is just an hour from Colorado Springs. Plan to stay up and view the night sky. Many of the Dark Sky Parks host guided Night Sky programs.**

13 Colorado Railroad Museum

Dip into Colorado's rich railroad history at this wonderful outdoor museum.

Cost: $$ Children 2 and under free
Hours: Open Tues–Sun from 9 a.m. to 5 p.m. Closed Mon and for some holidays, including Thanksgiving, Christmas, and New Year's Eve and Day.
Location: 17155 West 44th Avenue
Nearest Town: Golden
Denver Drive Time: 25 minutes via I-70
Accessibility: The museum's paved paths are wheelchair accessible and stroller friendly, and service animals are welcome for guests with special needs.
Bathrooms: Flush toilets located in the Depot entrance building; accessible restrooms inside the Museum Library
Gear Suggestions: Comfortable walking shoes, sunscreen, sunglasses, a hat, plenty of water, snacks to enjoy at one of the picnic benches dotting the railyard
Insider Tip: Don't miss out on this museum's special events. Every September, Thomas the Tank Engine rolls into the railyard for three weekends, offering young children an opportunity to take an interactive train ride with a life-size Thomas the Tank Engine. In May board the Dinosaur Express Train to follow dinosaur tracks around the railyard while riding a coal-fired steam locomotive. And for those looking to add extra oomph to the winter holidays, there's The Polar Express Train Ride, a sell-out, three-part extravaganza that brings the beloved children's book to life with theatrics, piping hot cocoa, and one seriously magical ride.

Explore

All aboard! The size of the equipment, the sounds of the trains—there's just something about a railyard that kids of all ages will usually connect with. Nestled inside the scenic town of Golden, Colorado Railroad Museum is all about preserving the state's rich railroad history. After opening its doors in Alamosa in the early 1950s with only a few pieces of equipment, the museum relocated to Golden in 1959 and expanded to include more than one hundred pieces of historic equipment. Today visitors will find narrow- and standard-gauge steam and diesel locomotives along with passenger cars and cabooses, all packed into a 15-acre railyard at the base of North Table Mountain.

Colorado Railroad Museum is one of only a few locations in the country currently operating steam locomotives, and the nonprofit organization maintains a fleet of four operational diesel locomotives. Train rides aboard vintage coaches and open-air excursion cars are available throughout the year, and special "Galloping Goose" motorcars are also operated on select weekdays. Train tickets can be purchased online or at the Depot. In addition to riding passenger cars from various eras, children can also jump inside stationary cabooses and blow the bells on some of the engines. Several cars are furnished with period furniture, appliances, and human figures positioned to depict those bygone days of rail travel.

When the ride's over, swing by the Roundhouse, a restoration facility where curious kiddos can watch experts tinker on trains. There's even a working turntable. From the Roundhouse, backtrack to the Depot, but be sure to stop to admire the Denver Garden Railway Society's model train layout. Between historic engines, kids will discover operating G-gauge model trains (weather and volunteer staff permitting). For those who don't know the model train lingo, G-gauge is the largest scale offered for model trains, and the size is ideal for outdoor use and children.

Back at the Depot, peruse a rotating lineup of exhibits to learn all about Rocky Mountain railroad heritage. There are two primary galleries that typically host three or four exhibits at a time; current and upcoming schedules are listed online at coloradorailroadmuseum.org. There's also a renowned research library containing rare archives, maps, and publications.

Don't forget to pop downstairs before you go: The Depot's lower level features miniature train sets from the Denver HO Model Railroad Club, and the layout is extensive. If your kids dig the model trains, help them make their own back home out of recycled egg cartons. Simply cut a row from the bottom of a paper egg carton, then let your child paint the "cars" one or more colors of their choosing. You can even embellish the train by adding wheels, and use miniature animals or figurines for passengers.

LEARN

Whether your child is learning about transportation, Colorado state history, or westward expansion, a trip to the Colorado Railroad Museum will bring classroom lessons to life.

- **Dramatic Play: Back home, line up several chairs in the living room, and play "train" with your toddler or preschooler. Older kids can help make and collect pretend tickets, and you can ask all participants where they're going and why.**
- **Book It: There's no shortage of picture books about trains, so be sure to head to your local library to check out a few themed stories. Golden Library is one of our favorite Jefferson County libraries. But if you're visiting the Colorado Railroad Museum with children ages 4 to 6, chug-a-choo to the organization's monthly Story Time & Craft. Check online for specific dates and times. In addition to being an in-person event, the story and craft are read and explained in a monthly video available through the Colorado Railroad Museum's YouTube channel.**

14 Colorado Wolf and Wildlife Center

Howl at the moon with your wolf pack.

Cost: $$$
Hours: Open Tues–Sun for guided tours only
Location: 4729 Twin Rocks Road
Nearest Town: Divide
Denver Drive Time: 105 minutes via I-25 to US 24
Accessibility: The site's pea gravel walkway would be difficult with a standard wheelchair or stroller. For those with mobility differences, golf cart tours are available in the summer months only. If you're visiting with an infant or toddler, consider using a baby carrier.
Bathrooms: Pit toilets past the visitor center
Gear Suggestions: Binoculars, a coat or windbreaker, sunscreen, a hat, plenty of water, a picnic lunch to enjoy post-tour. Sturdy, closed-toed shoes are highly recommended during tours.
Insider Tip: For a hair-raising adventure, don't miss Howl-O-Ween in October, when the center is all decked out for the holiday, and guides lead haunted tours. Or show up with your flashlight for a longer Full Moon Tour, hosted once a month on the Saturday closest to the full moon. Full Moon Tours start with refreshments and end with a nighttime hike to Chinook's Nature Trail, where Darlene Kobobel tells the story of how she founded the center.

Explore

Now's your chance to get up close and personal with some of the country's most misunderstood mammals. Back in 1993 Darlene Kobobel founded this sanctuary for rescued wolves and wolf hybrids that cannot live in the wild. The whole idea was to educate other animal lovers in a fun and interactive way. That mission continues to be accomplished through guided walking tours delivered by knowledgeable staff.

You'll catch your first glimpses of the wolves from the parking lot, as you descend a wide path toward the visitor center, where you can check in for your tour. Come a little early to view on-site foxes scurrying about in their habitats. Inside the gift shop, look for a kid-friendly "conservation corner" stocked with information on endangered wildlife plus Canidae skulls.

In order to walk with the wolves, you'll need to book—in advance, at wolf education.org—an hour-long tour that'll take your family through a series of 2- to 3-acre habitats constructed with native plants, trees, and rock formations. Standard tours take off at 10 a.m., noon, 2 p.m., and 4 p.m. in the summer months. After a brief history lesson, you'll follow your guide right up to the enclosure fences, where you'll get close enough to the wolves to smell their breath as they eat treats (mostly raw meat) out of your guide's hand.

While walking along a square-shaped trail system, ask children to count how many wolves they spy, and look for coyotes, too, along with red foxes and swift foxes. The whole time your guide will be spouting off fun, lesser-known tidbits about the animals.

Did you know that timber wolves are marathon runners? And the concept of an "alpha" is total bunk? Participants also learn that every wolf has a unique howl, and most visitors get to hear that fact firsthand during a guide-prompted, end-of-tour wolf howl-back, which is most children's favorite part of the adventure.

Longer 75-minute Feeding Tours (all ages welcome) are another option for those who'd like to see the wolves when they're most active, during dinnertime. And if you want to dig even deeper with your adolescent or teen, book a 20-minute Meet & Greet Encounter, an add-on experience that lets visitors walk into the enclosures of wolves (18 and up), coydogs (16 and up), and foxes (13 and up). Younger kids get a more intimate experience during one of the center's special tours for kids. Held one Saturday a month for ages 6 to 12, these tours follow the format of a standard tour while incorporating educational activities that let youth experience what it's like to be a wildlife biologist.

LEARN

For youth who are interested in animals, mammals, and/or apex predators, few experiences rival the opportunity to walk among Colorado wolves. Level up with one of the following activities.

- **Bust Myths: It's a myth that wolves howl at the moon. In fact, wolves aren't even nocturnal! They're crepuscular, meaning they're most active at dawn and dusk and generally sleep through the night. Like many animals, though, wolves can become hyperactive during a full moon, when they're able to take advantage of the extra light to hunt for food. Track the phases of the moon with your children for a month, and on the next full moon, go for a flashlight walk in your neighborhood, looking and listening for animals who might be out past bedtime. Permission granted to howl if you please. And remember, never hike on a trail between dusk and dawn. For more information about wolves and the myths they've inspired, check out Jamie's book *Mythbusting the Great Outdoors: What's True and What's Not?***
- **Reimagine the Classics: From *Little Red Riding Hood* to *The Three Little Pigs*, there's no shortage of children's books casting wolves as the bad guy. Read through a few of the classics, then ask your kids to evaluate these fictional stories in light of what they learned on their tour. Finally, see if your kids can rewrite one of their favorite age-old tales using their newfound knowledge of wolves.**

15 Coyote Ridge Natural Area

A special "Hidden Clues" trail makes this natural area extra fun for younger kids.

Cost: Free
Hours: Open daily 5 a.m. to 11 p.m.
Location: At the intersection of Taft Hill and Spring Mesa Roads
Nearest Town: Fort Collins
Denver Drive Time: 65 minutes via I-25
Accessibility: The dirt trail can accommodate a good jogging stroller. The interpretive loop found about a mile into the site is wheelchair accessible, and rangers will make arrangements for those with limited mobility to have vehicle access to the accessible trail loop. Call (970) 416-2815 or email naturalareas@fcgov.com for details.
Bathrooms: An outhouse is available near the cabin, about 1 mile into the hike.
Gear Suggestions: Sunscreen, sun-protective clothing, brimmed hats, sunglasses, binoculars, Rocky Mountain flora and/or fauna guidebook, a notebook and writing utensils, plenty of water, snacks or a picnic
Insider Tip: June through October the City of Fort Collins hosts a series of free educational activities and events; an event calendar is available at engage.fcgov.com/d/na. We recommend returning to Coyote Ridge Natural Area in the fall, with a flashlight, for Campfires at Coyote Ridge, a family-friendly program that includes a 30-minute guided hike along an unpaved trail, plus campfire stories and s'mores. Families with kids ages 16 and up might enjoy a Full Moon Walk. Offered near the full moon, when the area is bright with natural light, this special event includes a 2-mile-long interpretive hike.

Explore

If you're used to hiking in Boulder or Summit County, it might feel like you've left the state while gazing across the eastern plains in Coyote Ridge Natural Area. This welcoming nature preserve offers 2.2 miles of well-marked trail accessible from a parking lot on the west side of Taft Hill Road, just 10 miles south of Old Town Fort Collins.

For families with young children, the main event is a 0.25-mile "Hidden Clues" trail featuring a series of interactive panels that encourage children to sharpen their senses by detecting objects, sights, and smells they might otherwise miss. But you'll have to commit to a 2-mile out-and-back hike to reach this gem.

With a big "Welcome" sign, the parking lot servicing Coyote Ridge Natural Area is hard to miss. (If you're driving from Denver and you get to Harmony Road, you went too far.) The lot is spacious, but this natural area is a popular destination, so we recommend heading out early to secure a parking spot. If there aren't any available when you arrive, don't park in the horse trailer spaces, undesignated parking areas, or along Taft Hill Road. Wait for another group to leave, or have an alternate destination in mind.

From the Coyote Ridge Trailhead and "Welcome" sign, it's a straight shot into the natural area down a wide dirt-and-gravel path. Coyote Ridge's sole trail passes

through a broad meadow and montane shrubland of rabbitbrush, mountain mahogany, and three-leaf sumac.

During an easy, mile-long ascent toward the Hidden Clues Trail, you're liable to spy burrowing owls and plenty of prairie dogs. The rodents make their tunnels within an arm's length of the trail, and their abandoned tunnels provide habitat for tiny, spindly legged burrowing owls. With their mottled brown feathers, burrowing owls can be camouflaged in the prairie. Now's the time to get out those binoculars, and if you really want to up your odds of seeing an owl, arrive at dawn. Even if they don't spot an owl, your children will likely hear the bird's soft coo-coo and cackling calls. Familiarize yourselves with the calls before your visit by listening to samples on YouTube.

Coyote Ridge Trail rises up a hogback to an interpretive sign about snakes and other local wildlife. Read the sign, and always be rattlesnake aware, especially on a

THERE'S AN APP FOR THAT!

We're all for screen-free play, but sometimes technology really can enhance an outdoor experience. Agents of Discovery is a free educational gaming platform that encourages kids to explore the outdoors while solving educational challenges. To get started, download the Agents of Discovery app to your device, then search for the Natural Areas mission titled: "Celebrate 30 Years of Natural Areas." You can preload this mission before visiting Coyote Ridge Natural Area. Once you've reached the site, your kids can start completing their mission.

sunny trail like this one. Coyote Ridge is an important wildlife corridor, so you're likely to observe mule deer while you hike. Your kids might also spy coyotes, lizards, rabbits, deer mice, and foxes.

Down the trail, look for another interpretive sign with information on the area's prehistoric significance. This whole place was once submerged in water, and the hogbacks you're viewing were created from ocean deposits raised from sea level during the uplift of the Rocky Mountains about 65 million years ago. Some of the site's rocks still have fossils in them, and young paleontologists might try to find some during water breaks.

If your kids need it, there's an outhouse about a mile into the route. There's a water pump, too, but the water's not potable, so don't plan to refill your bottles here. You'll see a large cabin just past the outhouse; its shaded deck is the perfect place for a picnic lunch.

When you're ready, take a lap (or two!) around the Hidden Clues Trail. This short, interpretive loop encourages children to become "nature detectives" by observing their surroundings. This is a great time to bust out the nature journals and pens and pencils, and ask kids to spend some time recording their beautiful surroundings.

LEARN

From geology and natural history to wildlife biology, there's plenty to gain at this wonderful natural area.

- **Write On: In fact, many children lose significant ground in writing over long school breaks. Combat that by giving your kids plenty of opportunities to write. We love the way the Hidden Clues Trail at Coyote Ridge Natural Area puts kids in tune with undercover aspects of their everyday surroundings. Post-hike, ask your children to be nature detectives in their own neighborhood, jotting down notes about anything they hadn't noticed before. Ask them to use their notes to write a paragraph or short essay about anything special they unearthed.**
- **Keep Exploring: The quirky Fort Collins Museum of Discovery, 408 Mason Court, houses the Natural Areas Visitor Center in its lobby. There's a fee to enter the museum, but the visitor center is free and contains an interactive map and live black-footed-ferret exhibit.**

16 CSU Spur

See STEAM careers in action at this satellite CSU Campus.

Cost: Free
Hours: Mon–Fri 9 a.m. to 5 p.m., second Sat of every month 10 a.m. to 3 p.m. Closed Sun.
Location: 4777 National Western Drive
Nearest Town: Denver
Denver Drive Time: 15 minutes, via I-25 North and I-70 East
Accessibility: Numerous elevators in all three buildings make them easily accessible for wheelchairs and strollers.
Bathrooms: Full restrooms on each floor, gender-neutral restrooms, and designated lactating rooms. Water fountains include water bottle refill stations.
Gear Suggestions: No special gear needed, but comfortable walking shoes will keep everyone's feet happy as you explore the buildings.
Insider Tip: The CSU Spur campus is filled with enticing art installations. In Vida's lobby, step up to the 9-foot kitten known as Esperanza (which means "hope" in Spanish), and don't be surprised if you hear purring. The interactive art installation is more than adorable; it also gives visitors a lesson on the appropriate way to interact with a cat. Approach from the front and Esperanza purrs and meows. Watch out, though: If you stand behind her, she will warn you with a hiss and growl.

Explore

Denverites may recognize this location as home to the National Western Complex, a place many visit only once a year in January for the National Western Stock Show. However, a collaboration between the City of Denver, Colorado State University, and the National Western Stock Show brought CSU Spur to the neighborhood to create an educational destination that is accessible to as many families as possible. It brings new life, and families, to this underutilized area of the city with its interactive displays, rooftop gardens, and a chance to see veterinarians in action.

Spread across three themed buildings, CSU Spur engages the whole family in an exploration of various STEAM (science, technology, engineering, art, math) topics and careers. Terra connects visitors to growing things and plants, Hydro teaches about the water we depend on, and Vida includes a working veterinary clinic and equine rehabilitation center to focus on health.

Kids will have opportunities to get hands-on with interactive exhibits in each building. They'll also see scientists at work in labs surrounded by large viewing windows. The labs in Hydro and Terra aren't active every day, but you can still look through the glass for a glimpse at the equipment. If it's your first visit to CSU Spur, start at the information desk in the lobby of each building. Helpful staff have the lowdown on what is happening in the building that day.

It's really up to your child's interests, but we like to start in the Terra building. As you go up each floor, follow the story of the food we eat, from field to table, through

hands-on displays. At the top of Terra, delight the kids with a visit to a garden on top of a building. On a pretty day, take in the view of downtown Denver from four stories up. Now head back to the third floor to cross the bridge to Hydro.

As you explore the buildings, keep your eyes open for learning opportunities. Even the art on the bridge connecting Hydro and Terra, called Rotation Index, has a scientific story. Hint: If the weather changes while you are on campus, go back to the bridge to see how Rotation Index has changed.

In Hydro check out the giant map of the South Platte River and its tributaries, play in the water table, and visit the Backyard to expend some energy outside before heading to Vida.

Plan to spend the most time in the Vida building. As home to the Dumb Friends League Veterinary Hospital at CSU Spur and the Temple Grandin Equine Center, there is generally something to watch each day, including live pet surgeries or horses in the arena or equine rehabilitation center (arrive early and ask a staff member about the best chance to see surgeries). Next, when your little one is ready to use their imagination, visit Vida's mock veterinary clinic, where plush animals are waiting in a replica vet's office for a checkup. As you walk back to the parking lot, you'll catch a glimpse of the horses boarded in the stables.

The very best day to see CSU Spur at its most lively is on the second Saturday of every month, when the buildings host special hands-on activities and demonstrations.

LEARN

Art can bring complex ideas and concepts to life. Use the creative art installations around CSU Spur to help kids understand the importance of art in communicating concepts they are studying.

- **Start an Exploration Journal: Gift each child with a compact exploration journal and encourage them to write and sketch as they visit new destinations.**
- **Create Themed Art: Keep an eye out for the largest living "green" wall, with more than 1,620 plants; take in a sweeping view of the mountains and downtown; and hunt down "The Bale" art installation on the campus. When you get home, challenge the kids to make art inspired by what they saw or something they learned during the visit, perhaps a clay model of an animal or a painting of their own dream rooftop garden.**

17 Dedisse Park at Evergreen Lake

Learn about wildlife while enjoying Evergreen's central lake.

Cost: Free, though some activities such as boating and skating require a fee
Hours: The park is open daily from dawn until dusk. Check the Evergreen Recreation website (evergreenrecreation.com) for current boating and skating hours.
Location: 29612 Upper Bear Creek Road. The site's first-come, first-served parking can be tricky. On weekends only you can avoid the chaos by using the overflow lot at Stagecoach Park, 3229 El Pinal Drive, at the intersection of Stagecoach Boulevard and CA 74. From here, ride a free shuttle to the Lake House.
Nearest Town: Evergreen
Denver Drive Time: 35 minutes via 6th Avenue and I-70
Accessibility: Portions of the trail ringing Evergreen Lake are wheelchair accessible. A good jogging stroller is recommended for this destination.
Bathrooms: Drop toilets in the parking lot servicing the Lake House; portable toilets stationed at various points throughout the park
Gear Suggestions: KEEN sandals or similar water shoes, sunscreen, a hat, sunglasses, plenty of water, snacks or a picnic to enjoy at one of the site's many tables. If you plan to cast a line, bring fishing gear and a valid Colorado fishing license (required for all anglers ages 16 and up).
Insider Tip: Hearing a male elk's loud, wailing call—its "bugle"—is a quintessential Colorado experience. If you don't have time to make it up to Estes Park this fall, you can listen to the bull elk bugle at Evergreen Lake. During the rut (i.e., mating season), typically mid-September through October, elk will travel in herds through Evergreen, often visiting the public golf course abutting Evergreen Lake. Elk are most active at twilight, so plan to recreate at Evergreen Lake Park in the late afternoon, then hang out in the parking lot as night falls. Make safety your family's top priority. Bull elk are very aggressive, especially during mating season. Always view elk from a safe distance, and never approach a wild animal.

Explore

Just half an hour from Denver, measuring in at 40 acres, Evergreen Lake is surely the heart and soul of its namesake town. It's also the perfect place for a quick retreat into nature.

There's no set schedule, per se, but if you visit Evergreen Lake with your kids on a weekend day in the summer, you're liable to bump into volunteers from Evergreen Audubon who come to the park regularly on Friday, Saturday, and Sunday with handouts, visuals, and supplies to aid in educating families on a variety of nature topics.

Volunteers from the group Wild Aware routinely stop by Evergreen Lake in the summer, too, to educate parkgoers on local wildlife, often sharing ways humans and animals can coexist. You might also find a Colorado Parks & Wildlife booth with volunteers fielding questions about fishing. Since there's no event calendar available for these volunteer-run offerings, you'll just have to embrace their impromptu nature.

Some activities can, of course, be planned in advance. Fishing is a popular year-round activity at Evergreen Lake. (Yes, year-round: You'll see plenty of folks ice-fishing through the winter!) Summer's a great time to cast a line from the shore—the water's stocked with trout and tiger muskies. Anglers 16 and up need a valid Colorado fishing license, and there's a five-fish limit for those planning to keep their catch.

Boating is another beloved pastime. SUPs and other wakeless vessels are allowed on Evergreen Lake, and from early May to mid-September, the Lake House rents canoes, paddleboats, kayaks, and sailboats. It's totally fine to BYO boat; just don't forget to pay the day-use fee before launching. All personal devices must be inspected at a can't-miss-it checkpoint on the east end of the Lake House parking lot.

Always call the Boating Hotline at (720) 880-1391 before visiting Evergreen Lake since all boating is subject to weather closure. While we're talking logistics, some activities at Evergreen Lake require a waiver. If you're planning to boat or skate, why not complete the waiver online before your trip? It's available on the Evergreen Parks & Recreation website, at evergreenrecreation.com. There's a lot to do at Evergreen Lake, but swimming isn't an option. The town's drinking water comes from Evergreen Lake, so it's important to respect local regulations and keep children and dogs out of the water.

LEARN

Whether your child is a budding biologist or simply loves animals, Evergreen Lake is a perfect place to learn more about wildlife while investigating a unique mountain ecosystem.

- **Visit a Nature Center: If you're familiar with Evergreen, then you might remember when the Evergreen Lake House harbored Evergreen Audubon's wonderful nature center. A few years ago, the conservation-focused society relocated to the Church of the Transfiguration campus (27640 Highway 74). If you have time to spare, swing by Evergreen Audubon's new digs to learn more about the Bear Creek Watershed's natural environment. In addition to a variety of bird and animal displays, this year-round destination features an irresistible "Touch Table" stocked with real animal furs and antlers. More information is available online at evergreenaudubon.org.**
- **Take a Closer Look: Active families can hike—well, it's more like a stroll—the flat, 1.4-mile paved trail ringing Evergreen Lake. The trail includes boardwalks hovering just above the water, perfect places for viewing small wildlife, including local bugs, while taking in majestic mountain views.**

18 Denver Audubon Kingery Nature Center

There's no better place in town to learn about birds than this low-key nature center.

Cost: Free, though some programs require a fee.
Hours: Trails are open daily 5 a.m. to 10 p.m. Kingery Nature Center is open for events and programs only.
Location: 11280 Waterton Road (just past the intersection with Platte Canyon Road)
Nearest Town: Littleton
Denver Drive Time: 40 minutes via Santa Fe Drive to CO 470
Accessibility: The trails directly behind Kingery Nature Center are wheelchair and stroller accessible, but the paths to the ponds require an all-terrain chair and/or jogging stroller. For those seeking a quiet, low-sensory experience, weekdays are generally the best times to explore, but check in advance to make sure there's no special event planned during your visit.
Bathrooms: Drop toilets past the nature center
Gear Suggestions: Comfortable walking shoes, sunscreen, sunglasses, a hat, windbreakers, binoculars, nature-journaling supplies, a Colorado bird guidebook and/or Rocky Mountain animal checklist, plenty of water, a picnic
Insider Tip: Bird banding is a one-of-a-kind opportunity for families to see wild birds up close while scientists study them. Denver Audubon's popular bird-banding station is open every April and May, when guests can sign up for time slots to watch staff and volunteers apply numbered bands to the legs of birds. In addition to seeing various species up close, you'll learn a lot about local birds during their session, and your kids might even be called upon to release a banded bird. The ongoing project helps scientists track species distribution and movements, annual production, life span, and causes of death. The event sells out, so sign up online (denveraudubon.org/nature-center) early if you'd like to participate.

Explore

Located on the outskirts of Chatfield State Park, the Kingery Nature Center is one of the National Audubon Society's important birding areas. On the grounds surrounding the site's modest nature center, families might encounter any number of the 280 bird species that live in or migrate through the area.

First things first: This destination can be a little tricky to find. Plug the nature center into Maps on your iPhone, and you might end up on the north side of Chatfield State Park, between CO 470 and Chatfield Lake. This is wrong. Use Google Maps to view an accurate route to 11280 Waterton Road. If you're on Wadsworth Boulevard, coming from Denver, the parking lot servicing the nature center will be on your left, immediately after the stoplight where Wadsworth Boulevard branches off into Waterton Road and Glen L. Martin Boulevard. Veer left onto Waterton Road, then turn onto the first road you see, a bumpy dirt path ending at Kingery Nature Center.

After parking, follow a winding dirt path toward a welcoming stone building. If your kids are up for birding, a good place to start is the small garden on the west side

of the nature center (the one facing the parking lot). Staff set up bird feeders in this area, and you're liable to spy dusty blue Woodhouse's scrub jay, agile white-breasted nuthatches, black-capped chickadees, and downy woodpeckers, with their telltale red spots. Resident birds also love the free meals, so keep an eye out for dark-eyed juncos, spotted towhees, and white-crowned sparrows, to name just a few.

On the other side of the nature center, look for the impressive Native Plant Garden, welcoming all sorts of local and migratory winged wildlife, from birds to butterflies and bees. In 2016 this special garden was designated as a Habitat Hero "Gold" Garden, which means that the extensive landscape of native plants gives sanctuary to a variety of Colorado wildlife by providing food, water, and shelter.

While the grounds surrounding the nature center are open year-round, Kingery Nature Center is only unlocked when staff are present. If the nature center's open during your visit, you're in luck. Pop inside to peruse a handful of wildlife exhibits, insect collections, birding books, and a bird-themed gift shop. If you arrive on a day when it's closed, don't fret. Most activities are accessed outdoors.

In addition to interpretive signs about native plants and wildlife, kids can explore a flat riparian trail system extending past the nature center and leading to two ponds. Bring binoculars and a field guide to Colorado birds. Hugh Kingery's book *Birding Colorado: Where, How, and When to Spot Birds across the State* (FalconGuides) is an excellent resource.

Past the Lois Webster Amphitheater—named for one of Denver Audubon's founding members—you'll stumble onto two adjacent ponds. Use the dirt trail to take a short hike around the water, looking for aquatic birds such as osprey fishing at the pond. In the spring and summer, eye-catching yellow warblers nest around the water, which also attracts broad-tailed hummingbirds, beavers, foxes, coyotes, and bobcats. Most of these mammals are shy; look for their tracks while exploring.

Bring a nature journal and writing supplies, and ask kids to record what they see. Then enjoy snacks or a picnic lunch on the deck outside the nature center. Be sure to practice Leave No Trace rules by packing out whatever you bring in.

Throughout the year, Denver Audubon hosts a variety of workshops and special events at its nature center and nearby outdoor lab. From the annual Hootenanny in the fall to year-round homeschool science classes, most offerings are family friendly. A club for young birders encourages kids ages 7 to 15 to hone their skills during monthly excursions. For more details, and to sign up for a program, visit the organization's website at denveraudubon.org/nature-center.

LEARN

Sure, this destination is all about birds! But a visit to Kingery Nature Center can also help curious kids expand their knowledge of botany, conservation, and real-world careers in science and nature.

- **Be a Citizen Scientist: If your kids enjoy birding, consider participating in the Great Backyard Bird Count (birdcount.org). During this semi-annual citizen-science event, participants are tasked with counting birds in a specific area for a brief period of time, then submitting their findings using an app (eBird or Merlin). The program helps scientists worldwide better understand and protect birds.**
- **Digging It: Denver Audubon's Native Plant Garden is a great educational tool for families, with small signs listing the names of various Colorado plant species. Ask children to record their favorite flora, then consider bringing one or more native plants into your home garden. Harlequin's Gardens, 4795 26th Street in Boulder, is a premier place for buying native plants. The Colorado Native Plant Society (conps.org) runs online plant sales twice a year for those who'd like to purchase their plants online.**

19 Denver Botanic Gardens Chatfield Farms

Engage your senses in the colorful gardens on this historic farm.

Cost: $$ Children ages 2 and under free
Hours: Daily 9 a.m. to 4 p.m.
Location: 8500 West Deer Creek Canyon Road
Nearest Town: Littleton
Denver Drive Time: 44 minutes via CO 470 East
Accessibility: 2.5 miles of paved trails and 3 wheelchair-accessible footbridges; some wheelchairs available to borrow at the ticket booth on a first-come, first-served basis; wheelchair-accessible restrooms. Upcoming accessible amenities include a paved parking lot and new restrooms.
Bathrooms: Full restrooms with flush toilets near the Earl J. Sinnamon Center
Gear Suggestions: Sturdy shoes, long pants, hat, sunscreen, insect repellent, binoculars, picnic blanket, water, wagon or stroller
Insider Tip: Visit in the morning when the weather is cool to see the most activity around the Hildebrand Ranch and the farm gardens. This is when the animals will be most active and the gardeners will be working among the plants. Tour Chatfield Farms in the spring during bird migration and bring binoculars. A diverse range of bird species stop here on their journey.

Explore

If DBG at York Street is the refined city garden, Chatfield Farms is its more casual country cousin, taking families back to a time in Colorado history when farming sustained settlers from the East. Even before that, Native American tribes used the area for thousands of years as hunting, gathering, and camping grounds. Chatfield Farms maintains its strong ties to its history in the 700 acres of gardens, farm, and buildings visitors can explore today.

This botanic garden is set up to stroll any which way you choose using the 2.5 miles of paved and gravel paths winding throughout the gardens. For families with young kids, start with a visit to Butterflies at Chatfield Farms, where butterflies who call Colorado home, like swallowtails, monarchs, and painted ladies, can be found flittering among the curated gardens from Memorial Day weekend through Labor Day. Be sure to stop at the entrance door and wait for the guide to let you in or out. It will ensure that resident butterflies stay safely inside and potentially unwanted visitors stay securely outside. This butterfly oasis is a collaboration between Chatfield Farms and Butterfly Pavilion in Westminster, which provides an enthusiastic docent who is happy to answer all the kids' questions. Be sure to pick up a scavenger hunt board near the door to help identify the various species fluttering around.

Next, head west to the Hildebrand Ranch and Community Supported Agriculture (CSA) farm. In 1866 Frank Hildebrand settled this land near Deer Creek to farm and raise cattle. Today, you'll still find many buildings original to the ranch, including the farmhouse, a barn, and a woodshed. Walk around the ranch to visit rescued farm

animals—including a potbellied pig, miniature horses, goats, and chickens—and to view the many flowers, vegetables, and herbs growing on the farm.

Leaving the Hildebrand Ranch, head behind the white clapboard farmhouse and cross Deer Creek via a footbridge. Continue along the path until you reach a tree-house play structure. This is Deer Creek Discovery's children's play area. Kids can let loose to climb on the tree house and crawl into a small willow tent, as well as play in a small creek. A number of smaller paths nearby lead to a tractor and through a hidden glen of trees. As much a nature center as a botanic garden, Chatfield Farms is home to thriving riparian, prairie, and woodland habitats where birds, small mammals, and insects busily move about.

As you wind around the path to the chapel and schoolhouse (reserved for special events or kids' programs), step inside the *One Fell Swoop* willow sculpture made of sapling trees and branches collected from around Colorado. Installed in 2019 by artist Patrick Dougherty, the interactive sculpture will remain in place until it begins to naturally fall apart, reflecting nature itself. Kids will love the chance to play hide and seek in the many twists and turns of the sculpture.

Chatfield Farms currently does not have an education center, but a large renovation project is in the works to add new infrastructure like a paved parking lot, a visitor and education center, and a restaurant. In the meantime, pack a picnic to spend a playful day in this natural oasis.

LEARN

Art and science blossom side by side in the natural displays at Chatfield Farms. Plant a love for both with these garden-inspired activities.

- Support a Pollinator: Look for bees, butterflies, hummingbirds, and other species that pollinate the many plants at Chatfield Farms. What plants are they most attracted to? Plant a couple pollinator-friendly flowers near your home. Then observe the habits of these busy beings.
- Weaving with Nature: Inspired by the *One Fell Swoop* sculpture and natural elements around the garden and farm, find fallen elements of nature at home to make a small weaving. Craft a small loom from sturdy branches, tying or gluing branches in a square or rectangle. Then tie a few lengths of twine from the top of the frame to the bottom, about half an inch apart. What can you weave, over and under, through the strings? Try grass, flowers, long leaves, and stalks of herbs to make a nature weaving.

20 Denver Botanic Gardens York Street

Sow a seed of interest in the plant world with a visit to this city garden.

Cost: $$$ Children ages 2 and under free
Hours: Summer hours mid-May through Labor Day 9 a.m. to 8 p.m. Check the website for winter, spring, autumn, and holiday hours. Mordecai Children's Garden open Mar 1 through Nov 1 9 a.m. to 4 p.m.
Location: 1007 York Street
Nearest Town: Denver
Denver Drive Time: 10 minutes via East Colfax Avenue and York Street
Accessibility: Most of the indoor and outdoor gardens and facilities are wheelchair accessible. Check with Visitor Services for information on accessible routes. Wheelchairs are available to check out at no charge on a first-come, first-served basis. Sensory Processing and Autism Resource Kits (SPARK) are available to check out at no charge in the Helen Fowler Library. A photo ID is required.
Bathrooms: Full restrooms are available throughout the main garden and at the entrance to the Mordecai Children's Garden.
Gear Suggestions: Sunscreen, hats, sturdy shoes or sandals, water bottles to top off at the refill stations around the gardens. If you plan to play in the stream, bring a change of clothes and swim diapers for those who need them.
Insider Tip: Picnics are welcome in the main gardens and Mordecai Children's Garden, so pack a lunch or snack to enjoy at the picnic tables under the Mountain Shadows Pavilion or by the Home Harvest Garden. There are also two restaurants: The Hive Garden Bistro and Offshoots Cafe.

Explore

A visit to the 24-acre Denver Botanic Gardens at York Street is more than a walk through cultivated themed gardens: It's a tour of the world through plants. As you walk along the mostly paved paths around the gardens, everything from grasses found in the unique arid climate of Colorado to flowers, trees, and vegetation from all over the world flourish and change with the seasons. Hop on the main path as it guides you around the various garden spaces, but feel free to go where your interests, and the kids, take you. The Gardens Navigator Website, at botanicgardens.org, is a helpful tool to locate and identify thousands of plants found in the gardens and learn more about them.

In the main garden, children will enjoy following the trails to visit what my family likes to call the different "rooms," because of the arches and hedges that create a sort of doorway into themed gardens. Visit the sensory garden, step into the indoor Boettcher Memorial Tropical Conservatory, or watch the dragonflies skim the lily pad–filled ponds. Be sure to go inside the Science Pyramid, where you'll find colorful hands-on displays exploring the ways every living thing is connected.

Across from the main Denver Botanic Gardens entrance and attached to the parking garage, enter the Mordecai Children's Garden, designed to engage young children and families in the life of plants. Learn about native, high-altitude planting in this

kid-friendly garden. No need to be worried that your tot might grab a flower, as visitors are encouraged to touch and feel their way through this space. Wet and wild crowd favorites include Snowmelt Stream and Pipsqueak Pond, where budding botanists can hunt for insects hiding on water-loving flora.

Denver Botanic Gardens also offers an abundance of programs for children and families to dig deeper into the natural world. Check the website before your visit to see what's happening in the gardens that day. The popular Seedlings classes engage toddlers through 6-year-olds in hands-on activities around the gardens based on frequently changing themes. Little ones might pick a salad from the Home Harvest Garden or observe life in the Pipsqueak Pond. Whatever the theme, Seedlings classes often sell out, so register for these well in advance.

If you are visiting on a Saturday from March through October, head to the Helen Fowler Library to see if they are holding the Nature Tales Family Story Time. Young kids with a love of stories can borrow adventure packs and check out books from the library.

The Gardens Family Make and Take programs engage the entire clan with fun and educational activities like building a fairy garden or a pollinator feeder. You do need to register for these programs, but they are self-guided and self-paced. Denver Botanic Gardens provides the materials, inspiration, and space, then families are free to create.

LEARN

This is the place to inspire an interest in the varied plants, flowers, and trees that surround us. Set up experiments at home to cultivate young gardeners.

- **Grow Knowledge: Watching a plant develop from seed to first leaves is magical for little ones. Using just a paper cup and potting soil, plant and nurture a seed. Then, build lessons that explore what plants need in order to grow.**
- **Experiment with Nature: Engage older kids by setting up experiments using plants. Place one plant or seedling in a north-facing window and one in a south-facing window, or give one plant less water or added compost, or propagate a clipping from an existing plant, then observe how the different care affects each plant or seedling.**

21 Denver Chalk Art Festival

Colorful, temporary art activates downtown Denver streets in June.

Cost: Free
Hours: Varies by year. This annual festival runs for 2 days, usually on a consecutive Sat–Sun in June.
Location: Bannock Street, between 11th and 13th Avenues, in the Golden Triangle Creative District
Nearest Town: Denver
Denver Drive Time: Minimal; it's in the heart of the city.
Accessibility: Streets and sidewalks are wheelchair and stroller accessible, but this is *not* a low-sensory experience.
Bathrooms: Portable toilets available in the parking lot off of 12th Street, between Bannock and Acoma
Gear Suggestions: Sun protection, comfortable walking shoes, a camera, snacks, water
Insider Tip: This 2-day block party draws thousands of art lovers. To avoid parking woes, arrive early, or bypass parking entirely by taking the Light Rail.

Explore

Who says fine art belongs in galleries? At the annual Denver Chalk Art Festival, hundreds of artists spend one wild weekend transforming Bannock Street into a colorful museum in a tradition dating back to sixteenth-century Renaissance Italy when artists called Madonnari began using asphalt as their canvases in hopes that passersby might toss a few coins their way.

Denver's festival is a little more organized: Prospective artists must apply to participate, and those who are selected get a square of space in the Golden Triangle Creative District, 2 blocks south of Civic Center Park.

Longtime Denverites might notice that the festival's location has shifted. The Denver Chalk Art Festival got going in 2003 on the streets of Larimer Square. In 2020, during the pandemic, artists were required to pivot, conducting the beloved festival ad hoc, in driveways and on sidewalks around Denver. After a short hiatus, the formal festival is back, with a new home. If you're planning to visit and need

a landmark, the art can be found near the Denver Art, Kirkland, and Clyfford Still Museums. (The closest address is 123 West 12th Avenue.)

As far as free festivals go, this is certainly one of the most impressive. By Sunday night, the temporary exhibit will cover thousands of square feet of pavement, making the Denver Chalk Art Festival the largest of its kind in the Rocky Mountain region. Professionals and amateurs spend countless hours on their hands and knees, working inside 8-by-8-foot, 8-by-12-foot, and 12-by-12-foot boundaries to create original pieces of flat and three-dimensional artwork.

It's one of the most family-friendly festivals, too. Part exhibit, part street performance, the experience is hands-on and interactive. Spectators of all ages are encouraged to walk right up to their favorite artists and ask questions. In fact, visitors often come to the festival both days because they love to see the progression of the art throughout the weekend.

If you're attending with kids, peruse the pavement first before stopping at a special Kids Corner, where children who are feeling inspired can create their own temporary chalk masterpieces. As part of the festival's Youth Challenge, professional artists will coach children from local schools as they compete with one another on the block of Acoma between 11th and 12th Streets.

The whole weekend is set to the tune of live music from various bands, and food vendors are always on-site, too, dishing up pizza, barbecue, and other crowd-pleasers. The art might not last long—that's kind of the point!—but the memories your family makes at Denver Chalk Art Festival will stick long after the chalk washes away.

LEARN

Whether your kids are art lovers or art history buffs, this colorful festival is a fun way to bring creative learning into the outdoors.

- **Beautify *Your* Sidewalk: Why not stage your own chalk art festival at home? Grab a few boxes of sidewalk chalk, tape off squares on the sidewalk for each participant, and get busy. For older kids who want to take their work to the next level, there's no shortage of chalk art tutorials on YouTube. If there are other families on your block who might be interested, invite them to participate, and consider handing out prizes for winners in various categories. Want to level up? It's easy, albeit slightly messy, to make your own chalk from scratch using plaster of Paris, water, powdered tempera paints, and molds of your choosing. (Silicone ice cube trays in fun shapes make excellent chalk molds.) Mix water and plaster of Paris in a bowl in a ratio of 3:4, using three-fourths cup water for every cup of plaster. Add in as much tempera powder as you'd like, then pour the colorful goop into your molds and let it dry.**
- **Historical Perspectives: From Italian Madonnari to British screevers in the mid-1800s, there's a lot of history behind chalk art. Challenge older elementary students, adolescents, and teens do a deeper dive into the past while exploring the origins of the craft and how it developed through the ages.**

22 Denver Museum of Nature & Science

Gain a deeper understanding of the inner workings of nature at this family favorite.

Cost: $$$ Separate admission for museum, Gates Planetarium, Infinity Theater shows, and special exhibitions
Hours: Open daily 9 a.m. to 5 p.m., most Fridays 9 a.m. to 9 p.m.
Location: 2001 Colorado Boulevard
Nearest Town: Denver
Denver Drive Time: 10 minutes via East 17th Avenue
Accessibility: ADA-compliant parking and museum, elevators, wheelchair seating in the Infinity Theater and Gates Planetarium, braille maps, assisted listening devices for the Infinity Theater, American Sign Language interpreters for live programs and lectures with 1-week's notice, resources for guests with autism or sensory sensitivities, wheelchairs and strollers available to check out from the information desk
Bathrooms: Full restrooms with flush toilets throughout; gender-neutral restrooms and a caregiver's room with an armchair, sink, and electrical outlet in the family restroom inside Gems and Minerals, on Level 1
Gear Suggestions: Sturdy walking shoes, swimsuits and a dry change of clothes for playing in the spray ground behind the museum, open seasonally from late May to early September
Insider Tip: While a visit to DMNS can be pricey for a whole family, designated free days and free nights make it more affordable. Find a list of free days and free nights under Pricing and Discounts on the DMNS website, at dmns.org. If you plan to visit frequently, a family membership is the most economical option.

Explore

On any given day at the Denver Museum of Nature & Science, curious kids and their families scurry floor by floor to discover new exhibitions or revisit old favorites. It's not uncommon to see kids pulling their parents toward an anticipated exhibit, perhaps one they discovered on a school field trip or that they heard about from friends. It's that enthusiasm for investigating fossils, rocks, space, and the human body sparked by a visit to DMNS that makes it a cornerstone in many Colorado children's STEAM education.

The museum itself started with one man's spark of interest in the birds and mammals of the Rocky Mountains. In 1868 Edwin Carter, who came to Colorado as part of the 1859 Pikes Peak Gold Rush, retired to a Breckenridge cabin where he began his scientific study and collection of local birds and mammals. His collection of 3,300 prepared and mounted specimens eventually became one of the three founding collections of what was called the Colorado Museum of Natural History when it opened in 1908.

Today, the Denver Museum of Nature & Science, as it is now known, displays less than 1% of its total collection, with countless artifacts, fossils, and specimens stored in two levels of state-of-the-art storage below the museum. There's plenty to discover in

the three levels of exhibitions that visitors do see, covering topics from dinosaurs to the exploration of space.

Let the kids lead the visit. Little ones ages 3 to 8 years old could spend the whole visit in the Discovery Zone, learning science skills through play. Check out the hands-in water table, dinosaurs made for climbing, educational programming, a construction zone, and numerous other hands-on activities. Older children will be drawn to trips through Prehistoric Journey, Space Odyssey, and the Wildlife Halls. The popular Expedition Health takes visitors on an interactive climb to the top of a fourteener, tracking how our bodies change and adapt along the way. Don't expect to get through the whole museum in one visit, so be sure to hit your favorites first.

The interior exhibits at DMNS never fail to entertain and educate visitors, leaving them with a better understanding of some part of nature. A new outdoor play space, under construction as this book goes to press, will bring the same DMNS learning approach to a playful outdoor space. Until that opens, walk past the sculptures on the west side of the museum—a grizzly bear and Snowmastodon—and a dinosaur rising up from the elevator corridor of the parking structure. Wrap up any summer visit to DMNS with a frolic in the spray ground overlooking City Park. You'll be treated to stunning views of the city skyline and mountains behind.

LEARN

The kids will learn something with every step they take at DMNS. Here are a couple ways to enrich their learning experiences.

- Seek Out the Labs: DMNS staff and volunteers actively work on projects in scientific labs around the museum. Look for the Genetics Lab in Expedition Health, the Paleontology Prep Lab in Prehistoric Journey, and more, to interact with scientists and learn more about their projects and jobs in STEAM.
- Go on a Scavenger Hunt: Visit the DMNS website or Information Desk to find four scavenger hunts to create an adventure around the museum. Hunt for Colorado state symbols, museum treasures, and even hidden elves. Each list offers general locations and descriptions of the objects listed. The Hidden Elf Scavenger Hunt includes directions to lead kids on the quest for these crafty little tricksters. Use this one as a fun way for kids to practice following directions.

23 Denver Zoo

Learn more about the planet's animal inhabitants at this hometown favorite.

Cost: $$$ Children ages 2 and under free
Hours: Open daily 10 a.m. to 5 p.m., entry gates close at 4 p.m. A timed ticket reservation is required for entry. Select a timed entry window when purchasing a ticket online.
Location: 2300 Steele Street
Nearest Town: Denver
Denver Drive Time: 10 minutes via East 17th Avenue
Accessibility: Visit the Accessibility page on the website (https://denverzoo.org/accessibility/) to learn about the many accommodations Denver Zoo provides for mobility, dietary allergies, language, sensory considerations, and more. The zoo is a Certified Autism Center, with at least 80% of staff highly trained and certified in the field of autism. Nursing areas are available in family restrooms, the Wellness Room in Primate Panorama, and a Mamava Pod at the Gates Building Garden-level restrooms. The Wellness Room can also be used as a quiet space.
Bathrooms: Full restrooms with flush toilets throughout the zoo. All-gender and family restrooms available at the main entrance to the zoo; family restrooms also available at Kamala Café in Toyota Elephant Passage.
Gear Suggestions: Walking shoes, water bottles, hats, sunscreen; bring a wagon or stroller, or rent them at the zoo.
Insider Tip: Download the free Denver Zoo app for quick access to helpful information during your visit. The app is simple to use and gives visitors access to an interactive zoo map with the location of animals, food options, restrooms, and special attractions like the Conservation Carousel. Tap the icons on the map for more information and to see any closed exhibits. The app also has a spot to purchase tickets, view a schedule of animal talks and demonstrations, and learn about the personalities of some of the animals.

Explore

In 1896 Denver mayor Thomas S. McMurry received a gift that laid the foundation for Denver Zoo, one of the city's most beloved attractions. The gift? An orphaned American black bear cub that he named Billy Bryan. Billy was given a home in City Park and was soon joined by a collection of prairie dogs, bison, elk, and native waterfowl, some that roamed freely around the park. Today, the zoo is home to more than 3,000 fuzzy, furry, feathered, and scaly faces to visit representing 450 species—including many that are threatened or endangered—as well as innovative exhibits and interactive experiences to enrich how kids learn about animals from around the world.

Speaking of innovative exhibits, in 1918 Denver Zoo opened an exhibit that set off a shift in the animal enclosures of American zoos forever. Bear Mountain shed the bars and cages, typical in zoos of the time, to reflect a more natural habitat filled with rocks, native plants, and water. A moat cleverly hidden in the design established a safety barrier. Visitors to the zoo today can still walk past Bear Mountain—which is

listed on the National Register of Historic Places—though now it's home to cinereous vultures.

Denver Zoo continues to innovate. As you navigate the wide shaded trails around this 84-acre oasis, your family will see historic exhibits like Bear Mountain and Monkey Island alongside the more recent additions of Stingray Cove and the 22,000-square-foot state-of-the-art Helen and Arthur E. Johnson Animal Hospital.

With so many animals living at the Denver Zoo and miles of trails to navigate, you should pick up a map when you arrive, or use the one in the Denver Zoo app to find your kids' must-see animals. Take a moment to map out your visit, making sure to note the times and locations of the many daily animal talks. You could also take the frog's approach, hopping from one animal to the next as they spark your child's interest.

Whatever your preference, make time to ride the Conservation Carousel or Denver Zoo Railroad, set among the zoo's collection of legacy trees. To cool off on a hot day, stop for a 15-minute film in the 4D Experience theater. Seats are equipped with special effects that allow viewers to feel the action. These three attractions all require an additional ticket.

LEARN

As children move past wide-eyed wonder at the mere sight of a tiger or bear or elephant, enhance their zoo experience by learning more about animal biology and geography.

- **Learn about Animal Care: Pass through the lobby of Denver Zoo's state-of-the-art Helen and Arthur E. Johnson Animal Hospital and you might glimpse animals being cared for by the zoo's veterinary staff, thanks to the large viewing windows. Check the daily zoo schedule for Educator Talks at the animal hospital. Kids could learn about animal care or what it's like to be a zoo veterinarian.**
- **Travel the World: Visiting the zoo is a unique opportunity to study geography. As you learn about the different animals you see, make note of their country and continent of origin. At home, print a map of the world or individual continents, find the countries you noted, and have kids write the name of animals or draw their faces by the countries.**

24 Elk Meadow Park

Hear an elk bugle with your family.

Cost: Free
Hours: Open daily, 1 hour before sunrise to 1 hour after sunset
Location: 2855 Bergen Peak Dr. (Lewis Ridge Trailhead) or 32281 Stagecoach Boulevard (Stagecoach Trailhead)
Nearest Town: Evergreen
Denver Drive Time: 35 minutes via 6th Avenue to I-70
Accessibility: This park's rugged trails would be difficult with a wheelchair or stroller.
Bathrooms: Outhouses at the trailheads
Gear Suggestions: Comfortable walking shoes; layers; including a windbreaker; sunscreen; sunglasses; hats; high-energy snacks; plenty of water; Nuun electrolyte tablets; binoculars; a nature journal and writing supplies

Insider Tip: Time your trip right. September and October are the best months to view elk in Colorado. During this short mating season—it's called "the rut"—bull elk can be spotted at the forest edge, preparing to battle other males. If you're lucky, you'll hear suitors bugling, or calling out to females. Bugles usually start with a deep call that becomes a high-pitched squeal before ending in a series of grunts. We cannot overstate the importance of safety when viewing elk. Never approach an elk. These massive hoofed creatures can weigh up to 900 pounds, and they're aggressive and unpredictable. Don't worry, with the binoculars you packed, your kids will still get a great view of local elk, without taking an unnecessary risk.

Explore

By some estimates, Colorado is home to 280,000 elk, making our Centennial State the elk capital of North America. There's really nothing quite like watching a herd of wild elk move about in their natural habitat. And yes, you've guessed it: As the name suggests, Elk Meadow Park is one of the most likely places to see elk in the foothills of Jefferson County.

Two trailheads service Elk Meadow Park. Both the Stagecoach and Lewis Ridge Trailheads offer access to this park's beautiful, secluded dirt hiking trails, and it's easy to get from one trailhead to the other via the Meadow View and Sleepy S Trails.

The climb to the park's picturesque high point, Bergen Peak (9,708 feet), is a challenge. When visiting with young kids, you might opt for the Meadow View Trail Loop, a laid-back option combining five trails: Sleepy S, Elk Ridge, Meadow View, Founders, and Painter's Pause. (Don't worry, everything is well marked, and the route isn't as complicated as it sounds. Grab a trail map from the kiosk at the Lewis Ridge Trailhead; you'll figure it out.)

Viewing elk can be a year-round activity in Colorado. The large ungulates are grazers surviving on grass, shrubs, wild fruits, leaves, and occasional nibbles of bark. The evergreen forests and deciduous trees at Elk Meadow provide shelter and nourishment to local populations. When visiting, look for elk on the outskirts of the park's central meadow.

Timing is everything with wildlife viewing. Dawn and dusk are the best periods to observe animals, but you've got to be thoughtful if you're planning to hike with your kids in the late afternoon or early evening. Know exactly where you're headed, and unless you really know what you're doing, be 120% sure you won't be caught on a trail with your children after dark.

Located about 0.6 mile beyond the park's Lewis Ridge Trailhead, the Carol Karlin Overlook is a perfect place for safe animal watching. For the most direct route to the overlook, park in the lot off Bergen Peak Drive. Walk to the kiosk at the Lewis Ridge Trailhead, and begin hiking north. In 180 feet bear right at the first trail intersection to merge onto Painter's Pause Trail. Follow the dirt path to reach a well-marked, sunny lookout.

Similar to fishing, wildlife viewing requires patience. Pack plenty of snacks as well as drawing supplies and a portable game such as Spot It! Junior. A few activities like these can do wonders in the kid-patience department.

Always—we repeat, always—view elk and other large wildlife from a safe distance. If you're close enough for a selfie, you are way too close. As a general guideline, wildlife watchers should give all animals at least 25 yards of personal space. For predators such as bears and wolves, and aggressive ungulates like elk and moose, make it 100-plus yards.

LEARN

Animal lovers and burgeoning wildlife biologists will get a lot out of an active trip to Elk Meadow Park.

- Classify Ungulates: The Latin word *ungulate* translates to "hoofed animal" and is used by zoologists to describe several groups of mammals. Ungulates can be odd-toed (think horses and rhinos) or even-toed (deer, sheep, pigs, camels, giraffes, et cetera). Where do elk fit? Back home, with the help of a computer, print and display images of a wide variety of ungulates, then ask your kids to classify the animals as odd- or even-toed. Challenge older children to match ungulates with images of their tracks. Sometimes the differences are subtle.
- Meet and Greet: Wildlife viewing can be disappointing since there are no guarantees of spotting an animal in its natural habitat. At the Denver Zoo, at 2300 Steele Street in downtown Denver, your kids are sure to see a wide variety of ungulates up close, from Asian elephants and Bactrian camels to black rhinos, cape buffalo, eastern bongo, lesser kudus, zebras, llamas, red river hogs, and more. In addition to live elephant demonstrations offered daily at no additional cost beyond your entry ticket, families can also pay for an exclusive encounter with the zoo's reticulated giraffe herd. During the experience, giraffe experts will help families get to know each member of the herd while spouting off facts about their unique personalities and biology. For more information and to purchase tickets online, visit denverzoo.org.

25 El Pueblo History Museum

Take a hands-on journey through southern Colorado's fascinating past.

Cost: $ Members, kids, and active military get in free.
Hours: Open daily 10 a.m. to 4 p.m. The museum is closed on Thanksgiving, Christmas Day, and New Year's Day.
Location: 301 North Union Avenue
Nearest Town: Pueblo
Denver Drive Time: 110 minutes via I-25
Accessibility: The one-story indoor facility is ADA compliant with barrier-free entrances and accessible toilets. Wheelchairs and strollers are available to check out at the Museum Store desk (first-come, first-served). This low-key museum will generally deliver a quiet experience for children with sensory differences. Groups with disabilities and/or special needs cost $4 per participant at the time of this writing, and caregivers and staff are free. To make a group reservation, call (719) 583-0453.
Bathrooms: Flush toilets near the main entrance
Gear Suggestions: Comfortable walking shoes, a camera, nature-journaling supplies, snacks, refillable water bottles
Insider Tip: Plan to visit in the summer when the museum's replica 1840s adobe trading post is open, typically from Memorial Day through Labor Day, weekdays only, though it varies by year based on the availability of tour guides. When open, guides take guests on informational tours through this one-of-a-kind outdoor space, walking families through several re-created rooms, including a kitchen, family living quarters, and an area specifically for trappers and fur traders. There's also the trading post itself, giving kids an idea of what trading was like in nineteenth-century Colorado.

Explore

There's always something fresh and innovative to discover at El Pueblo History Museum, one of several satellite museums within History Colorado's wonderful collection. El Pueblo History Museum opened its doors in 1959, across from the Colorado State Fairgrounds, at 1001 Beulah Avenue, for visitors interested in learning more about southern Colorado's unique past. There's plenty to see at the museum, but the story of its relocation in the 1990s to El Pueblo Trading Post is itself a fascinating tidbit of local lore.

The Arkansas River Valley was one of the first areas of Colorado to be settled by European colonists. Beyond its proximity to the Santa Fe Trail, the area offered fertile soil and relatively mild winters. It's no wonder, then, that the El Pueblo Trading Post was Pueblo's first permanent settlement, built in 1842 on the banks of the river. By the early 1850s, another trading post had popped up nearby, and it seemed like a village might even be forming. In those early days, El Pueblo was a bustling business where European and Mexican traders hooked up with Native American tribes, including the Utes. But that didn't last long.

On Christmas Eve in 1854, Ute chief Tierra Blanca led an attack on El Pueblo. Most of the twenty people at the trading post were killed, and after the attack the area was abandoned, practically overnight. Eventually El Pueblo's adobe walls crumbled.

The settlement of Pueblo grew from El Pueblo's ruins, and the old trading post was demolished, its location nearly lost beneath a growing city. It wasn't until 1989 that anthropology professor William G. Buckles rediscovered the historic site with a class of students from the University of Southern Colorado (now CSU-Pueblo). Following Buckles's discovery, the City of Pueblo and the Colorado Historical Society worked together to relocate the museum to the site of the historic El Pueblo Trading Post.

The museum you see today was completed in 2003, and the complex includes a main building with three exhibit halls plus several event spaces, along with a reconstruction of the El Pueblo Trading Post that highlights life in the mid-1800s. If possible, plan to visit when the trading post will be open because it's a real treat to walk around the re-created business center.

After entering through the museum's main doors, located on the south side of the building, you'll check in at the front desk and gift shop before taking a deep dive into the town's regional history. If your kids are anything like mine, they'll want to start with the site's hands-on activities. There's always something to touch and manipulate, though the offerings will vary depending on which exhibitions are on display during your trip. While younger children engage in a more tactile study of the era, older kids can peruse the exhibition hall walls, which are filled with photographs and informative descriptions keyed to current historical displays.

Between the two largest exhibition rooms, you'll find a tepee paying homage to the area's indigenous inhabitants, typical of what the Ute, Cheyenne, and Arapaho would have used.

LEARN

If you're looking for a bucket-list endeavor, might we suggest making it a goal to visit all of History Colorado's museums and historic sites in a single year?

Having entered the Union in 1876, Colorado might be a newer state—and yet the Centennial claims a rich and complex history with few dull moments. In addition to the El Pueblo History Museum, History Colorado operates ten museums and historic sites across the state. Most of us are already familiar with the History Colorado Center, at 1200 North Broadway in downtown Denver. (If you haven't been yet, this massive, hands-on history museum is a must-see with kids of all ages.) In addition to the Center for Colorado Women's History and Grant-Humphreys Mansion, both in downtown Denver, there are lesser-known sites such as the Healy House Museum & Dexter Cabin (Leadville) and the Fort Garland Museum & Cultural Center in Costilla County, where visitors explore life in a nineteenth-century military fort. The Ute Indian Museum in Montrose celebrates the Ute peoples' persistence. For a full list of museums within the History Colorado network, visit historycolorado.org/museums.

26 Fiske Planetarium and the Colorado Scale Model Solar System Trail

Travel through space without leaving planet Earth.

Cost: Free to walk the trail; $$ for planetarium shows; children age 3 and under free
Hours: Public planetarium shows Thurs–Sat evenings, matinees Sat–Sun afternoons. Box office and planetarium exhibit space open 30 minutes prior to shows.
Location: 2414 Regent Drive
Nearest Town: Boulder
Denver Drive Time: Approximately 35 minutes via I-25 North and US-36 West
Accessibility: ADA-compliant seating available. Call at least 24 hours in advance to reserve these seats. Assistive listening devices available at the ticket window for the hearing impaired. The Scale Model Solar System Trail is wheelchair accessible.
Bathrooms: Full bathrooms with flush toilets in the planetarium when open
Gear Suggestions: Walking shoes, hat, and sunscreen for tracking the Scale Model Solar System Trail
Insider Tip: To view the stars up close and off of the planetarium screen, visit a free public open house at Sommers-Bausch Observatory, next door to Fiske Planetarium. Held most Fridays when CU classes are in session and the skies are clear (8 p.m. fall and spring semesters and 9 p.m. summer semester). The open houses give visitors a chance to look at the twinkling stars through a telescope. View a schedule of open houses on the Sommers-Bausch Observatory website (www.colorado.edu/sbo/).

Explore

Whether a child is just learning to sing "Twinkle, Twinkle Little Star" or they are starting to identify constellations in the night sky, planetariums open a window to the solar system. Fiske Planetarium, on the University of Colorado Boulder campus, hosts educational (and entertaining) programs in their 65-foot-diameter dome. It's the largest planetarium between Chicago and Los Angeles.

As part of the College of Arts & Sciences, Astrophysical & Planetary Sciences Department (phew!), Fiske is a learning and project zone for CU faculty and students. But when the planetarium isn't being used for collegiate pursuits or local school field trips, the general public is invited to fulldome films, star talks, and even laser shows.

To find the right show for your family, visit the Fiske calendar online at www.colorado.edu/fiske/. It offers descriptions of each show, including a recommended age range. Plan to arrive 30 minutes before your show to explore the exhibits that fill the planetarium lobby. Sit in a model of astronaut Scott Carpenter's *Aurora 7* Mercury space capsule and see an astronaut's view of the Earth. Glimpse Fritz, the planetarium's original projector, and—your kids are going to love this—take a picture of your body's thermal energy with the FLIR thermal camera display. Then settle in the comfy reclining seats for a trip through the solar system on the dome above. Star

shows, fulldome films, and live talks include plenty of time for inquisitive kids to ask the astronomers and educators questions about space or the planetarium.

Before or after the show, impress the kids with a walk from our sun to the dwarf planet Pluto in less than half a mile. The Colorado Scale Model Solar System Trail starts across from Fiske's front doors, by the display with a gold orb in the center and a blue plaque below; this depicts the sun. As you walk from one display to the next, you'll be traveling our solar system, with the planets and the distances between them scaled down 10 billion times smaller than the actual size. The trail travels along tree-shaded pedestrian walkways through the CU campus, and interpretive signs share interesting scientific information about each planet, their moons, and the history of our solar system.

As you reach Pluto, cross to the other side of the sidewalk to see a plaque dedicated to Ellison Onizuka, a CU Boulder alumnus who was one of seven crew members killed when the space shuttle *Challenger* exploded just after its launch on January 28, 1986. Older kids may be interested to learn that CU Boulder has a strong connection to space exploration, with twenty CU Boulder scientists, faculty, and alumni who have been astronauts on NASA space missions.

LEARN

Studying the solar system expands your child's universe. Use a visit to the planetarium and Colorado Scale Model Solar System Trail to propel an interest in space. Here are some activities to continue the lesson at home.

- **Build Your Own Model Solar System: If the kids haven't already constructed a model solar system for school, take inspiration from the Scale Model Solar System Trail and make one together. Use Styrofoam balls or clay to create the sun and planets, then hang them in the correct order orbiting the sun. Find cool solar system resources, activities, and informative videos at solarsystem.nasa.gov.**
- **Make a Cotton Ball Constellation: Long ago, humans looked to the night sky and saw how some groups of stars looked like particular shapes, for example, a hunter, a bear, or a lion. They named the group of stars, or constellations, after those shapes: Orion the hunter, Ursa Major the Great Bear, and Leo the lion. Although light pollution in the city can make it difficult to see full constellations in the night sky, re-creating the constellations from cotton balls and straws will help children visualize the concept. Make the activity delicious by using marshmallows instead of cotton balls.**

27 Florissant Fossil Beds National Monument

Glimpse petrified and fossilized remains of nature from long ago.

Cost: $$
Hours: Open daily 9 a.m. to 4:30 p.m.
Location: 15807 Teller County Road 1
Nearest Town: Florissant
Denver Drive Time: 2 hours via I-25 South and US 24 West
Accessibility: Parking lot, visitor center, theater, and 0.4-mile Ponderosa Loop trail are wheelchair accessible. Introductory film includes subtitles, audio description, and assistive listening devices upon request; assistive listening devices and audio guides also available for the indoor exhibits.
Bathrooms: Full bathrooms at visitor center. Toilets also available at Hornbek Homestead and Barksdale Picnic Area.
Gear Suggestions: Walking or hiking shoes, hats, sunscreen, insect repellent, binoculars, journal or sketchbook
Insider Tip: Picking up or taking any fossils found in Florissant Fossil Beds is illegal. If you find something that looks significant, leave it where it is and tell a park ranger. If the kids are itching to hunt and find their own fossils, travel a bit down the road to Florissant Fossil Quarry, where, for a per person fee, you can dig through a tray of rocks to find your own fossil to take home.

Explore

Look out across the grassy valley of Florissant Fossil Beds National Monument. You are standing where an ancient lake once flourished. Plants, insects, fish, birds, and mammals of the Late Eocene epoch filled the water, air, and groves of redwood trees around this lake.

You are also in the shadow of once-active volcanoes. Over thousands of years, volcanic eruptions and environmental changes buried the plant and animal life under deposits of ash, mud, and lava, preserving fossilized remains beneath the earth's surface. As wind, erosion, and time changed the face of Colorado and swept away layers, these shadows of ancient life around the lake emerged.

In the late nineteenth and early twentieth centuries, scientists and settlers came into the area, as did tourists, intent on taking their own souvenir fossils. By the time Florissant Fossil Beds gained its National Monument status in 1969, untold numbers of fossils and petrified tree remnants had been taken from the area. Apart from the fossils in the visitor center and the few petrified tree stumps visible around the park, the remaining treasures of Florissant lay hidden below the earth's surface. That makes Florissant a valuable place to engage kids' imaginations and talk to them about the importance of preservation.

At the beginning of your visit to Florissant Fossil Beds, pick up a copy of the *Junior Ranger Activity Book* at the visitor center. This will help guide your time at the

park. Once the visit to the fossil beds is completed, kids can return to the visitor center, say the pledge, and earn a badge. Florissant Fossil Beds also offers *Junior Paleontologist Activity Books*. (Both booklets are available to download on the park's website.)

While you are in the visitor center, watch the 18-minute film about the history of the park and the development of the fossils. Then explore the exhibits to see real fossils found at Florissant.

If time is limited, be sure to take the easy 1-mile Petrified Forest Loop to view the massive petrified tree stumps. (Just imagine, scientists believe that when these trees died, they were 250 feet tall and likely 500 to 700 years old.) This trail through the bed of ancient Lake Florissant features interpretive signs to help visitors visualize life in and around the lake. If there is more time, ask the ranger at the visitor center to recommend one of the longer hikes that fits with your family's interests and abilities.

Florissant's other treasure is in the sky above the park. Although close to Colorado Springs, the southern Front Range of the Rockies blocks much of the light from the city. In 2021 Florissant Fossil Beds National Monument was designated an International Dark Sky Park. If you have an opportunity to stay overnight in the area, look for the Night Sky program during the summer months hosted by volunteers from the Colorado Springs Astronomical Society.

LEARN

You are literally standing on history when you visit this national monument. Many important fossils are preserved beneath the kids' feet, so incorporate these activities to enrich your visit.

- Make a Fossil: Real fossils take millennia to form, but you can speed up the process for a simplified lesson in fossils. Use clay, plaster of Paris, or salt dough to create your own fossil impressions. Gather natural items around your home and yard, such as shells, leaves, flowers, or even plastic dinosaurs, roll out the clay, and press the items into it to make an impression. Let the clay dry.
- Imagine a Different Scene: Hike one of the trails that begin at the visitor center and pass over what was once an ancient lakebed. Pretend to explore underwater and talk about what things you might see based on the fossils you observed in the visitor center.

28 Fossil Creek Reservoir Natural Area

Experience Colorado's untouched beauty while enjoying outstanding birding.

Cost: Free
Hours: Open daily from dawn to dusk
Location: 3340 Carpenter Road (The entrance into the natural area is on Carpenter Road, approximately a mile west of I-25, or 2 miles east of Timberline, depending on where you're coming from.)
Nearest Towns: Fort Collins and Loveland
Denver Drive Time: 60 minutes via I-25
Accessibility: The paved Heron Loop Trail, which passes one of several viewing piers, accommodates standard wheelchairs and standard strollers. The site is most crowded on weekends, between 10 a.m. and 4 p.m. For a quiet, low-sensory experience, visit on a weekday morning.
Bathrooms: Flush toilets inside the building on the west end of the parking lot
Gear Suggestions: KEEN sandals or similar shoes that work for walking near water, sunscreen, a sun hat, plenty of water, snacks
Insider Tip: The City of Fort Collins publishes a variety of free lesson plans and activity pages for families interested in interacting with nature at their own pace. Go to fcgov.com/naturalareas and click on the "Learning Library" tab to access a trove of DIY activities, including a handy Bird Observation Lesson Plan.

Explore

If you're a longtime Fort Collins resident or Colorado native, then you might remember when this site opened as Fossil Creek Regional Open Space. The City of Fort Collins and Larimer County purchased the site together, and originally the county managed it. As programs matured, it made more sense for Fort Collins to oversee the open space, at which point the site's name changed to reflect new management.

Take note: You'll have to leave Fido at home for this trip. The Fort Collins Natural Areas Department has one main priority: conservation of natural resources. (Though public recreation is certainly a big benefit!) Based on the city's mission, trails inside this natural area are designed to minimize human impact on wildlife, and that's why pets and bikes aren't allowed inside Fossil Creek Reservoir Natural Area. Water recreation, including boating, fishing, and swimming, is also a no-no. But who cares about any of that? What you're here for is the birding.

Fossil Creek Reservoir Natural Area is designated as an Important Bird Area by the National Audubon Society, mainly because it provides crucial habitat to bald eagles and other raptors, as well as a wide variety of songbirds, shorebirds, and waterfowl. To view the site's feathered residents, you'll want to hop onto one of several short hiking trails and head toward the water.

From the parking lot, you'll have easy access to the Sandpiper and Cattail Flats Trails, both mellow, out-and-back routes crossing a rolling prairie and ending at the reservoir. Sandpiper Trail is a 0.4-mile (one way) path to a sheltered wildlife-viewing area; at 0.75-mile (one way), Cattail Flats Trail is a slightly longer hike ending at

another wildlife-viewing area. Both routes provide access to great birding opportunities on the shore of the tree-lined reservoir, but for some reason I personally prefer Sandpiper Trail. The 0.25-mile paved Heron Loop Trail is perfect for those visiting with wheelchairs and/or strollers.

A camera, sketchbook, and art supplies are highly recommended. It's impossible not to feel inspired while looking out over the water, and if creativity strikes, you'll want to make sure your kids have the right tools to capture the incredible scenery.

If you're planning to do some birding, then binoculars are a must. You might also want a spotting scope, which lets you zoom in on wildlife just a little bit more. Both shelters are outfitted with interpretive signs containing information about resident and migratory birds. While these placards are a good jumping-off point, serious birders will also want to pack a Colorado bird guidebook. Hugh Kingery's book *Birding Colorado: Where, How, and When to Spot Birds across the State* (FalconGuides) is an excellent resource.

It would be a real shame to go all the way to Fossil Creek Reservoir and not set aside time to visit Twin Silo Park, 5552 Ziegler Road, a crowd-pleasing playground at the intersection of Kechter and Ziegler Roads in Fort Collins. My kids could spend an entire day horsing around on the ropes and cargo nets leading to a giant slide connecting two 48-foot farm silos. With community gardens, an orchard, paved walking trails, pickleball courts, and a BMX park, there's plenty to do until your stomach rumbles—at which point you might as well head to Old Town Fort Collins, the city's charming downtown shopping district, for a bite to eat.

LEARN

In addition to birds, Fossil Creek Reservoir provides habitat for a variety of mammals, including coyotes, foxes, and deer, making the natural area a perfect destination for young naturalists.

- **Become an Expert: Teach your kids that scientists classify all living things by domain, kingdom, phylum, class, order, family, genus, and species. Free classification charts are easy to find online with a simple web search. Back home, have children pretend to be wildlife biologists as they classify plush toy animals and/or animal figurines.**
- **Start Here: If you and your kids are new to birding, this natural area is the perfect place to hone your craft. Pack snacks and plenty of patience so you can spend an entire morning in nature, looking for the site's feathered inhabitants. Bring a guidebook and Colorado bird checklist, and see how many birds you can cross off as you explore. Remember to respect every animal's need for personal space.**

29 Fountain Creek Nature Center

Stroll a wetland trail and learn how water travels from the mountains to the Gulf of Mexico.

Cost: Free
Hours: Tues–Sat 9 a.m. to 4 p.m.
Location: 320 Pepper Grass Lane
Nearest Town: Fountain
Denver Drive Time: Approximately 80 minutes via I-25 South
Accessibility: Wheelchair-accessible nature center; Terrain Hopper off-road mobility vehicles available to borrow through the El Paso County Community Services Department Trailability program, to make trails more accessible.
Bathrooms: Full bathrooms inside the nature center
Gear Suggestions: Walking shoes, sunscreen, hats, insect repellent
Insider Tip: Look for QR codes along the trail and scan them to learn more about the natural areas around the nature center. Hear about everything from the plants, animals, and people who have lived in the area or currently call the area home to the impact of water pollution and ways to keep water clean. The audio tour is also available on the Fountain Creek website to listen to on your phone or at home.
communityservices.elpasoco.com/nature-centers/fountain-creek-nature-center

Explore

Fountain Creek, this nature center's namesake, begins its life west of Colorado Springs in Woodland Park, then flows 74.5 miles before merging with the Arkansas River on its journey to the Mississippi River and eventually the Gulf of Mexico. Along the way, Fountain Creek flows past the nature center, creating an opportunity for kids to learn more about our waterways and the habitats around them.

To start your visit, take a moment at the balcony viewing platform just south of the nature center. Find Pikes Peak in the distance. Snowmelt from Pikes Peak flows into Fountain Creek, and this is the water that makes the journey to the Gulf of Mexico. It's hard for kids to fathom that water from the top of the mountains can reach the ocean, but this view creates a visual connection to bring the lesson to life.

Descend the hill on the 0.7-mile loop trail to enter a lush wetland habitat filled with plants and animals and a trail around a cattail-lined pond. Although it may be hard to see in the summer, Cattail Marsh Pond is the center of this habitat. If you follow this trail around the pond, it connects to the Fountain Creek Regional Trail on the southwest side. The regional trail stretches from the north to the south end of the park and is just under 3 miles long.

Back on the loop trail, look for wildlife like great blue herons, turtles, and white-tailed deer that regularly visit the marsh and woodlands. Turn your attention to the plants that support this habitat. Cattails are abundant around the marsh and provide important food and shelter for birds and waterfowl, as well as fish and insects. Red-winged blackbirds build their nests in the cattails. See if you can spot them.

As you continue on the trail, look for Grandfather Cottonwood. A sign below this massive shady tree tells a Native American story of how the stars become part of the sky. The cottonwood tree plays an important role in this ancient tale.

Begin or end a visit indoors at the nature center for engaging hands-on displays about the five ecosystems found at Fountain Creek. A watershed table helps kids understand more about water flowing along the ground, while a birdcall display and the Beak Buffet help visitors understand more about what occupies the sky above the nature center. Monarch butterflies also flit through the area, making a stop here on their migration to Mexico. Watch for monarch chrysalises nurtured in indoor displays. Another favorite spot in the nature center is the Naturalist Nook, a corner stocked with books, artifacts, and costumes to encourage self-exploration.

Through the exhibits, kids and adults also gain a better understanding of how each of us can care for the planet at home through recycling, sustainability, and keeping the water clean. Don't leave without taking in the view of the pond, woodlands, and Pikes Peak from the nature center windows. Use the binoculars nearby to scan for wildlife and get an up-close glimpse.

Fountain Creek hosts a variety of low-cost programs and special events for kids, adults, and families, as well as kids' camps. Check for programs and events on the website.

LEARN

Fountain Creek Nature Center hosts an impressive guest list of birds, animals, and invertebrates throughout the year. In addition to identifying bird visitors, kids can also learn about monarch butterfly migration.

- **Identify the Birds: Listen quietly as you walk through the woodlands, meadows, and marsh area and you will hear numerous birdsongs. The Cattail Marsh Wildlife Area around the nature center hosts more than 270 species of birds. Use a phone app like Merlin to record and identify birdsong and calls you hear.**
- **Hunt for Milkweed: The area around Fountain Creek Nature Center is a certified and registered way station or sort of rest stop for monarch butterflies. The habitat provides milkweed, nectar, and shelter the monarchs need as they migrate through North America. Work together with the kids to identify the milkweed plants.**

30 Four Mile Historic Park

Denver's 12-acre history park brings the American West to life.

Cost: $$ Children ages 6 and under free
Hours: The history park is open year-round from 10 a.m. to 4 p.m. June–Dec guests can visit Wed–Sun; Jan–May the site's open on weekends only, Fri–Sun.
Location: 715 South Forest Street
Nearest Town: Denver
Denver Drive Time: Minimal; it's in the heart of the city.
Accessibility: Wheelchairs and jogging strollers will work on the site's gravel trails, but take note that it might be a bumpy ride. For a quiet, low-sensory experience, visit the history park during general admission hours, and avoid free days and special events.
Bathrooms: Flush toilets inside the museum and on the far end of the history park
Gear Suggestions: Sun protection, comfortable walking shoes, a camera, snacks, water
Insider Tip: Admission is free on the fourth Friday of every month. These days are designated as "Living History" days, and interpreters often dress up to bring various aspects of Denver's western past to life. Guided tours of the historic Four Mile House are also available on these special days and during general admission.

Explore

In an age of 24-7 digital media, who wouldn't benefit from a little old-fashioned family fun? From barns, stables, and an authentic root cellar to a tucked-away tepee, Denver's 12-acre history park brings the past to life, connecting visitors to local Colorado history and the spirit of the people who settled the area.

The centerpiece of the history park is a two-story white cabin known as the Four Mile House. Back in the 1800s, there were a number of so-called mile houses, places that offered services to those traveling along the Cherokee Trail, a California-bound path following an older route created by Indigenous Peoples. The Four Mile House is significant because, well, it's still standing!

Two brothers, Samuel and Jonas Brantner, built Denver's oldest standing structure in 1859. After some bad luck trying to find gold in Cherry Creek, the Brantner brothers sold the Four Mile House to Mary Cawker, who then ran it as a true mile house. The cabin was a welcome sight for weary travelers looking for rest and a home-cooked meal before heading into Denver. Having stood the test of time, the home was designated a Denver landmark in 1968 before being added to the National Register of Historic Places the following year.

Today, parkgoers are invited to peruse the home and its period furniture during guided tours (check online for details; fourmilepark.org). Guests aren't admitted into the Four Mile House without a guide since it's chock-full of artifacts.

You won't need a docent for anything else in the park: The rest of the grounds can be viewed at your family's leisure. Other popular attractions include re-creation buildings such as a bee house, summer kitchen, and privy—and don't miss the prairie

schooner and restored stagecoach, which kids are more than welcome to climb into. Beyond all of the historically accurate replicas, Four Mile Park is also a working farm. If you keep exploring, you're bound to run into horses, pigs, goats, and chickens before stumbling upon the site's outbuildings, where "blacksmiths" and "quilters" can be seen whiling away the hours.

This is definitely a tactile learning destination, and the site maintains a large collection of touch items, many located at the farm-chores station behind the schoolhouse, where kids can wash old clothes using wash tubs and washboards, then hang them to dry on a line. There's also a makeshift creek on the edge of the property, complete with gold panning (no additional cost).

Four Mile's year-round programming is another draw for families. There are a handful of special events throughout the year, including a Pumpkin Harvest, a Christmastime soiree, and an egg hunt. They're all fun, but Four Mile's annual Independence Celebration takes the cake, with live music, food trucks, and historic demonstrations.

Festivities are fantastic, but sometimes it's the quiet moments that move this mom the most. There are plenty of secret nooks hidden throughout the park. Don't be surprised if your favorite family moment involves little more than a blanket under a shade tree, a simple picnic lunch, and giggly, gadget-free conversation.

LEARN

Whether your kids are studying westward expansion, the Colorado Gold Rush, historic architecture, or Colorado state history, this fabulous destination makes it easy to imagine a life before smartphones.

- **Make Your Own Timeline: The indoor museum preceding the history park contains a wealth of historical information. And on the "About" page on Four Mile Historic Park's website, fourmilepark.org, families will find a fascinating timeline with detailed information about the Four Mile House and other events during the period. After gathering information, encourage kids to create their own timelines of nineteenth-century life in Denver.**
- **Home on the Range: Back home, extend the experience by partaking in some bygone homesteading tasks. Bake a loaf of bread with your kids, and while the dough's rising, try churning butter. You could also do a load of laundry the old-fashioned way, washing clothes by hand in a bucket, then hanging them to dry in the sun. At the very least, your children will walk away with a better appreciation for modern conveniences. End your day with a fireside read-aloud. We highly recommend a Laura Ingalls Wilder book.**

31 Garden of the Gods

Take in the iconic sandstone rock formations for a lesson in geology.

Cost: Free entry to park and visitor center; fee for the Geo-Trekker theater show, but children under age 5 and SNAP cardholders get in free.
Hours: Park open daily 5 a.m. to 9 p.m. Nov 1 through Apr 30, 5 a.m. to 10 p.m. May 1 through Oct 31. Visitor & Nature Center open daily 9 a.m. to 5 p.m. in winter months, 9 a.m. to 6 p.m. Memorial Day weekend through Labor Day weekend.
Location: 1805 North 30th Street
Nearest Town: Colorado Springs
Denver Drive Time: 70 minutes via I-25 South
Accessibility: The Visitor & Nature Center is ADA compliant and has three non-motorized wheelchairs available to borrow on a first-come, first-served basis. The summer shuttle is also ADA compliant.
Bathrooms: Clean, modern restrooms in the Visitor & Nature Center. Park restrooms located in the main parking lot and at the Trading Post.
Gear Suggestions: Good walking shoes, hats, sunscreen, plenty of water
Insider Tip: A *Junior Ranger Activity Guide* is available in the gift shop (for around $2) and offers kids a variety of activities to do in the park, like Nature Hike Bingo, along with puzzles and questions to help enrich the visit.

Explore

Yes, Garden of the Gods park can be busy, but it is also possible to find a quieter time to take in the red sandstone formations rising from the earth, free of heavy traffic and crowds. Just ask the folks at the information desk inside the Visitor & Nature Center, and they'll tell you that weekdays in the early morning or after dinner can offer the chance you need to push the stroller, let the kids explore in a quieter atmosphere, and capture a solo selfie with the rocks. (As a bonus, these are also cooler times to visit the park in the summer.)

Speaking of the Visitor & Nature Center, this is the place to start a visit. The 17,000-square-foot center at the east side of the park near Gateway Road explores the history, people, geology, and, perhaps most fun for the kids, the wildlife and plant life of the park through modern, hands-on displays.

It was 1859 when the surveyor Rufus Cable first visited the area and declared that it was "a fit place for the gods to assemble." It's doubtful that he ever dreamed kids would be able to watch a computerized video depicting continental drift (watch as Colorado moves into place through 600 million years) or sit in a theater designed like a sci-fi exploration vessel and watch a movie about how the rock formations came to be. But the center is filled with learning opportunities for modern kids.

An attention-grabbing wall of animals that call the park home anchors the exhibit area of the center, where kids can solve park mysteries and identify animal prints and, that enduring kid-favorite, scat. On the lower level of the center, the Geo-Trekker theater plays a 15-minute movie that blasts viewers on a ride through 1 billion years in the park's history. Tickets can be purchased at the kiosk near the entrance to the Geological Time Tunnel, which leads to the theater.

When you are ready to explore the park, pick up a park map from the information desk or download the free Garden of the Gods app for a park map, a map of the trails, and an audio tour. Use the trail map or ask the information desk folks to help you find the best trail for your family's interests and abilities. The Perkins Central Garden Trail is an easy 1.5-mile round-trip paved walking path perfect for families with young kids or strollers. Just be aware that this is also likely to be the most traveled (busiest) trail. The various trails wind past different red rock formations, all of which have names listed on the park map. Look for Kissing Camels, Pulpit Rock, and Three Graces, and don't forget to point out Pikes Peak, which rises above the park in the west.

LEARN

Colorado is a wonderland of geological mysteries for kids (and many adults, too). Walk this garden of stunning rocks and help kids devise topics for their own research.

- **Inquiring Minds: The Garden of the Gods may bring up questions. Where did the rocks come from? Why are they red? Who named them? Take this as an opportunity to guide kids into finding their own answers. When kids ask if anyone ever lived here, write the question down and say, "Let's try to figure that out. Where do you think we could look for that answer?" Then set off on your research.**
- **Rock On: As the family explores nature, take in the view. Ask kids what large rock formations or outcroppings of mountains look like to them. Does it look like a person dancing or maybe a dog carrying a ball? Let the kids give the rocks their own names.**

32 Golden History Park

The past comes to life at this authentic outdoor museum.

Cost: Free
Hours: Open daily 5 a.m. to 11 p.m., with some restrictions
Location: 11th and Arapahoe Streets, adjacent to the Golden Hotel
Nearest Town: Golden
Denver Drive Time: 25 minutes via I-70 or 6th Avenue
Accessibility: Both the history park and indoor museum typically offer quiet, low-sensory experiences. All-terrain wheelchairs and jogging strollers will work on Golden History Park's wide, dirt and gravel trail.
Bathrooms: Flush toilets available inside the Golden History Museum, and portable toilets are set up along Clear Creek.
Gear Suggestions: Sun protection, comfortable walking shoes, snacks, plenty of water
Insider Tip: Golden History Park is extra fun in the summer on special "Homesteader Days," when buildings are open to the public and costumed interpreters deliver a legit living history experience. Consult the organization's website, goldenhistory.org, for more details.

Explore

If you'd wound your way up Golden Gate Canyon Road back in the early 1900s, you might have passed the Pearce Ranch, where English hard-rock miner Thomas Pearce homesteaded one of the largest ranches in the area with his second wife, Henrietta. Generations of Pearces lived in the Pearce/Helps Cabin, but the historical dwelling and its outbuildings were almost lost entirely in the 1990s when developers planned to replace them with new housing.

Community members rallied to preserve local history, and over a four-year period, dedicated volunteers relocated a handful of the ranch's original structures, reconstructing them log by log at Golden History Park. Today, the outdoor museum gives families a glimpse into high-altitude ranching life at the height of the Pikes Peak Gold Rush.

Situated in the heart of downtown Golden, the Golden History Park is wedged between 11th Street and Clear Creek, the latter a beautiful freshwater stream drawing tubers, swimmers, anglers, and artists. Since the living history attraction abuts the Golden Hotel, it's easiest to navigate to 800 11th Street (the hotel's address). Street parking is usually available along 11th, but if you're having trouble finding a spot, you can park across the water, at the Golden Visitors & Information Center, 1010 Washington Avenue.

Once you've arrived, a short 0.2-mile trail loops you past two 1800s-era cabins, along with several additional structures: a working blacksmith shop; two-seat outhouses; the root cellar, which was the frontier version of a refrigerator and storeroom; and the obligatory chicken coop, heritage chickens and all.

Bring a quarter to feed the fowl, and take plenty of time to peer inside building windows as you explore the grounds. The Pearce/Helps Cabin, with its distinctive dovetail notching, is decked out with period furnishings ranging from smaller trinkets—a coffee grinder, for example—to large-scale items such as a bathtub and pump organ. There's even a working cookstove. The park also includes a rose garden, vegetable garden, and small orchard behind the one-room schoolhouse.

Living history makes my family thirsty, so we always like to meander over to Washington Avenue, Golden's western-themed main street, for a fresh-brewed iced tea at the Windy Saddle Café. Within a 2-block walk, you'll find a variety of saloons, breweries, and restaurants, including a food hall off of 12th Street—plus frozen yogurt and ice cream shops for a sweet end to your adventure.

To really tap into the town's rich history, cross Clear Creek via one of the footbridges, and follow a paved walkway to the Golden History Museum, 923 10th Street (also free). After snapping a family photo in front of the colorful "Greetings from Golden" mural, head indoors to browse several gallery spaces, including a hands-on "touch gallery" designed as a general store and diner in partnership with the Children's Museum of Denver. Ask for a scavenger hunt at the front desk, and be sure to pick up a Golden History Park brochure, where you'll find more details about the antiquated homestead you've just explored.

LEARN

Whether your kids are studying westward expansion, the Colorado Gold Rush, historic architecture, or Colorado state history, Golden History Park brings elements of the past into real time.

- **High-Level Thinking: While walking the premises, ask children to compare historical structures with our modern-day buildings. What amenities did European settlers and miners rely on? Have any of the buildings become outdated? Why? This activity hones analytical thinking and observation while developing speaking skills.**
- **Writing: Encourage children to journal about their surroundings. There are plenty of places to sit and write, and creative students might even want to start outlining a short story about a family living on the Pearce Ranch at the turn of the century. Both fiction and nonfiction can be used on this writing assignment, and for kids who really want to level up, make a pit stop at the Golden Library (jeffcolibrary.org/locations/gn), where librarians can help your curious children check out a few books about life in the olden days.**

33 Hiwan Heritage Park and Museum

Visit a historic summer camp and play among stately conifers.

Cost: Free
Hours: May through October, Tues–Fri noon to 4 p.m., Sat–Sun noon to 4:30 p.m. Closed Mon. November through April, Thurs-Fri noon to 4 p.m., Sat-Sun noon to 4:30. Closed Mon-Wed.
Location: 28473 Meadow Drive
Nearest Town: Evergreen
Denver Drive Time: 40 minutes via US-6 and I-70 West
Accessibility: First level of the house tour is accessible, then a video can be set up to show the full tour. ADA-compliant parking.
Bathrooms: Full restrooms on-site, ADA-compliant bathrooms
Gear Suggestions: Walking shoes
Insider Tip: Each October, Hiwan Heritage Park hosts Hiwan Halloween, a not-too-scary, outdoor (weather-permitting) festival in the park. Families dressed in costume come for free crafts, games, and treats, plus a look at the historic buildings.

Explore

Even when Denver was young, folks were escaping the city heat and heading into the mountains for a chance to connect with nature. Mary Neosho Williams, a wealthy Civil War widow from New York, and her daughter, Josepha Williams, found their connection to nature as they camped in canvas tents nestled among pine trees, near where the Hiwan Heritage Park and Museum stands today. This park mixes Colorado history with a short nature walk, and on the right day, an elk sighting.

In the late 1880s, Mary and her daughter, Josepha, ventured west so that Josepha could attend Gross Medical School in Denver. Dr. Jo became one of Colorado's first female physicians, specializing in treating patients suffering with tuberculosis. In 1893 Dr. Jo purchased the more than 1,000 acres where she and her mother loved to camp during summers and named it Camp Neosho. Dr. Jo and Mary commissioned local carpenter, Jock Spence, to modify the existing log cabin on the land to suit their summer retreat needs.

Eventually, Jo married, Charles W. Douglas, and they had a son, Eric. In 1914-1918, Jo and Charles commissioned Spence to construct major additions to the main house. Dr. Jo lived out her life at her beloved Camp Neosho. After her death in 1938, the camp had a second life as a home and cattle ranch owned by the Buchanan family. In 1974, the Jefferson County Historical Society advocated that Jefferson County Open Space purchase the buildings and grove to avoid demolition by rampant development in the community.

Today, families can tour the historic house and a cool, peaceful ponderosa pine grove that Dr. Jo loved so dearly. The restored home reflects the style of Dr. Jo's family, including artifacts reminiscent of her husband and son's passion for collecting

American Indian art. Sign up for a free guided tour of the house to see elements of the original barn structure, a 1930s/1940s–style kitchen, and the dining room wall that was built around an existing tree.

After the house tour, visit the Housekeepers Cabin in the back and, from there, cross the bridge and head up the stairs to the Stone House. When it's open, the Stone House has hands-on activities, books, and games for kids.

The Stone House also marks the beginning of the rustic Forestry Trail through a grove of native gramma grasses, wildflowers, and conifer trees. The trail is short, just 0.1 mile long, but it's a pleasant walk in the fresh air through meadow, forest, and across a small creek. It ends near a replica of the tents used at Camp Neosho.

Nearby, covered and uncovered picnic areas are a pleasant place to relax as the kids check out a prairie schooner and chuckwagon or run around and play on the cluster of tree stumps.

If you visit without a tour of the museum, there is a self-guided tour around the property. Pick up a reusable map in the box to the right of the museum's front door. As with many other Jeffco Parks and Open Space locations, there is a booklet available to enrich the visit for young kids and families. Once kids complete the exploration activities, they can say a pledge and earn a badge. The *Junior Historian of Hiwan Heritage Park* booklet is available inside the museum, or it can be printed from the museum's website at jeffco.us/1251/Hiwan-Heritage-Park.

LEARN

The shaded park around the museum makes a pretty outdoor classroom. See what lessons about nature your child can pick up around the museum. These activities will get you started.

- **Read the Rings: On the Forestry Trail, look for the interpretive display with tree "cookies" or slices of trunks from fallen trees. Each cookie teaches viewers something different about the life of a tree, from reading the growth rings to uncovering different trauma the tree may have experienced during its lifetime. It's a valuable example of how trees are impacted by their surroundings.**
- **Make Journey Cake: There were no minimarts along the trails for travelers of long ago, so they had to pack foods that would keep for days . . . and sometimes longer. Journey cakes traveled with the early settlers, like Mary Neosho Williams and Dr. Jo, as they came west to Colorado. Find a recipe online for the bread and give it a try. The basic recipe includes just cornmeal, salt, and water—ingredients that were easy to pack or find along the trail. Pack your journey cakes for a picnic by the prairie schooner at Hiwan. Talk about why the settlers might need to make such a simple bread, and what wild foods or plants were available to them as they traveled west.**

34 Hudson Gardens & Event Center

Learn beekeeping at Littleton's free botanical garden.

Cost: Free
Hours: Garden open daily from sunrise to sunset. Welcome Center & Gift Shop open daily 9 a.m. to 4 p.m.
Location: 6115 South Santa Fe Drive
Nearest Town: Littleton
Denver Drive Time: 20 minutes via Santa Fe Drive
Accessibility: The paved and crushed-gravel trails looping through the garden are ADA compliant and can accommodate wheelchairs and strollers.
Bathrooms: Flush toilets inside the gift shop and just off the Mary Carter Greenway, behind Nixon's Coffee House
Gear Suggestions: Comfortable walking shoes, sunscreen, a hat, sunglasses, plenty of water, snacks, nature-journaling supplies, a notepad and writing supplies
Insider Tip: This fabulous public garden is just a hop-skip from the Mary Carter Greenway, where families can go for a mellow hike alongside the water. If it's open, Nixon's Coffee House is a great place to re-up on fluids and fuel before or after a family hike.

Explore

There's so much more to this destination than pretty flowers. With the Rocky Mountains for a backdrop, Hudson Gardens is a nonprofit organization featuring 30 acres of display gardens, along with gentle trails, open spaces, nature-based play structures, water features, and plenty of peaceful nooks for those needing a few quiet moments immersed in nature.

The main entrance is off Santa Fe Boulevard, and unless there's an event when you arrive, you should find ample parking in one of the lots preceding the main entrance. Stop in the gift shop for a quick bathroom break if needed, and to view books, toys, seeds, home decor, and local confections, all themed around gardening and the site's other big offering: beekeeping.

That's right! Hudson Gardens is home to a very special apiary with twenty beehives owned by community beekeepers. The bees pollinate plants inside Hudson Gardens and in the surrounding community. Several times a season—check online for specific dates and times (hudsongardens.org)—families can drop by the apiary anytime between 9 a.m. and noon for a free Meet the Beekeeper class. In addition to observing live, active beehives, families will get a chance to see local beekeepers use various management techniques. You'll also have a chance to pick an expert's brain.

The apiary is located on the west side of Hudson Gardens, just beyond the big red barn. It's easy to locate the rows of wooden bee boxes by following the paved path that circles through the garden. Maps are available on the organization's website, and if you come when the gift shop's open, you can always ask for directions.

Feeling inspired? Hudson Gardens takes the concept of a community garden to the next level with its Community Beekeeping program. The Hudson Gardens' Community Apiary exists to raise awareness about honeybees and gain support for their conservation. All on-site beehives are maintained by individual beekeepers who apply for the program on an annual basis, and anyone's allowed to apply, regardless of previous beekeeping knowledge and/or prior experience. Much like with a community vegetable garden, new community beekeepers can learn from more experienced beekeepers. Members can also attend apiary mentorship sessions.

Of course, bees aren't the only buzz at Hudson Gardens. There's lots to see and discover during your visit, including a water lily pond, rose garden, the Colorado

Garden, vegetable and herb plots, and Bob's Pond Water Garden, which showcases the incredible diversity of our planet's aquatic plants. All of these spaces can be accessed via the sole paved trail running through the property.

The trail picks up on the left side of the gift shop. Follow the path west, walking slightly downhill, to reach the adorable Hobbit Hole play area preceding Turtle Pond. From here, walk in either direction to loop around the site, and be sure to stop for some birding at Songbird Garden, just south of Monet's Place, a perfect spot for a quick snack and forest bathing. Between the vegetable and herb gardens, and the community beehives, you'll find another nature play area, called Sticks and Stones, made from repurposed logs and stones.

As you explore, challenge your kids to find all eighteen sculptures spread across the gardens. Look, too, for the G-Scale Garden Railroad, with a miniature town mimicking the Colorado landscape. The train is a seasonal attraction, running from April through September, but Hudson Gardens is a year-round destination. If you love Hudson Gardens as much as we do, return for their signature events, a magical jack-o'-lantern display in October, and winter holiday lights.

LEARN

In addition to learning about gardening in Colorado, guests of all ages can study bees and other pollinators while grasping the need to support native ecosystems.

- **The Birds and the Bees: After visiting Hudson Gardens, it's hard not to wonder what you can do at home to support local bee populations and other pollinators, including native butterflies and songbirds. Colorado State University Extension provides Coloradans with free online resources covering a variety of environmental topics. To learn all about pollinators and how your family can create a pollinator habitat, visit extension.colostate.edu/topic-areas/insects/creating-pollinator-habitat-5-616/. Hudson Gardens partners with CSU Extension Master Gardeners to provide hands-on gardening workshops; check online for a current listing of classes.**
- **Walk with a Guide: For bird-loving families, guided bird walks are offered monthly at Hudson Gardens through an Audubon Master Birder. During the walks, guests learn all sorts of useful birding tips to employ on subsequent self-guided expeditions.**

35 Itty Bitty Art Project

Art comes in all sizes in the western-themed town of Golden.

Cost: Free
Hours: Downtown Golden and the Clear Creek Trail can be accessed 24-7. Golden parks, including Parfet, are open daily from 5 a.m. to 11 p.m. unless otherwise posted. The Golden Visitors & Information Center is open weekdays from 9 a.m. to 5 p.m. and 10 a.m. to 4 p.m. on weekends.
Location: 1010 Washington Avenue (Golden Visitors & Information Center)
Nearest Town: Golden
Denver Drive Time: 25 minutes via 6th Avenue
Accessibility: The Art Tour follows a route using mostly paved trails and sidewalks that are wheelchair and stroller accessible.
Bathrooms: Flush toilets inside the Golden Visitors & Information Center; portable toilets available at various points along Clear Creek
Gear Suggestions: Comfortable walking shoes, sunscreen, a hat, sunglasses, water, snacks to enjoy at one of the many benches along the Art Tour routes, a Frisbee or ball to use at Parfet Park, simple art supplies
Insider Tip: Safety first! Clear Creek runs straight through Golden, offering visual appeal and opportunities for some serious outdoor recreation. During your visit you'll see people of all ages tubing down Clear Creek, often in inner tubes they've rented from local outfitters. Tubing can be lots of fun, but keep in mind that water conditions vary by day. If you decide to tube with your children, read through the rules outlined on Visit Golden's website, at visit golden.com/plan-your-visit/creek-info. Always wear safety gear when tubing—life jackets, helmets—and look for colored flags along Clear Creek. These flags correspond to the safety levels on "Creek Warning Flags" signs. Never get into the water on red and double-red flag days; kids under 18 shouldn't swim and tube on yellow flag days.

Explore

Clear Creek rushes through Golden, offering tubers and kayakers a wild ride. Now art lovers are in for a thrill, too, as they hunt for tiny pieces of art scattered in clandestine locations along Clear Creek Trail, Washington Avenue, and the paved path inside Parfet Park. Dubbed the Itty Bitty Art Project, this whimsical art walk challenges families to take a closer look at cracks in the concrete, old tree stumps, water drains, and more.

The project launched in 2022, when ten local artists working with the Golden Public Art Commission decided to shrink down the town's typical public art scene, essentially creating an outdoor art show of miniature paintings and sculptures in some pretty unexpected places.

Your first stop should be the Golden Visitors & Information Center, 1010 Washington Avenue, where you'll grab a free *Itty Bitty Art Walk Tour* brochure. The pamphlet opens to a map your kids can use to hone their navigational skills while scouring

nearby trails and sidewalks for small pieces of art hidden in plain sight. Go ahead and try not to smile when you discover the dinosaur bending around a pillar!

As you walk with your children, observe the sheer creativity behind this unique project. Animation guru Daniel Morrison, for example, puts sprinkler heads and weird water distribution faucets to good use by creating a funny-looking alien. He also squeezed a miniature train into some wall cracks near the Golden Library, a fun stop-off with a wonderful kid's room.

For her three-dimensional piece *The Golden Herd*, artist Judith Cassel-Mamet placed small toy bison and trees into brick, then colored in a blue sky. On the

Washington Avenue bridge over Clear Creek, Anne Fitzgerald's *Take Flight* was a big hit with this writer's children.

After a very successful first year, the Itty Bitty Art Project expanded into Parfet Park in 2023, where new artists have added even more miniscule art. But take everything you're reading here with a grain of salt: This artwork isn't meant to be permanent. Rather, it's an ephemeral venture somewhat similar to the Denver Chalk Art Festival (see chapter 21). If the art fades, breaks, or is vandalized, that's it. It's gone. So please don't be disappointed if the Itty Bitty Art Project has transformed into something new by the time you're reading this book. Instead, embrace the unpredictable nature of art and life. (Isn't that what parenting's all about, anyway?)

If you're looking for something a little more permanent, Golden also runs a more traditional public art scene, with over two dozen large-scale sculptures and murals created to capture the spirit of the West. From cowboys and gold miners to wild mustangs, vivid paintings and three-dimensional statues can be found all around town. For a relaxing stroll, you can follow the route outlined in the free *Golden Public Art Walking Tour* brochure, also available at the Golden Visitors & Information Center.

LEARN

Art is certainly the most beautiful component of STEAM education, and in Golden you'll find plenty of real-life lessons in immersive artwork, creative uses of space, and even city planning when you stop to consider the role public art plays in beautifying the town.

- **Do Your Homework: Of course we're going to recommend that your kids start their own Itty Bitty Art Project back home! Challenge young artists to create miniature artwork out of simple supplies. Then, place their tiny masterpieces in out-of-the-way spots where observant neighbors will be pleasantly surprised.**
- **Dive Deeper: If you'd like to learn more about the artists behind all of the itty-bitty art, visit the City of Golden's website, cityofgolden.net/play/recreation-attractions/public-art/itty-bitty-art. Here you'll find links to artist websites. Why not ask your child to research the local creative behind their favorite piece of tiny art?**

36 Johnson-Habitat Park

Discover a natural play area along the revitalized South Platte River Greenway.

Cost: Free
Hours: Open daily 7 a.m. to 10 p.m.
Location: 610 South Jason Street
Nearest Town: Denver
Denver Drive Time: 10 minutes via I-25 South to South Santa Fe Drive exit
Accessibility: Wheelchair-accessible trail to the river and around the park, picnic shelter
Bathrooms: ADA-compliant portable toilet
Gear Suggestions: Hats; sunscreen; tennis shoes; and shoes that can get wet, for exploring near the water

Insider Tip: A colorfully painted building rising from the tall grass on the southeast end of the park is the headquarters for SPREE (South Platte River Environmental Education). This program through the Greenway Foundation offers nature-based events, summer and school-day-out camps, field trips, and stewardship opportunities that engage kids and families in the habitats along the South Platte River. Find program listings on the Greenway Foundation website, thegreenwayfoundation.org/events.

Explore

You would never know it today, but the area along the South Platte River at Johnson-Habitat Park was once the site of a city dump. For nearly 100 years—up until 1965—visitors to the area were more likely to see household trash than wildlife floating in the water and sitting along the banks. Then Denver's Great Flood of 1965 spurred a flood of change to the areas around the South Platte River. Starting in 1974 with Denver mayor Bill McNichols, a decades-long improvement of the riverfront area was set in motion to make the area a safer, more attractive place.

Decades later, the Greenway Foundation has worked to bring life back to this sliver of land near I-25 and South Santa Fe Boulevard, giving families a space to interact with nature without leaving the city.

Parking for Johnson-Habitat Park is on South Jason Street and West Exposition Avenue, with a few off-street parking spots on Exposition Avenue. The South Platte River Trail runs around the outside of the park, so keep your eyes open for walkers, joggers, and bicyclists as you cross the paved trail. Though the area is still surrounded by warehouses and businesses, you just need to walk through the tall grasses growing around the park perimeter to discover a transformed natural play zone.

Every part of this park was developed as a space to learn about and interact with nature. Kids can climb in and around synthetic boulders and tree stumps, dig in a

sand pit, and walk a trail down to the western bank of the river. It's OK to dip your toes into the water and wade a bit, but hold off on swimming, according to the folks working on water quality.

The same trail that takes you to the water winds its way through the compact park, offering some (fading) interpretive signage about the history of the area and the habitat. In the center, a flat grassy area is great for kicking around a ball, running, or picnicking on a cool day. Though the park does not have much shade, there is a picnic shelter on the north end with two tables. As you explore the trail, keep your eyes open for hidden paths through the grass. You'll know you've found them when you see animal tracks embedded on the sidewalk. Follow these paved paths as they wind through the tall grasses and give you a feeling of wandering.

At the top of the park, kids can play on a climbing web and multilevel fort. Look for the mosaic forget-me-not flowers embedded in the concrete nearby; beside them you'll see two ringed planters that introduce the various plants around the park, like forget-me-nots, columbines, and cattails.

LEARN

There's a lot to see, hear, smell, and touch at this urban park. Visit on a sunny day to kick off a sensory study.

- Go on a Sensory Scavenger Hunt: From the grassy hillsides to the banks of the South Platte River, Johnson-Habitat Park is full of engaging sensory experiences. Give kids the lead to tell you what they hear (tumbling water), see (dragonflies), and feel (spikey grass) as they explore different spaces.
- Make a Sun Print: Children can create a unique addition for their nature journal with just construction paper and found nature objects. Ask kids to collect fallen bits of nature with interesting shapes. (Always check the rules at parks and nature centers before picking or taking any nature element.) Arrange the objects on top of a sheet of construction paper and attach them with clear tape. Set the paper in the sun with the natural elements facing up, and leave it there for a few hours, or until the paper fades considerably. Then remove the tape and observe the shadows left behind. If you would like a more vibrant print, look for special solar paper at an arts-and-crafts store.

37 Joy Park and Adventure Forest at the Children's Museum of Denver at Marsico Campus

Play in the coolest backyard in town.

Cost: $$$ Children under age 1 free
Hours: Open daily 9 a.m. to 4 p.m. Closed Thanksgiving Day, Christmas Eve, Christmas Day, and New Year's Day.
Location: Children's Museum of Denver at Marsico Campus, 2121 Children's Museum Drive
Nearest Town: Denver
Denver Drive Time: 10 minutes via East Colfax Avenue and I-25 North
Accessibility: Wheelchairs, noise-canceling headphones, grip assists for tools in certain exhibits, and ADA-compliant workstations. View the *Museum for All* accessibility guide to read about the various ways the museum and outdoor spaces are accessible. The Nest is a sensory studio in the museum inspired by the work of Dr. Winnie Dunn, who identified four groups of sensory types and their different needs.
Bathrooms: Plenty of bathrooms inside the museum
Gear Suggestions: Sunscreen, hats, plenty of water. When the river is flowing (generally throughout the summer), bring a swimsuit, towel, and change of clothes.
Insider Tip: Watch for Joy Park free nights throughout the summer season when the Joy Park stays open for play from 4:30 to 8 p.m. (or dusk) with no admission cost.

Explore

The Children's Museum has long been one of Denver's favorite indoor spaces for kids to play, learn, and test their limits. While working on a renovation that doubled their indoor exhibit space in 2015, they also turned focus to the outdoor space behind the museum. The resulting 60,000-square-foot Joy Park is *the* place for young kids to play outside—and learn—on a nice day.

As you ascend the hill in Joy Park, kids will encounter a number of quintessential Colorado activities to try out. They can dig in sand dunes, climb on giant straw bales, splash and wade in the stream (seasonal), and even soar on a kid-friendly zip line—all activities the Children's Museum team developed to emphasize both the body and brain benefits of time spent in nature.

At the top of Joy Park is the ultimate adventure course for kids at least 5 years old or 44 inches tall and their adult. You may have seen the top of the 500-foot-long Adventure Forest rising up from behind the museum as you passed by on I-25—it's hard to miss it. At its highest point, the "Tippy-Top Lookout" is at exactly 5,280 feet elevation with exciting panoramic views of Denver. But that's jumping ahead; first, kids have opportunities to test their limits as they climb high, scramble across a spiderweb-like net, swing on a rope, cross a glass bridge, and slide down a 70-foot

slide. If it sounds like a challenge, it's meant to be. The course is designed to give kids a chance to take calculated risks, falter, face a fear, or maybe feed their inner thrill seeker—it's a very Colorado frame of mind. As they travel along, there is also a story woven into the art throughout the structure. Look for hints to help decode a secret language and reveal more about the story.

Helmets are required for all climbers, and they are provided for everyone at the beginning of the adventure. Anyone navigating the course should also wear sturdy, closed-toed shoes. A parent is required to accompany any child doing Adventure Forest in order to check in. If you have a younger child along, too, it's OK to give permission for your older child to climb independently while you stay just below and watch.

If you can, though, get in there and join your child. It may be your only opportunity to crawl through a tunnel looking down on I-25 or take in the city views at the top, because the museum does not allow adults without children on Adventure Forest. Be assured, it's just as fun for grown-ups and definitely worth it to see your little one push through challenges to come out braver on the other side.

LEARN

Visiting Joy Park and Adventure Forest ignites a creative spark for outdoor fun. Though kids will probably be worn out after a day in this big backyard, you could work on this activity over time.

Encourage your child to use what they find around their own house and backyard to build a miniature Joy Park at home. Start by asking what inspires your child. Is it books? Physical activity? Engineering? Puzzles? Tap into their ideas to set up an unplugged play area. Here are some starter ideas:

- **Plant a small garden and watch it grow.**
- **Set up a small obstacle course with trees to run around, patio chairs to crawl under, and challenges with a jump rope and Hula-Hoop.**
- **Put up a tent or lay out a blanket for a reading, art, or just daydreaming space.**
- **Build structures with twigs or rocks.**
- **Make a simple sandbox and add a couple kitchen items you no longer use, like thrifted bowls, baking tins, spoons, and measuring cups.**

38 Junkyard Social Club

Delve into life-size science at Boulder's "rebel museum" and adventure playground.

Cost: $$
Hours: Tues–Sun 10 a.m. to 6 p.m.
Location: 2525 Frontier Avenue
Nearest Town: Boulder
Denver Drive Time: 40 minutes via I-25 and US 36
Accessibility: The club is ADA compliant, and sensory kits are available for families who'd like them.
Bathrooms: Flush toilets inside the main building
Gear Suggestions: Comfortable closed-toed shoes, refillable water bottles, coffee mugs
Insider Tip: From board and card games to role-playing games, the Junkyard's monthly game night is a great way for families to connect. No need to pre-register: Just swing by with your children and grab a table. Check the organization's website (junkyardsocialclub.org) for specific dates and times.

Explore

Yes, this eclectic community hangout and kid-friendly playground is, essentially, a junkyard. Located in the heart of Boulder, Junkyard Social Club is a vibrant destination anchored by its 6,000-square-foot "adventure playground." The unique outdoor arena is equipped with shaded, upcycled play structures, swing sets, and a sand pit, along with funky art installations and colorful murals.

It all started in 2020, when four Boulderites hatched an idea for a nonprofit community space that would bring some artistic grit back to town. The founders began diverting junk from local landfills, and after securing a space in a former print warehouse, they assembled the ultimate upcycled play space.

Instead of hands-on learning, it's full-bodies on at the Junkyard, where the absence of commercially manufactured play equipment leads to a whole new level of creative play and learning. All ages are welcome, but children 10 and under will be most thrilled by the outdoor playground as they run, jump, and climb.

Beyond the large-scale play structures, visitors will discover tons of "loose parts" scattered throughout the site. Loose parts can be anything from pine cones to wooden planks, buckets, clamps, pipes, and even small pieces of rope, and they're essential to the Junkyard experience because they create unexpected, unstructured opportunities for children to build, invent, and investigate their surroundings.

Basically, anything goes. Your child is welcome to engineer a gondola with ropes and pulleys, or design mini-golf holes, or build a fort, or create mini-parachutes to launch off of the play structures. My 3-year-old turned the sand area into a restaurant and spent the morning making pretend food for customers. All this to say, your kids

will know exactly how to use the available materials as they engage in their own scientific discovery.

Roll-up glass garage doors lead from the outdoor playground to an indoor space that's also pretty neat, with a supplemental play structure and jungle gym, quiet nooks for reading and relaxing, and tons of tables and desks where kids can grab available art supplies and get creative. Don't miss the art and game lounge upstairs.

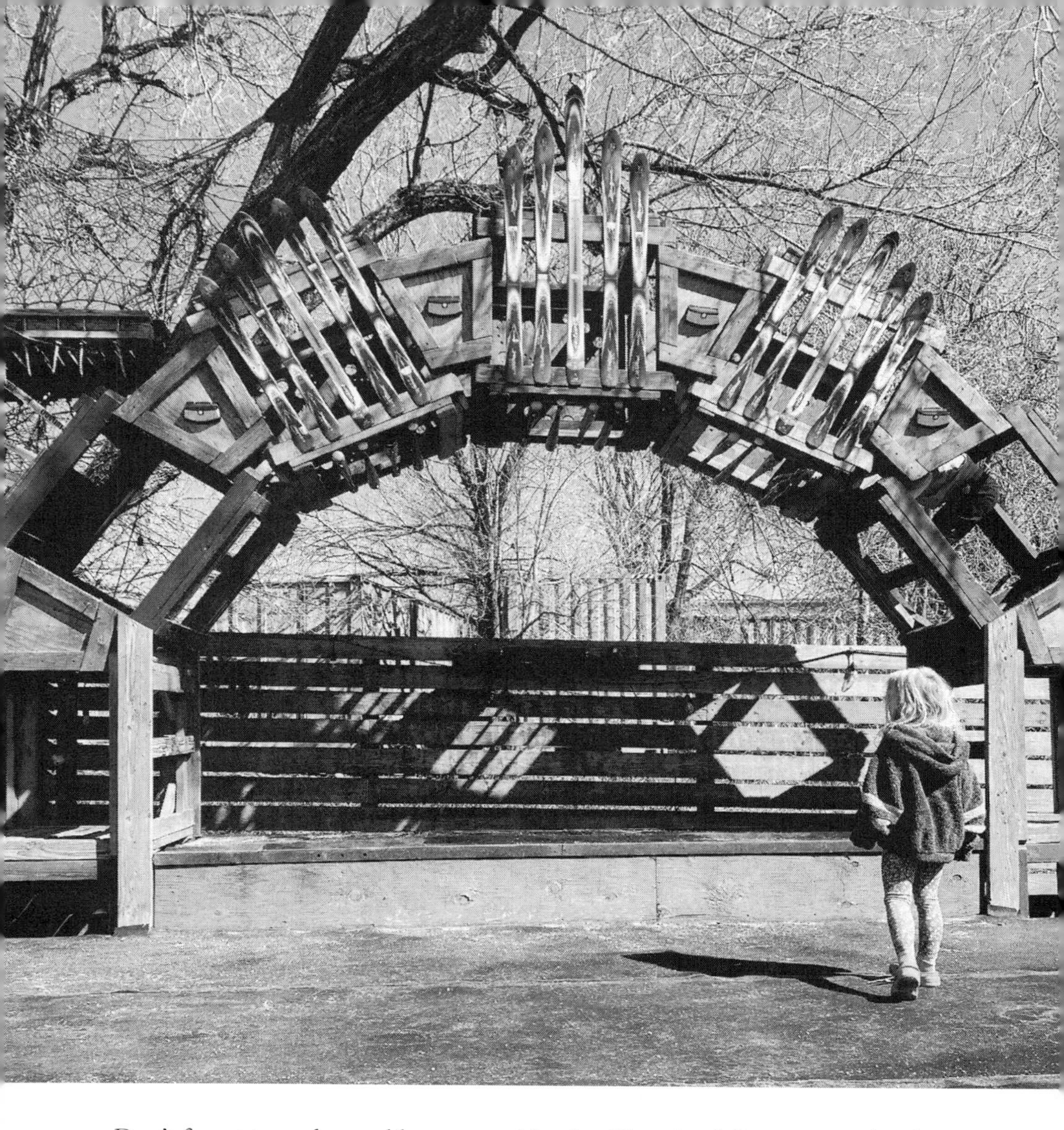

Don't forget to pack reusable mugs and bottles: There's a full-service coffee shop and cafe brewing local beans and serving up snacks and small bites such as paninis and burritos. An on-site bar opens in the afternoons and on weekends. In addition to being open for general admission and quirky play, the Junkyard offers tons of camps and workshops, including homeschool classes, plus weekly special events. As an organization dedicated to STEAM education, the Junkyard also runs a number of ongoing classes ranging in theme from robotics to life-size science. Offerings change with the season, so check online for current listings.

LEARN

STEAM-based learning rules at the Junkyard, true, but this special destination is also a great place for children to learn about waste reduction, upcycling, and conservation more generally.

- Get Inspired: Back home, let your kids scour the house for rubbish that they can repurpose into their own creative masterpieces. With a hot-glue gun and a little ingenuity, it's easy to turn yesterday's trash into a sculpture or three-dimensional mural.
- Extend the Fun: Want to take your garbage education one step further? Couple this play-based experience with a trip to the Garbage Garage Education Center, located at the Larimer County Landfill, at 5887 South Taft Hill Road in Fort Collins. Now's your chance to find out how a landfill works while learning just how much trash a city generates . . . and where all that garbage goes. Drop in Tuesday through Friday, between 10 a.m. and 2 p.m., for a family-friendly tour of the educational center. After walking through the site's "Mountain of Trash"—i.e., a tunnel-like hallway covered in discards from the nearby landfill—families can peruse the building and learn about alternatives to tossing waste. Classes end with a craft, and off-site virtual programming is available for those who can't make it all the way up to Fort Collins. For more details, visit larimer.gov/solidwaste/education/edcenter.

39 Lair o' the Bear Park

Hike along the tumbling Bear Creek at this family-friendly park.

Cost: Free
Hours: Open daily, 1 hour before sunrise to 1 hour after sunset
Location: 22550 Colorado State Highway 74
Nearest Town: Idledale
Denver Drive Time: 30 minutes via US 6 West and CO 470 East
Accessibility: Within the park, Bear Creek Trail is a natural-surface path, mostly flat, and hiking stroller or all-terrain stroller friendly for a 2-mile roundtrip hike, from the main trailhead to the Donafon Castle (private property).
Bathrooms: Toilets and ADA-compliant toilets at trailhead, no sinks
Gear Suggestions: Walking shoes, hats, sunscreen, water, insect repellent, swim shoes, dry change of clothes, towel, picnic

Insider Tip: This trail is consistently busy, so arrive early for the best opportunity to get a spot in the parking lot. Also check the main homepage for Jeffco Parks at www.jeffco.us/964/Parks, and link to the park's individual page for up-to-date information. Hikers, runners, picnickers, and mountain bicyclists all start filling the lot at the trailhead as early as 7 to 8 a.m. in the summer. There are a couple other parking pullouts along the road, but you will walk a bit on a shoulder before you reach the trailhead. Another option is to park at Little Park just east of Lair o' the Bear. (Turn left off of 72 West/Bear Creek Road onto Miller Road.) Bear Creek Trail connects to the parking lot here. The stretch of trail between Little Park and the boundary of Lair o' the Bear Park can often be a little quieter.

Explore

When it's time to step up from hikes around the neighborhood park, this Jeffco Open Space park in the foothills near Idledale is a win for kids and grown-ups alike. The pleasant, mostly shaded Bear Creek Trail extends the length of the park, meandering along the cool, tumbling waters of Bear Creek.

Throughout the park, Bear Creek Trail connects to a number of shorter trails ranging in difficulty from easy to challenging, but most are doable for families depending on your preference and time. You will see kids of all ages along the trails, including tots in carriers strapped to their parents' backs and tweens navigating the trails on foot or bike. Lair o' the Bear is family friendly in so many ways that it often shows up on lists of best Denver-area trails for families. That also makes it busy, but it's well worth the trip.

If you have to pick one trail for a visit to Lair o' the Bear, start with Bear Creek Trail. For 2 miles roundtrip, this flat, natural-surface path rewards kids with three bridges, a tiny creek crossing, a view of the privately owned Dunafon Castle, and an array of interesting plants, insects, and birds to watch. The trail itself is peppered with picnic tables, some near the water, so definitely plan a stop for a snack or lunch. Bear Creek Trail is not a loop, though, so plan to turn around before the kids wear out. You'll need to double back to finish your hike and reach the parking lot where you

started. If the kids are up for a longer hike, Bear Creek Trail extends into adjoining parks for a 12.6-mile round-trip hike.

As you travel Bear Creek Trail, watch for signs marking the Creekside Loop. This quiet hike-only trail (no bikes allowed) takes you up to the water's edge. Old cottonwood trees shade the trail, and low banks make it easy to dip your feet in the water. (*A note on safety:* Water levels in Colorado creeks can rise and fall and water

can move quickly, so keep a close eye on children around the water's edge.) Fishing is also allowed in the creek as long as you follow the Colorado Parks and Wildlife rules and regulations.

The side trails that connect to Bear Creek Trail are well marked with signs. For an easy route with a slight elevation gain (216 feet) and a pretty view of a valley, find the

Bruin Bluff Trailhead. This 1.5-mile hike takes you past ponderosa pines and dainty wildflowers before winding back to Bear Creek Trail.

As you hike and pass the castle, Bear Creek Trail crosses into Corwina Park. At this point the trail becomes a more challenging climb that is still reasonably kid friendly, depending on your child's interest and experience. (Note that this climb also leads to the start of Rutabega Ride, a bike-only directional trail, so you will likely have bikes around you on the trail. Use proper trail etiquette and be on the lookout for others.) It's not uncommon to see families on this part of Bear Creek Trail, venturing up to Panorama Point for a view of Kittredge, the surrounding Evergreen area, and, on a clear day, Mount Evans. If you are lucky, you may also see chipmunks scurrying across the boulders around Panorama Point. On the hike up and down, the trail passes through a shady mountain forest with marvelous large rock formations along the way. Any of these trails is sure to spark your child's inner naturalist.

LEARN

Any hike can become a journey into the daily lives of insects, birds, and plants if you look at things in a new way. Encourage children to adopt a new perspective as they observe nature in this laid-back park.

- **Look Low, Look High: As you hike the mountain trails, it's easy to focus on the destination ahead. Instead, make a game of looking high and low. What plants and insects do you see on the ground near the trail? What creatures are soaring above or busy in the trees? A game of I Spy could get things started.**
- **Start a Digital Wildflower "Collection": Did you know that in many parks and nature preserves, picking flowers, collecting rocks, and taking other natural elements isn't just discouraged, it's unlawful? These actions can damage vital habitat for plants, animals, birds, and insects. Instead of picking wildflowers, take a picture and compile the photos in a scrapbook or in your nature journals. Children can look through field guides to identify and label the flowers they find.**

40 Littleton Museum

Wander through two living history farms that reflect Littleton's western heritage.

Cost: Free
Hours: Tues–Sat 9 a.m. to 5 p.m., Sun 11 a.m. to 5 p.m.; last entry at 4:40 p.m. Closed Mon. and major holidays
Location: 6028 South Gallup Street, adjacent to Ketring Lake
Nearest Town: Littleton
Denver Drive Time: 20 minutes, via Broadway and Littleton Boulevard
Accessibility: The indoor portion of the museum is wheelchair accessible; however, the pathways in the historic farms are gravel, so there may be mud or ice depending on the time of year. It is advised to call ahead to inquire about the condition of the pathways. Wheelchairs and strollers are available to be checked out at no charge on a first-come, first-served basis. Glasses for generic color-blindness are available for both kids and adults. Sensory backpacks for both children and adults are available for check-out at no cost from the reception desk with an ID.
Bathrooms: Bathrooms inside the museum and a family restroom located across from the Research Center
Gear Suggestions: Dress for the weather. Bring sunscreen, hats, and sturdy shoes or rain gear to explore the historic farms.
Insider Tip: Check out the Daily Programs on the website to see what will be happening on the farms each week. Special museum events also give visitors a glimpse into various parts of life in Littleton during the 1800s. Look for Sheep to Shawl, Draft Animal Day, and the Harvest Festival to see the historic farms filled with demonstrations and activities.

Explore

From the Pikes Peak gold rush of 1859 right up to the end of World War II, agriculture was at the heart of Littleton's history. This now-sprawling city just 20 minutes south of downtown Denver grew out of one man's love for the location.

In the mid-1800s, New England engineer Richard Sullivan Little took a job out west to survey for a series of irrigation ditches that would bring water from Denver to the farms outside of the city. Scores of Pikes Peak gold seekers had moved into the area in hopes of striking it rich, and farms and businesses were springing up to provide goods and services for the growing population. Little knew the area would not only be ideal for agriculture, but also therapeutic for his wife's asthmatic condition. So, he brought his family west and the Littles settled near where historic Littleton sits today. With other settlers, they began building the community.

Today, the Littleton Museum, near Littleton Boulevard and Gallup Street, shares the many stories of the area from prehistory to present day. Inside the modern main museum building, you'll have an opportunity to peruse displays of local artifacts, photos, and documents alongside art exhibits and hands-on exhibits for the kids.

Pass through the museum doors to step into two living history farms, one an 1860s homestead and one an 1890s urban farm. Under the canopy of old cottonwood trees, each farm features historic buildings that are open to the public and represent what life would have been like for early settlers in Littleton. Although the museum is not on the original location of the Little family farm, the historic buildings nestled between Ketring Park and peaceful Ketring Lake make visitors feel as if they've been whisked back to a slower pace of life.

Explore the farms to encounter lively barns with resident animals like pigs, oxen, and sheep, and a mouse-hunting calico cat named Chloe, who keeps an eye on the 1860s farm. Though we visit the museum frequently, we love to watch their social media for the animal videos and pictures, especially in the spring when they post the arrival of lambs and piglets.

The property also features growing gardens, an orchard, a school, and a blacksmith shop. Historic interpreters dressed in period-appropriate costumes work around the farms, gardens, and schoolhouse to provide a glimpse into daily life for the families who lived in these eras. They are also enthusiastic about answering visitors' questions.

Explore the museum's website, at museum.littletonco.gov, for a list of daily farm programs each week. Kids might just encounter the blacksmith working in the forge, settle in for a lesson in the 1860s schoolhouse, or learn about frontier chores, gardening, or baking.

LEARN

The slice of historic life on display at this living, breathing museum creates endless ideas for learning.

- **Watch the Seasons: With gardens, an orchard, and farm animals all tended at this museum throughout the year, this is a fun spot to observe the changing seasons. Visit once a season (it's free!) and talk about how things look the same or different. In the summer kids may see thriving crops behind the 1860s homestead and then the same plot turned to an empty patch after fall harvest. The spring means baby animals and the annual sheep shearing, while costumed interpreters may use the colder winter weather to demonstrate baking techniques.**
- **Dig Deep: The Learning Resources area of the Littleton Museum website is full of educational videos, activities, and projects for families to do at home or during a visit. Watch interpretive videos on historic methods of cooking and baking, farm life, or farmer talks. Teachers and homeschool families can also download curriculum ideas under Teacher Resources. Borrow an idea from these resources, or research your own historic activity and spend a day living like early settlers.**

41 Lookout Mountain Preserve and Nature Center

Climb to the top for a hike through a mountain meadow.

Cost: Free
Hours: Fri 11 a.m. to 3 p.m., Sat–Sun 11 a.m. to 4 p.m. Closed Mon–Thurs. Trails open 1 hour before sunrise to 1 hour after sunset.
Location: 910 Colorow Road
Nearest Town: Golden
Denver Drive Time: 30 minutes via US 6 West
Accessibility: Main floor of the visitor center is wheelchair accessible
Bathrooms: Full bathrooms in visitor center when open, additional bathrooms on the exterior of the building available when closed.
Gear Suggestions: Sturdy walking shoes, hat, sunscreen, insect repellent, water
Insider Tip: Lookout Mountain is visited by walkers, hikers, tourists, motorists, and bicyclist, so be on alert and share the road. Buffalo Bill's Grave is just up the road from the preserve and nature center. Stop here to catch a captivating view of Golden below, towering mountains to the west, and Denver in the distance.

Explore

When you take in the views and a breath of fresh air at the top of Lookout Mountain, it's easy to understand why this spot, just a quick drive from Denver, makes "must-see" lists for out-of-town visitors. Even longtime Coloradans enjoy the break from city energy to walk among ponderosa pines and listen to the rustling aspens—without the bumper-to-bumper mountain drive. This spot, at an elevation of 7,377 feet, is also home to a peaceful, interactive place for families to learn more about the plants and wildlife on the mountain.

Lookout Mountain Preserve and Nature Center spreads out across 100 acres of forest and grassy mountain meadow, and the lodge-style nature center building is a welcoming starting point for a visit. Step inside to explore educational exhibits about the plants found in the area and to view a display of animal specimens that call the mountain home, including deer, bears, foxes, birds, and coyotes. Along with introducing the park's inhabitants, this exhibit teaches visitors how to live in harmony with wildlife, including tips for sharing natural areas at home and in the wild.

If the kids endlessly stream animal videos, make time to watch the animal cam. Though you may not glimpse the bigger wildlife during your visit, the loop on-screen provides an opportunity to see pictures and videos of animals caught on cameras around the preserve. For off-screen bird-watching and other animal watching, there is a viewing room with floor-to-ceiling windows and comfy chairs. You never know what might walk by as you scan the forest through the windows—we watched a doe and her fawn graze just beyond the nature center's back door.

While younger siblings explore the hands-on nature activities in the playroom, older sibs may want to seek out one of the friendly volunteer naturalists or rangers. When the kids start asking questions—so many questions—about the exhibits, these folks are full of answers. Rangers can also provide kids with a Jeffco Open Space Junior Ranger booklet featuring activities to help connect them to nature during their visit. Kids who finish the activities in the book can track down that friendly ranger again, recite the ranger oath, and receive a badge.

Once you're equipped with an introduction to Lookout Mountain, it's time to hit the trails. Lookout Mountain Nature Center's two loop trails are perfect even for young children. Pick up the easy half-mile Forest Loop Trail just behind the center. Walk through the forest of conifers and wildflowers and watch for deer and squirrels. Just past the footbridge, hikers have the opportunity to veer off onto the Meadow Loop Trail, adding 0.7 mile to the hike. If you are looking for a longer or more challenging hike, Lookout Mountain Trail picks up across the street from the nature center, with a connection to Buffalo Bill Trail and Windy Saddle Park Trailhead.

Lookout Mountain is on Lariat Loop, one of Colorado's popular scenic byway drives. On summer weekends, the area buzzes with hikers, bicyclists, and tourists, so if you have the chance, visit on a weekday.

LEARN

High atop Lookout Mountain, children can learn lessons about sharing natural spaces.

- **Be a Good Neighbor: Colorado wildlife can be found sharing the park near your house or even your backyard. Explore the exhibits to uncover ways to peacefully cohabitate with the birds, insects, and animals.**
- **Identify the Conifer: The Rockies are full of trees that produce cones, have needle-like leaves, and stay green all year round—these are called conifers. That is a simple explanation to identify a conifer, but did you know there are eight main families of conifers, including, pine, spruce, fir, juniper, and redwood, and 615 species of conifers within those families? Learn how to identify the conifer families and species that share Colorado's mountains. *Hint:* Take a close look at their cones and needles.**

42 Majestic View Nature Center

Inspect ponds and prairie habitat full of activity at this suburban nature oasis.

Cost: Free
Hours: Tues–Fri 10 a.m. to 3 p.m., Sat closed for programs only, Sun–Mon closed
Location: 7030 Garrison Street
Nearest Town: Arvada
Denver Drive Time: 25 minutes via I-70
Accessibility: Accessible nature center and paved trails including the gravel Cattail Trail and 0.1-mile Prairie Trail, both starting near the nature center
Bathrooms: Indoor restrooms when the nature center is open, port-o-lets near the playground on the east side of the park and by the nature play area in the parking area for the CSA farm
Gear Suggestions: Walking shoes, hat, sunscreen, binoculars to view birds
Insider Tip: The astronomy pad near the nature center parking lot has a concrete slab for setting up telescopes. The area around it uses only amber lighting to reduce light pollution and create better conditions for sky viewing. Standley Lake Stargazing hosts astronomy nights on-site throughout the summer for stargazing. Visit standleylakestargazing.com for dates and times.

Explore

This natural area tucked in an Arvada neighborhood at the end of Garrison Street lives up to its name with inspiring majestic views all around. It's no wonder that animals and humans have been drawn to the area for generations. Elk, bison, and deer once roamed the peaceful shortgrass prairie. Then in the late 1800s, when an irrigation canal came to the area, it became rich farmland. Fast-forward a century and Majestic View is an exciting place to take the family to inspect plants of the wetlands or the lake filled with frogs and fish.

Majestic View is a large city park with a playground and recreational area, as well as grassy spots for kids to run and play. But the big draw for families is the 80 acres of protected nature zones. Once a farmhouse, the 3,000-square-foot nature center features a collection of hands-on displays like mounted wildlife, a turtle tank, and the watershed table. Everyone will learn a little something about how to be a good steward of nature. Bring a picnic lunch or snack to eat on the shaded nature center deck and refill your water bottles out front at the water station with a spigot for humans, one for dogs, and one for filling water bottles.

Inside, a kid-size beaver dam will keep little ones occupied for a while, which is great because there are a couple of comfy parent-size chairs nearby. Be sure to check out the Beaver Pond Residents display. Did you know that a beaver is called a keystone species? Their presence in a wetland habitat has a profound impact on an array of other species, from insects to birds. They also have a remarkable ability to restore degraded wetland habitats. Kids will learn all about these busy ecosystem engineers as they build their own structures with wood blocks and rock pillows.

Don't miss the wildlife monitor for a sneak peek at wildlife roaming the park, from a variety of hidden trail cameras. Craft tables nearby are stocked with glue, crayons, and other art supplies, along with sample project ideas to get kids creating.

Once you've had a playful introduction to the area, it's time to head out to explore 25,000 square feet of demonstration gardens and 80 acres of wetlands and prairie. This is the time to pull out the binoculars. As you leave the nature center, go left down the paved Interpretive Trail. Just after a curve in the trail, turn left onto a narrow gravel footpath. This is the Oberon Lake path. It's a great place to look for

Majestic View's many winged visitors. Great blue herons, American kestrels, red-winged blackbirds, and even the American white pelican are known to make stops here to rest during their migration. The path ends at the lake, lined with cattails. This is an interesting spot to look for turtles and dragonflies, and to teach kids to use their senses to observe nature.

Now backtrack to the paved trail and look for the Cattail Trail on the south side of the nature center near Garrison Street. This trail guides hikers through wetland grasses and shortgrass prairie back to the main road. A newer portion of the trail has a packed-dirt surface and gives hikers amazing views of the lake and wildlife resting areas. This trail meets up with a paved trail that travels the perimeter of the park via Holland Court and 72nd Avenue.

Majestic View's popular children's programming offers camps and classes for pre-K kids through fifth graders, including a monthly playdate in the nature play area at the end of Prairie Trail. Find, and register for, current programs on the website (majesticviewnaturecenter.arvada.org) or look for the What's Happening board by the entrance to the nature center for upcoming activities.

LEARN

Look beyond the sweeping vistas at this nature center to see the world with microscopic eyes. Teach kids to deconstruct the big picture in order to study nature's individual building blocks.

- **Name the Peaks: Stand on the Interpretive Trail at Majestic View and look west. On a clear day you'll see a lineup of Rocky Mountain peaks in the distance. Pick up a park map at the nature center, unfold it, and look across the bottom for a photo identifying the individual peaks and their names. Use this as a starting point in learning the location of Colorado's peaks.**
- **Get to Know Ecosystem Engineers: Inside Majestic View Nature Center, learn about the beaver's job title of ecosystem engineer. Through the daily work of building their dams, these creatures build microhabitats that support a plethora of other species. Are there other birds, animals, or even insects with this important job? Ask the nature center staff or read up on ecosystem engineers to uncover the answers. Kids can construct a simple web diagram that illustrates species who benefit from the beavers' work. Ask them: Who cohabitates in the beaver dam? What about the ponds created by their dams?**

43 Marjorie Perry Nature Preserve

Experience one of Metro Denver's best-kept secrets.

Cost: Free
Hours: Open daily from sunrise to sunset
Location: Off the High Line Canal, south of Belleview Avenue, between Colorado Boulevard and South Holly Street
Nearest Town: Greenwood Village
Denver Drive Time: 20 minutes via I-25
Accessibility: You'll need a good jogging stroller or all-terrain wheelchair to access Marjorie Perry Nature Preserve via the flat and bumpy dirt trail servicing the area. While the High Line Canal Trail can get busy, especially on weekends, the preserve itself generally offers a quiet, low-sensory experience.
Bathrooms: Portable toilets at the trailhead at 4200 East Belleview Avenue.
Gear Suggestions: KEEN sandals or similar shoes that work for walking and water play, sunscreen, sunglasses, bucket hats, binoculars, nature-journaling materials, plenty of water, a picnic lunch, books to read pondside, bikes if you're riding into the preserve
Insider Tip: Go on a wildlife safari. Begin your adventure before 9 a.m. In addition to avoiding the bikers on the High Line, you'll up your odds of spotting wild animals if you head out early. Remind children to walk quietly through the preserve, and help them maintain their patience by playing quiet games such as a whispering version of I Spy. Always give wildlife at least 25 yards of personal space. Make it 100 yards or more for predators such as coyotes. If you're close enough for a selfie, you're way too close.

Explore

Forest bathing has swept the United States, and if you're looking for a few peaceful moments of total nature immersion, few in-town spots rival Marjorie Perry Nature Preserve. There are multiple ways to access this under-the-radar destination. The quickest route into the 52-acre open space is via the trailhead at 4200 East Belleview Avenue Park in the lot off of Belleview, then walk east to reach the High Line Canal Trail, at which point you'll go south, away from Belleview, until arriving at your destination. This short, partially shaded route is about 0.5 mile each way. The trail's wide, and the scenic landscape makes for a gorgeous city hike with kids of all ages.

But it can also be fun to bring bikes and Striders and ride into the preserve, where single-track trails cut through the natural habitat. For a pretty 4-mile trek, access the High Line at its Dahlia Trailhead. There's parking past Arapahoe Tennis Club, at 4450 South Dahlia Street. Turn left onto the trail. At mile 33, use the underpass to cross East Belleview Avenue, then follow the dirt path to a secluded refuge anchored by two idyllic ponds.

The preserve is an incredible wildlife habitat hosting mammals, birds, raptors, reptiles, and amphibians, all thriving in the middle of Greenwood Village. Animals come

to the area for water, of course, and the natural vegetation. As you explore the area, look for red foxes, striped skunks, raccoons, coyotes, cottontail rabbits, and fox squirrels. Even if you can't spy all of these mammals, you might see their tracks or scat as you walk. Greenwood Village's website has a special page devoted to Marjorie Perry Nature Preserve: greenwoodvillage.com/352/Marjorie-Perry-Nature-Preserve. Look for a "Mammals" link near the bottom of the page, where you'll find images of the mammals who call the preserve home, plus pictures of their tracks.

Bird-watching is another fun activity to enjoy inside the preserve. How many songbirds and raptors can you spot? The song of the yellow warbler is something to hear, and listen for mallards quacking, too, and chickadees chirping, as you search for the telltale red breast of a robin who might be fluttering between the cattails and cottonwoods. If you're lucky, you and your kids will catch a glimpse of a hawk overhead, swooping down, occasionally, for a deer mouse. And if you're out early enough, you might see a white pelican wandering alongside one of the ponds. Have

your binoculars ready, and consider bringing a Colorado birding book to help with identification.

There are some interesting insects to discover near the water, namely dragonflies and butterflies, and as you walk from pond to pond, look for interpretive signs, offering up educational tidbits about the flora and fauna that make up a wetland habitat, plus information about conservation.

LEARN

From habitats and ecosystems to conservation, there's plenty for kids to glean while exploring this serene spot.

- Get Artistic: Have your kids ever tried plein-air painting? The French term means painting outdoors, and the preserve is an excellent place for budding artists to capture nature's beauty. Bring along simple art supplies, including watercolors or acrylics and thick paper, and let children spend time turning their surroundings into a work of art.
- Connect with Nature: The preserve is named for a naturalist, outdoorswoman, and conservationist who spent most of her long, vibrant life in Colorado after moving to the state when she was 3 years old. In the spirit of the late Marjorie Perry, learn more about local conservation efforts. Greenwood Village's website, greenwoodvillage.com, has an informative fact sheet on preserving water quality in wetlands habitats. Located at 1200 Broadway in downtown Denver, History Colorado Center has some excellent exhibits on water conservation tucked away in a second-floor exhibition room. And there's no shortage of books on the topic available at local public libraries.

44 May Natural History Museum

Dig deep in this vast collection of tropical insects.

Cost: $$ Children ages 5 and under free
Hours: Open daily May 1 to Oct 1, 9 a.m. to 6 p.m., last admission at 5:30 p.m.
Location: 710 Rock Creek Canyon Road, Colorado Springs. Look for Herkimer, the world's largest beetle and the museum's mascot Hercules beetle—who is 10,000 times the size of an actual beetle and bigger than a Volkswagen Beetle—at the turnoff to the museum.
Nearest Town: Colorado Springs
Denver Drive Time: 90 minutes via I-25 South
Accessibility: The museum is wheelchair accessible, and if you need quiet space to reset, the museum is surrounded by a peaceful, shady outdoor setting.
Bathrooms: Bathrooms are available near the gift shop.
Gear Suggestions: Comfortable walking shoes, sun protection, plenty of water. In the spring bring a fleece jacket or coat since the collection room housing the displays is not heated, in order to preserve specimens.
Insider Tip: When you purchase your tickets, ask at the desk for a copy of the scavenger hunt. It has some questions that will even challenge the observation skills of adults. If you complete the hunt, there is a small prize waiting for the kids.

Explore

John May was just a teenager when he dreamed up a plan that would support his family through the Great Depression during the 1930s. May's father was a naturalist, and a newly unemployed park ranger, who had begun collecting tropical insect specimens during his time in South Africa during the Boer War. May saw an opportunity to take his father's stunning collection on the road, giving viewers a look at insects of a size most Americans of the time had never seen. Under the tutelage of a German cabinetmaker, May learned to build custom airtight cases and stands to display and protect every butterfly, moth, spider, beetle, and stick bug in the collection.

After years of touring with the collection, the family decided to settle in Colorado, where the dry climate was a perfect match for preserving the delicate insects. True to his hardworking nature, May constructed a museum outside of Colorado Springs to house the collection, which is where you'll find the world's largest private collection of insects today.

Only a small percentage of the collection is actually on display, but considering the specimens number over 100,000, visitors will see an eye-popping 7,000 insects of all shapes, sizes, and, uh, creepiness. Some specimens are more than one hundred years old, some have since gone extinct or have never been seen again, and some are now illegal to trade. The best of the best are on display.

The 6,000+-square-foot museum isn't loaded with hands-on displays or computerized learning modules, but the collection is the main draw. There is also a small theater space showing an episode of the television show *Strange Inheritance* that tells the story of the collection. If you have little tykes or kids with specific interests, ask at the desk about other age-appropriate entomology videos they can cue up on the video screen.

Step into the collection room filled with the same display cases made by John May, some propped on stands and some lining the walls, which will guide you along. (Very little ones may need a boost for a good look into the cases.)

A small exhibit case at the beginning includes details about the collection's origins (along with a list of near-death experiences in the lifetime of the collector James

May). At the end, view an exhibit of insect collector's gear and one on pinning the specimens for display, before spilling into a small gift shop with fun and educational toys, books, and gifts with an insect theme. Remember to bring a lunch or snack to eat at the picnic tables before you head home. The remote natural setting is also perfect for hunting down your own insects.

LEARN

This museum opens kids' eyes to the variety and staggering size of tropical insects. Here are some ways to extend what they've learned at the museum.

- **Lesson Learned: Look closely at each specimen. You'll see a tiny slip of paper with part of the bug's scientific name handwritten by John May's daughter, Lynda. We may just call them bugs, but they also have far more interesting scientific names. These names are based on the science of grouping and organization of biological things called taxonomy. Swedish professor, scientist, and doctor Carl Linnaeus first created the system of organizing and scientific naming of living things in the eighteenth century. His hierarchy of categories is still used today: kingdom, phylum, class, order, family, genus, and species. Use this naming system as a springboard to talk about how living organisms are different or the same. Keep it simple with young children. Compare scaly things versus feathered things and things with fur, for example.**
- **Level Up: Using the same hierarchy, challenge middle and high schoolers to research the classification hierarchy of various species they see in the museum.**

45 Meadow Music at Chautauqua Park

Boogie down while becoming an eco-activist.

Cost: Free thanks to ongoing support from the City of Boulder Open Space and Mountain Parks (OSMP) division
Hours: They vary; check the Jeff & Paige website, jeffandpaige.org, for this year's concert schedule.
Location: 900 Baseline Road
Nearest Town: Boulder
Denver Drive Time: 40 minutes via I-25 and U.S. Route 36
Accessibility: Shows are wheelchair accessible. Jeff & Paige concerts tend to be loud events routinely drawing crowds of 400 or more. Families are welcome to lay out blankets away from the main stage, but the experience isn't low-sensory.
Bathrooms: Flush toilets located below the Chautauqua Dining Hall
Gear Suggestions: Comfortable shoes, sunscreen, a windbreaker or light jacket, plenty of water, a picnic, blankets or low-profile chairs
Insider Tip: Most families discover Jeff & Paige through their Meadow Music program, but the summer concert series is just one of the band's many offerings. The husband-wife duo perform year-round, up and down the Front Range, and most of their public shows are free. Check out their website, jeffandpaige.org, for a current schedule, and look for the band at local parks, nature centers, and libraries.

Explore

Jeff Kagan and Paige Doughty know that STEM is way more fun when you break out the guitar. The husband-wife music duo met in graduate school, while studying environmental education, and it is fair to say their love was sustainable. The two founded their signature Meadow Music Program in 2005, and they've been performing at Chautauqua Park ever since, introducing kids to the various ways we can all care for the stunning natural landscape that surrounds us in Colorado.

In addition to funding Jeff & Paige's award-winning summer concert series, Boulder OSMP also provides staffing for every Meadow Music event. A typical show at Chautauqua kicks off with an easy, 0.2-mile ranger-led hike geared toward toddlers and preschooler's. Hikes are stroller friendly, and guests in wheelchairs can use a fire access road to reach the "summit," where a ranger pops out in full costume, dressed up as the animal of the day.

The animal of the day might be a coyote, bear, or mule deer, and there will also be a color of the day, which varies based on what wildflowers are blooming in Boulder. When the hike ends, the real fun begins. Families roll out blankets, and Jeff & Paige begin their high-energy performance, featuring dozens of original songs tuned to environmental education.

Concerts are visual and extremely kinesthetic. In addition to colorful costumes and bold dance moves, science- and nature-themed skits are performed between sets

with the goal of bringing eco-issues to life. By the third song, most children have joined a kid-friendly mosh pit that forms near the stage. You can expect lots of audience interaction and participation throughout the show. From songs about Colorado wildlife and ecosystems to eating local and biking to school and work, the band covers topics in science, nature, and sustainability, with language perfectly pitched to little ears.

Things usually begin to wind down after an hour, but everyone's invited to stick around after the show for nature-based play on the nearby playground, located on the east side of the lawn. There's also a wonderful Ranger Cottage near the trailheads that's definitely worth a visit. All are welcome at Jeff & Paige events, but be aware that Meadow Music is specifically designed for kids ages 2 to 8. Registration is not required for Meadow Music events; just show up and enjoy time outdoors listening to live music with your kids.

LEARN

Meadow Music's all about making environmental education accessible for young kids. And there's no need for the learning to stop once the music ends.

- Start a Band: Of course we are going to suggest that you and your kids go home and start your own eco-minded band! If you don't have instruments on the ready, why not infuse an extra STEM component into the project, and make a few out of upcycled materials? Then get to work writing and composing your own nature-themed songs about wildlife, conservation, sustainable living, or whatever else strikes your fancy. If you and your kids need some additional fodder, check out a few environmental books at your local library, and learn more about the subject before finalizing your lyrics.
- Visit Jeff & Paige Online: The Jeff & Paige YouTube channel is packed with short, educational videos for families, offering a robust online learning community. Many of the band's YouTube videos include scientific lessons coupled with hands-on activities young children can do at home with a caregiver while learning more about nature and the environment.

46 Mines Museum of Earth Science

A hidden gem for learning about rocks, minerals, and Colorado's mining history.

Cost: Free
Hours: Mon–Sat 9 a.m. to 4 p.m., Sun 1 to 4 p.m.
Location: 1310 Maple Street, inside the General Research Lab (GRL) building on the campus of Colorado School of Mines
Nearest Town: Golden
Denver Drive Time: Under 30 minutes via 6th Avenue
Accessibility: Wheelchair accessible from the back entrance, with elevator between two floors; museum materials available in Spanish
Bathrooms: Bathrooms on each floor of the GRL building
Gear Suggestions: No special gear needed, but bring good walking shoes if you want to explore the campus or the Mines Geology Trail.
Insider Tip: There are six burros hidden throughout the museum. Find five of the burros during your visit and kids will get a small prize. Ask to see a sample of the burro at the front desk.

Explore

Folks likely know that the Colorado state flower is the blue columbine, and the state animal is the Rocky Mountain bighorn sheep, but here's one to stump the kids: What is the Colorado state rock? Or the state mineral?

The Mines Museum of Earth Science is the perfect place to explore the rocks, gems, and minerals of this state so connected to the Rocky Mountains. This museum is the official keeper of Colorado's State Mineral Collection, where visitors can view more than 2,000 dazzling and significant items in the bright, open museum space (the total collection includes more than 40,000 items).

Start a visit at the front desk for some ideas from the student scientists on duty that day. They are also a great resource for any questions kids may have throughout the visit. Explore on your own or stream the ten-stop "Best of Mines Museum" audio tour on your phone for around $2. Groups of four to fifteen visitors may also schedule a guided tour of the museum that can be adjusted for the ages in the group. (There is a per person fee for guided tours, and they need to be booked by museum staff at least one week in advance.)

The main level gives everyone a chance to explore the cases on Colorado mining history and tools, and oodles of rocks, minerals, and gemstones from Colorado and the Western Hemisphere. A safe filled with gold coins minted in Denver sits at the top of the stairway leading to the lower level.

At the bottom of the stairs, walk through Blaster's Mine to see what it might feel like in an underground mine. Explore the dark cave for the fluorescent mineral exhibit, which is a kid favorite. As you leave the mine, you'll see another museum favorite, Miss Colorado's crown (as long as she isn't wearing it at an event that day).

Kids may be able to identify some more symbols of Colorado as they view the sparkling design. Do you see mountains, columbines, aspen leaves?

The lower level is also a place for fans of dinosaurs and space exploration. View the museum's collection of 500-million-year-old fossils and touch an Apatosaurus leg bone. Then shoot into outer space with a glimpse of two moon rocks collected during Apollo missions and a display of meteorites from around the state. One of the meteorites was found in an eastern Colorado farmer's field. He brought the rock home and used it as a doorstop for years before the family had the museum examine the rock to determine that it was indeed a meteorite. Once a quarter, the museum invites any visitors to bring their own rocks for identification.

The museum gift shop is curated with educational toys, gifts for kids and adults, and rocks, along with an outstanding collection of children's books with rock and earth science themes.

LEARN

If you are constantly finding carefully collected rocks in your kiddo's pockets, this museum will inspire them to learn more about their discoveries.

- **Become a Rock Hound: Rocks are like tiny treasures. Take a walk around town, your neighborhood, or even your backyard to collect rocks of different colors, shapes, and textures, and learn to identify them. Are they smooth or rough? All one color or many colors? Can you scratch them? Are they magnetic? Borrow a library book or use an online guide to figure out the type of rocks your child finds. Be aware, though, that collecting rocks in some locations, like national parks, is prohibited.**
- **Borrow a Lesson Kit: The museum offers three different hands-on educational kits for lessons in rocks and minerals. Anyone may check out the kits for up to three weeks. Reserve the kits on the museum website (mines.edu/museumofearthscience/).**

47 Morrison Natural History Museum

Mastodon-size fun awaits at this hands-on learning center.

Cost: $$$ $1 per person admission for EBT cardholders
Hours: Open daily 10 a.m. to 5 p.m., with last call for ticket sales at 4 p.m. The museum is closed on Jan 1, Thanksgiving Day, and Dec 24 and 25.
Location: 501 Colorado Highway 8
Nearest Town: Morrison
Denver Drive Time: 25 minutes via Sixth Avenue West and CO 470
Accessibility: The site is wheelchair accessible, and strollers are permitted, though a baby carrier is an easier choice if available.
Bathrooms: Flush toilets past the gift shop
Gear Suggestions: Comfortable shoes, snacks to enjoy at the picnic tables outside the museum
Insider Tip: Don't forget to pop into the laboratory after your tour. Since Morrison rocks are still producing new finds, potential fossils are shipped to the museum on a regular basis. Hence, guided tours always end on the second floor, at an on-site laboratory, where visitors are invited to "work on the rocks," using real paleontology tools to remove sand from rocks scientists are actively studying. It's an incredible, unforgettable experience.

Explore

At first glance this two-story museum might seem small, but some humongous treasures are tucked away inside. The town of Morrison is famous for its iconic dinosaur discoveries. In fact, the first Stegosaurus fossil was unearthed in Morrison in 1876 at the nearby Dinosaur Ridge.

In 1874 the first T. rex tooth was found in the nearby town of Golden. With so much local paleontology happening, it's no wonder everything inside Morrison Natural History Museum pertains to Colorado fossils. (Well, almost everything! The wooly mammoth, an extinct species that lived during the Pleistocene, wouldn't have roamed quite so far south.)

While it's fine to visit the museum anytime it's open, first-timers are advised to show up at the top of the hour for a guided tour (included with admission). Departing from the main desk and lasting 45 minutes to an hour, tours are recommended because the museum's four exhibition halls were designed to be viewed with a docent.

From the Jurassic and Cretaceous periods to the last ice age, you'll get a chance to view many of the critters that have called Colorado home through the ages as you peruse rare and recent fossils and adorable infant dinosaur tracks. Our family really enjoys the oddball characters, like a 30-million-year-old, 600-pound Archaeotherium staff members lovingly refer to as "the warthog from Hades."

The museum keeps a special collection of ice age survivors, which are live animals, including snakes, lizards, turtles, and salamanders. If you're lucky, you'll show up at feeding time (no schedule is posted; the animals eat based on their needs). Kids

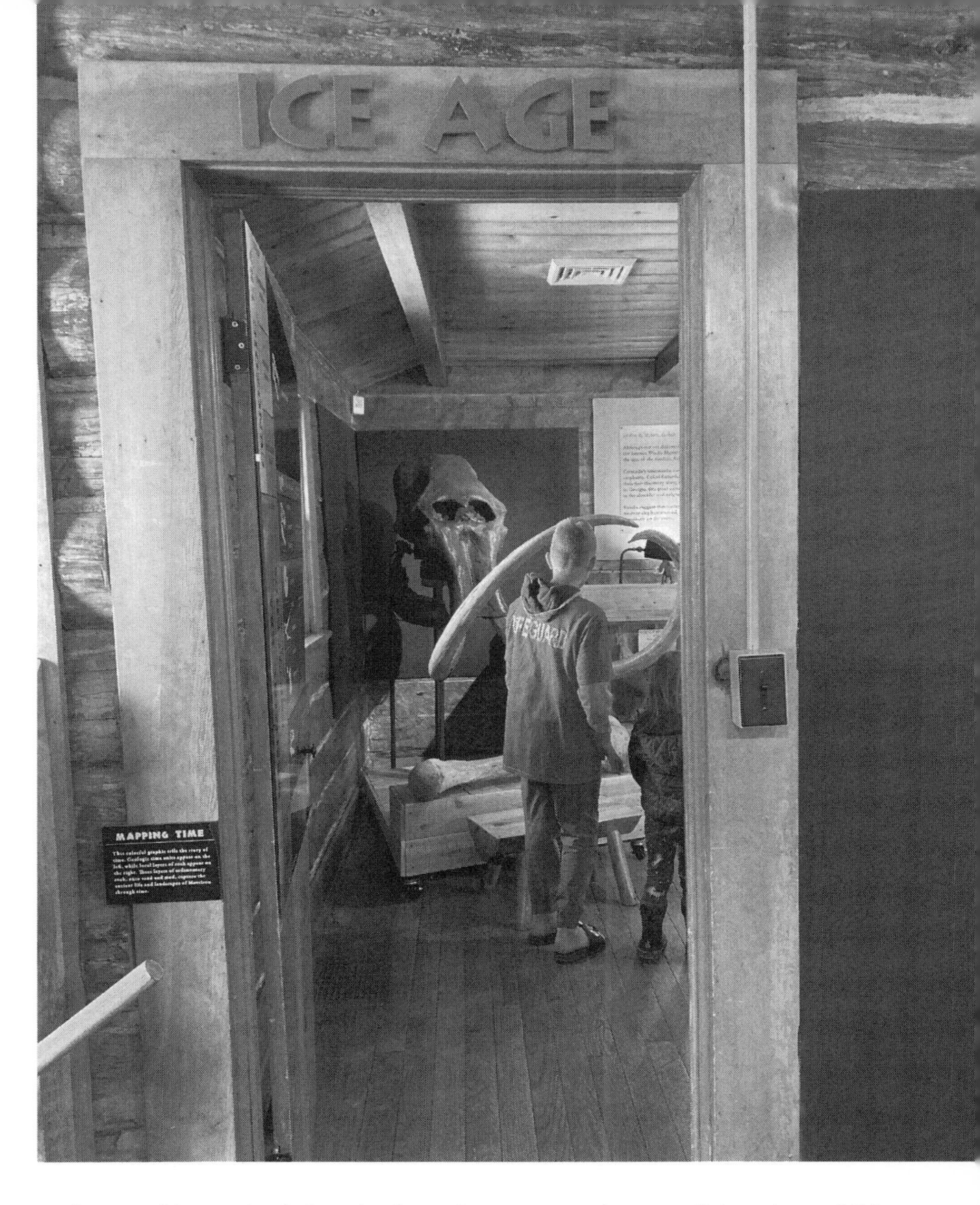

can't pet resident animals, but they're welcome to touch most of the other exhibits. Yes, you read that right! As long as your children are gentle, Morrison Natural History Museum is a hands-on facility, and touch-based learning starts at the entrance with a massive Tyrannosaurus rex skull.

Unlike at other museums, staff encourage tactile learning because guests get a much better idea of size and sharpness if they explore with their hands. From teeth and bones to footprints, the vast majority of the items on display are casts of bones. Don't worry, you'll know which items are off-limits because they're behind glass.

After the tour younger children will love digging for "bones" in the Fossil Dig Pit, which is essentially a gigantic sandbox with a 15-foot faux dinosaur buried inside. Curious guests are welcome to bring their "finds" inside, and museum staff will help identify the specimens.

While you're exploring alfresco, check out the Time Garden, a collection of rocks that'll walk you through 1.3 billion years of Earth history, and the Jurassic Garden, where you'll discover scouring rush, ginkgo trees, and other plants similar to those that grew in Colorado 150 million years ago. Both gardens are on the south end of the museum's property, and if the weather's nice, you can follow the narrow dirt Time Trail—it picks up directly behind the museum—about a quarter mile up to a scenic overlook. Why not pack a picnic lunch to enjoy the Paleo way from outside and immersed on all sides by stunning dinosaur history?

LEARN

What kid doesn't like learning about the science of fossils? For those studying paleontology, rocks and minerals, or prehistory more generally, Morrison Natural History Museum is the kind of place that'll bring textbooks to life.

- **Delectable Dinos: Learning will be much more delicious if you bake sugar cookies imprinted with dinosaur tracks. Back home, prepare your favorite sugar cookie recipe, then let your kids use toy dinosaurs (available for purchase in the gift shop if you don't have any on hand) to make footprints. Before baking, add a dusting of cinnamon over the tracks for effect.**
- **Measure Up: To get a real sense of size and scale, ask your child to research some of their favorite dinosaurs, focusing on how tall and/or long they were. Outside, use sidewalk chalk to measure your child, then see how they stack up, using string and sidewalk chalk to mark the height/length of one or more dinosaurs.**

48 Morrison Nature Center at Star K Ranch

Discover a hidden wetland trail in an unexpected area of Aurora.

Cost: Free
Hours: Wed–Fri noon to 4 p.m., Sat–Sun 9 a.m. to 4 p.m., closed Mon–Tues. Call ahead to verify nature center hours, as they may vary seasonally. Trails open daily from dawn to dusk.
Location: 16002 East Smith Road
Nearest Town: Aurora
Denver Drive Time: 25 minutes via I-70 East
Accessibility: Accessible nature center building
Bathrooms: Full bathroom inside the nature center (when open) with diaper-changing station and water fountain
Gear Suggestions: Sturdy walking shoes, hats, sunscreen, insect repellent
Insider Tip: Ask for an activity book at the desk inside the nature center. The booklet suggests activities to do during your visit as well as when you get home. The booklets change frequently so there is a new reason to pick them up each time you visit.

Explore

Driving through the industrial neighborhood of Aurora on Smith Road, between Chambers Road and Airport Boulevard, you would never guess that it's also home to one of Metro Denver's lush natural areas. It's a lovely surprise as you turn onto Laredo Street and find yourself in a hidden wetland that's home to giant shady cottonwoods, red-tailed hawks, and a nature center filled with opportunities for families to play and learn.

One local man, Virgil "Pop" Stark, knew the beauty of this area. He bought the property in 1950, built a house on it, and called it his retirement home. Pop hosted his friends at the ranch, where they fished from the ponds and threw parties alongside his animal friends, a singing cat, a lazy sheepdog, and a pond full of alligators. Members of Pop's family lived on the ranch until 1992, when they moved to Denver after negotiating the sale of the property to the City of Aurora in the 1980s. A decade later, Pop's house and garage became the Morrison Nature Center and the land around it a peaceful oasis in a bustling city.

In the parking lot you'll be greeted by *Steel Stampede*, a striking art installation by sculptor Douwe Blumberg depicting a herd of life-size horses galloping through the prairie grasses.

As you step inside the nature center, look to your left. This cozy room with a couch, fireplace, books, and a sensory table was part of Pop's original home and is a peaceful spot for quiet playtime. Explore the nature center displays and meet the ambassador bull snake who slithered into the nature center one day and stayed. There's also a 60-year-old western box turtle, a tiger salamander, and a Woodhouse's toad. Tinker with the hands-on interpretive exhibits, many of which change out seasonally so there is always

something new to see. Imaginative kids can also dress up in the nature center's costumes or put on a puppet show. Before heading out to the trails, check the resource wall for self-guided tour brochures and activity sheets. If the nature center is closed, self-guided tour maps are available at the kiosk near the trailhead.

Anchoring the 250 acres of riparian woodland around the nature center is the quiet 0.75-mile Wetland Loop Trail. Wind around cattail-filled ponds and through cottonwood groves using the self-guided sensory tour for kids. (There is also one for adults with a focus on the property's history.) As you reach numbered posts along the trail, match the number to interpretive descriptions in the brochure. Take time to look for birds, amphibians, and maybe even a beaver dam. The Animal Sightings board in the nature center will let you know which species have recently visited the area.

For a longer walk, extend the Wetland Loop with the 0.9-mile Creekside Trail or the Sand Creek Greenway Trail, which also connects to the High Line Canal Trail.

Morrison Nature Center offers a variety of low-cost programs to give children a deeper connection with nature and wildlife, including a monthly Junior Naturalist series, full-moon hikes, and "nature at night" guided walks to see a different side of the natural areas.

LEARN

It's a surprise to find a lush nature center like this one hidden in the city. Help children channel their inner detective to reveal exciting nature discoveries.

- **Hone Your Observation Skills: Pick up a copy of the Morrison Nature Center Scavenger Hunt inside the nature center to see what you can find around the trails and wetlands. There is also an Urban Nature Scavenger Hunt to reference as you explore closer to home.**
- **Learn the Different Grasses: Shortgrass prairies once dominated the eastern plains of Colorado. Did you know that Colorado has a state grass? It's called blue grama grass and you can identify it by the soft, eyebrow-like bristles at the end of its stems. Check out the display on grasses inside the Morrison Nature Center and learn how to identify different species.**

49 Mount Falcon Park West

Hike to a crumbling castle surrounded by unforgettable mountain vistas.

Cost: Free
Hours: Open daily, 1 hour before sunrise to 1 hour after sunset
Location: 21074 Mount Falcon Road
Nearest Town: Indian Hills
Denver Drive Time: 45 minutes via 6th Avenue West to Kipling Street to US 285
Accessibility: The direct route to the Walker Home Ruins is doable with a good jogging stroller or all-terrain wheelchair.
Bathrooms: Drop toilets 0.1 mile past Mount Falcon West Trailhead
Gear Suggestions: Comfortable walking shoes, sunscreen, a hat, sunglasses, plenty of water, snacks, binoculars, nature-journaling supplies

Insider Tip: Did you know that feeding wildlife is against the law in all Jefferson County Open Spaces, including Mount Falcon Park? The fine for this violation is $100. If you're found taking, collecting, or otherwise gathering natural resources, including items such as rocks and wildflowers, that's another $100. Every park has its own rules and regulations, and before visiting a new place, it's always a good idea to brush up on local expectations. For a full rundown, visit the destination's website, and do a little sleuthing to figure out which entity manages the land you're planning to visit. Jefferson County Open Space manages Mount Falcon Park, and their park regulations are posted online at www.jeffco.us/1583/regulations.

Explore

In addition to well-marked trails and views for days, Mount Falcon Park claims several "secret" structures bursting with Colorado history. It's important to know that two trailheads service the 2,249-acre park. While it's possible to reach the site's historic ruins via the closer-to-Denver Mount Falcon Morrison Trailhead, this option requires a pretty challenging 5.8-mile out-and-back hike with 2,000 feet of elevation gain along the rugged Castle Trail. With kids, especially younger ones, we prefer to park in the Indian Hills lot servicing the Mount Falcon West Trailhead, located at the end of Mount Falcon Road.

There are actually two parking lots near the trailhead. Try the upper lot first. If it's full, you can always backtrack to the lower lot. Follow a wide dirt-and-gravel path past a stately stone pavilion to reach a kiosk and outhouses. As you walk, be sure to tell preschool and grade-school children that they're on a mission to uncover the park's hidden gem, the crumbling shell of a real-life castle!

A little less than 0.5 mile into the route, you'll reach the Castle-Meadow Trails intersection. Most hikers turn left at this junction to descend directly to the Walker Home Ruins. In another 0.5 mile, you'll arrive at Mount Falcon's main event, the remains of entrepreneur John Walker's turn-of-the-century mountaintop mansion. The old castle will be to your left, off the trail just a bit, so task your kids with finding it once you reach the next trail intersection.

Take some time to read about the massive home and its builder, John Walker, a self-made millionaire originally from the Pittsburgh area. Walker dabbled in many things: In addition to being a magazine guru—he edited *Cosmopolitan*—and automobile entrepreneur who co-founded the Locomobile Company of America, Walker might have also been one of the greatest conservationists in Colorado history. Few Denverites know this, but he's responsible for the way much of the Front Range looks today.

When Walker relocated to Colorado in 1905, he began developing the Riverfront Park area in downtown Denver. He purchased over 4,000 acres of land, including what is now Mount Falcon Park. While searching for the perfect place to build a family home, Walker preserved thousands of acres of land. He gifted forty of them to the Jesuits. You guessed it: They built Regis University on their property.

By 1909 Walker had finally found the right place to settle down. He hired Italian stonemasons to build a chalet with a whopping ten bedrooms, eight fireplaces, and a music room, library, and servants' quarters. The ruins you're viewing are the remains of his extravagant home. Hard times followed the construction of Walker's castle. John's wife, Ethel Walker, died in 1916, and two years later lightning burned down the whole place, forcing Walker to leave the area.

Walker's personal tragedy wasn't totally in vain. According to the interpretive sign preceding the ruins, Walker's vision for land preservation eventually became the foundation for Denver Mountain Parks and Jefferson County Open Space.

LEARN

History lovers have so much to gain from a hike to the Walker Home Ruins, which comes with life-size lessons in everything from architecture and land development to entrepreneurship, conservation, and more.

- Hands-On History: Walker had his hands in a bit of everything! He boosted farming in Colorado by introducing irrigated alfalfa as a crop, and he invested in the Stanley Steamer steam-powered automobile. Ask older children to research Walker and create a timeline and/or fictional story based on his life. Young kids in need of tactile learning opportunities can ride in a Model T—not exactly a Stanley Steamer, but still—at History Colorado Center, 1200 Broadway in downtown Denver, where guests learn more about life in early 1900s Colorado while exploring the museum's first-floor Destination Colorado Exhibit, with tons of hands-on displays.
- Walk On: Mount Falcon Park has other secrets, too, so if you have time, keep exploring. Pick up a map at the trailhead, then let kids develop their navigational skills while they attempt to find the park's three main structures—the castle ruins plus a shelter and lookout tower. Remember that first trail intersection you hit? If you go straight through it, you're on Tower Trail, which takes you to the immaculately maintained Eagle Eye Shelter, a scenic overlook near a boarded-up well. A little farther up the trail, your kids will stumble on Lookout Tower, with a staircase leading to the best views in the park.

50 Mount Sanitas History Hike

Hike straight through Colorado history on this classic Boulder trail.

Cost: Free
Hours: Boulder OSMP trails are open 24/7; the Centennial Trailhead parking lot is open daily from 5 a.m. to 11 p.m.
Location: 301 Sunshine Canyon Drive
Nearest Town: Boulder
Denver Drive Time: 40 minutes via I-25 and US 36
Accessibility: You'll need an all-terrain wheelchair and good jogging stroller for the flat portion of Mount Sanitas Trail. Summiting the mountain requires use of East Ridge and/or Sanitas West Valley Trails. Both trails have high foot traffic and traverse the ridge leading to the Mount Sanitas summit. The terrain is very rugged, with boulders and projected rock outcrops.
Bathrooms: Outhouses at the far end of the Centennial Trailhead parking lot
Gear Suggestions: Binoculars, comfortable walking shoes, sunscreen, a hat, sunglasses, a windbreaker if attempting to summit, plenty of water, snacks, nature-journaling supplies
Insider Tip: There are multiple ways to access Mount Sanitas Trail, but the easiest way in for those who don't have neighborhood access is via Centennial Trailhead. From Boulder, take Broadway north to Mapleton Avenue. Turn left (west) onto Mapleton, and drive for 0.9 mile to reach the Centennial Trailhead parking lot, located on the left (south) side of the road. From this lot, you'll backtrack, on foot, to get to the Mount Sanitas Trailhead and welcome sign.

Explore

From the Centennial Trail parking lot, look for a green sign reading "Trail to Pedestrian Crossing for Mt. Sanitas." Following the arrow on the sign, walk past the outhouse, and in about 200 feet turn left to carefully cross Mapleton Avenue at the crosswalk. After passing a Mount Sanitas trail marker, go through the opening in the fence. Don't worry, you're on the right track! Follow the dirt path uphill, and hike straight through a four-way trail intersection. Before you know it, you will have arrived at the Mount Sanitas welcome sign, and your hike through history will have officially begun.

Ask school-age children to read aloud the name of the area's towering summit. If they pronounce the mountain "sa-KNEE-tis," emphasizing a long "e" sound, give them a quick social studies lesson as you hike along Mount Sanitas Trail, the wide and flat gravel path wedged between Mount Sanitas and a hogback ridge.

John Harvey Kellogg—yes, *that* Kellogg, the cereal guy—was a Seventh Day Adventist practicing medicine at the turn of the century, presenting the once novel idea that diet plays a role in one's overall health. In 1894 Dr. Kellogg opened the Boulder-Colorado Sanitarium and Hospital. Tuberculosis sanatoriums were cropping up all across Colorado, but treatment at Kellogg's place was spa-like. In fact, by 1904 people with communicable diseases were prohibited at the Boulder-Colorado Sanitarium and Hospital, which operated its own dairy and a natural foods factory.

Because the name Sanitas is derived from the word "sanitarium," the correct pronunciation is "SAN-eh-tis," emphasis on the first syllable.

At the intersection of the Sanitas Valley and Dakota Ridge Trails, see if your kids can nail this mountain's correct pronunciation before ascending Dakota Ridge via a rocky course offering bird's-eye views of the draw below.

You're using the same trail Kellogg's sanitarium guests once traversed. To get his clients outdoors, Kellogg built several stone structures throughout the area. For a fun twist on a scavenger hunt, see if your kids can find ruins as you hike. Hint: Look for a smokestack just past the Sanitas Valley and Dakota Ridge trail junction. It was part of the original sanitarium, along with a nearby stone shelter and the remains of an archway.

Dakota Ridge Trail continues for another 0.8 mile, passing some interesting rock formations before reaching a scenic overlook and three-way trail intersection. Brochures for the Boulder-Colorado Sanitarium and Hospital promoted not just the hospital's facilities but also its on-site activities, including burro rides up Mount Sanitas.

A pamphlet from 1902 read, "Nearly everyone can reach the peak by taking his time." That's still true today! But if your kids aren't quite ready for a burro-free ascent, you can always turn left at the trail post and enjoy an easy, mile-long stroll back down the Sanitas Valley Trail.

To summit the 6,863-foot mountain, turn right onto the Sanitas Valley Trail. Sanitas Valley Trail becomes East Ridge Trail, a fully exposed, difficult path gaining nearly 1,000 feet of elevation in less than a mile. Near the summit, portions of the trail are difficult to follow. This is a very popular hiking route, so follow somebody who seems to know what they're doing, and tread carefully over exposed rocks and around steep ledges.

Those who summit earn incredible views. To make the hike a loop, walk across the peak and descend on the Mount Sanitas West Valley Trail. Whichever route you chose, don't forget to turn right at Mapleton Avenue to get back to your car.

LEARN

Rich in history, this outdoorsy destination is a great place for local history buffs to brush up on the past, of course, but there are also opportunities to learn about human health and diseases as well as earth science.

- **Well Read: If you're digging the sanitarium history, there's much more to learn at Boulder's stately Carnegie Library for Local History, 1125 Pine Street, where you'll find more historical information, along with bulletins, photographs, and personal histories. Check the library's website, boulderlibrary.org/locations/carnegie, for current hours and details on how to book an appointment. In addition to learning about the sanitarium, ask older kids to research tuberculosis and other diseases that ran rampant in the 1900s. Isn't it incredible how our knowledge of communicable diseases has changed in a little over a century?**
- **Rock Out: For budding geologists and rock hounds, there's a lot to love about the area's natural surroundings. In addition to a craggy summit, this hike traverses a hogback, which is the technical term for a long, narrow ridge with a thin crest and steep slopes. You'll also get a great view of the five large, numbered Flatirons along the east slope of Green Mountain. Rockhounding is a kid-approved activity that involves searching for, and sometimes collecting, rocks. Gary Warren's book *Rockhounding Colorado* (FalconGuides) is an excellent starting point for newcomers. With younger children, spend time learning about the rock cycle, then make your own rocks using glue, sand, pebbles, and a disposable cup. A quick internet search will turn up directions for at-home rock making, and there are also tutorials online for creating edible rocks.**

51 Museum of Outdoor Arts

Make art part of everyday life at Marjorie Park.

Cost: $$ Check online for free days and group rates
Hours: Open weekdays by appointment
Location: 6331 South Fiddlers Green Circle
Nearest Town: Greenwood Village
Denver Drive Time: 25 minutes via I-25
Accessibility: This outdoor museum usually offers a quiet, low-sensory experience, and the paved trail looping around the art is wheelchair and stroller accessible.
Bathrooms: Flush toilets available at Fiddler's Green Amphitheatre
Gear Suggestions: Comfortable walking shoes, sun protection, water, snacks or a picnic lunch
Insider Tip: Marjorie Park is currently open during museum events and by appointment only. Don't let that deter you and your kids from experiencing this one-of-a-kind site. Anyone can make an appointment to tour the art. Call (303) 806-0444 to schedule your visit, or alternatively, you can schedule by email at info@moaonline.org.

Explore

Alice's Adventures in Wonderland meets *The Secret Garden* in this quaint gated museum, where a winding path weaves through a fantastical series of bronze sculptures inspired by Alice's journey. The whole gang's here, including the Mad Hatter, Cheshire Cat, and Queen of Hearts. Interspersed between beloved Lewis Carroll characters, you'll find Italian lion statue replicas dating back to the 1500s and plenty of newer art, too, some created by students through a residency program.

The Museum of Outdoor Arts owns and operates this gorgeous venue, maintaining over forty pieces of art from its permanent sculpture collection. The best thing to do is grab a *Self-Guided Art Tour* pamphlet at the ticketing counter near the main entrance gate on the north side of the park. The guide provides an overview of the art inside Marjorie Park, and it also lists several sculptures in public spaces outside the gates. Look for notes on audio links available through a free dial-in audio tour. To take the tour, call (303) 353-1714, then enter "1" plus the three-digit code listed in your guide.

The pamphlet offers an opportunity to learn more about the park, too. Originally named Samson Park after a beloved Yorkshire terrier, the greenspace was renamed in 2015 in memory of co-founder Marjorie Madden. Madden, a fine artist with an affinity for nature, designed the park with her husband, developer John W. Madden.

The Maddens started their project back in the 1980s, as John W. was developing Greenwood Plaza, a Greenwood Village business district he aimed to embellish with original art. An inaugural collection of 19 acquisitions has grown to

include more than 150 pieces of art spread throughout Greenwood Plaza, Denver, and Englewood. In fact, about 25% of MOA's collection is located in and around Englewood, between Santa Fe Drive and South Broadway, and West Dartmouth and West Hampden Avenues. The result is a fine art museum without the typical walls and stuffy vibe.

Marjorie Park itself is a magical, hands-on place where guests can run around and interact with their surroundings. Go ahead and let your kids touch the art as they explore. Hands-on learning engages both the left and right sides of the brain, and interacting with sculptures that have been thoughtfully placed throughout a green-space offers up an interesting chance for children to consider the intersection of art and their natural surroundings.

Who knows? Maybe your child will develop a deeper sense of place while roaming the grounds. At the very least, parents can let their imaginations wander as they tour a beautiful English-style garden. It's every bit as relaxing as it sounds!

If the weather's nice, and you feel like taking a bigger walk, explore Greenwood Plaza, too, and see how many of the nearby sculptures you and your kids discover. They're listed on the *Self-Guided Art Tour* pamphlet you picked up on your way into Marjorie Park.

LEARN

From fine art to city planning, there's plenty for kids to learn while exploring Marjorie Park's pristine grounds.

- **Get Analytical: Art analysis involves thinking about the features of the artwork you're viewing, then speculating about what the artist might have been trying to convey through their work. Liven up your tour of the park by asking your child questions as you walk. Which sculpture is your child's favorite? And what did they like about it? These are just starting points for good conversation that develops both critical thinking and public-speaking skills.**
- **Artful Home: The Museum of Outdoor Art's founding mission is to make art part of everyday life. So why not give your yard, patio, or balcony an MOA-inspired upgrade? Have fun finding the perfect piece of three-dimensional art to add to your favorite outdoor space. Scouring antique and/or thrift stores for the perfect piece can be a fun way to spend an afternoon with the whole family. Better yet, challenge adolescents or teens to create something special.**

52 National Center for Atmospheric Research Mesa Laboratory

Touch a cloud at the NCAR in Boulder.

Cost: Free
Hours: Open 8 a.m. to 5 p.m. on weekdays, 9 a.m. to 4 p.m. on weekends and holidays
Location: 1850 Table Mesa Dr.
Nearest Town: Boulder
Denver Drive Time: 40 minutes via I-25 to US 36
Accessibility: The front-door entrance accommodates those with accessibility needs, and wheelchairs are available at the front desk. The lab doesn't offer designated quiet hours, but for those requiring a low-sensory experience, the best times to visit are weekdays from 9 a.m. to 9:50 a.m. and 2 to 3:30 p.m. There's also a 2-hour-long Sensory Tour for blind and low-vision guests available with advance notice. More accessibility information can be found at https://scied.ucar.edu/visit/accessibility.
Bathrooms: Flush toilets inside the laboratory
Gear Suggestions: Comfortable shoes, snacks, refillable water bottles, sunscreen if you plan to explore the outdoor component
Insider Tip: Super Science Saturday is an annual public science celebration planned by the UCAR Center for Science Education. The event draws thousands of guests of all ages to the Mesa Lab every fall for a fun day of scientific exploration. Dates and times change from year to year; more information is available on the educational prong of NCAR's website, at scied.ucar.edu.

Explore

Designed by architect I. M. Pei as a place where scientists with different expertise could come together to collaborate and study the Earth as a system, the Mesa Laboratory serves as the headquarters for the National Center for Atmospheric Research, NCAR for short, a nonprofit supporting local and national science communities.

Set against Boulder's iconic Flatirons, Mesa Laboratory's futuristic, concrete-and-stone architecture beckons passersby. Inside, a multilevel visitor center will seal the deal for your kids with a series of tactile exhibits and games built to inspire budding scientists in meteorology, climatology, and space-weather topics.

After grabbing a map of NCAR's exhibits near the front desk, head over to the NCAR theater, just past the Weather Gallery, to view one of several short films available for guests of all ages (open captioning available). After the show, plan to chase your kids around the museum while they touch clouds, view a tornado created by crosswinds, steer a virtual hurricane, and tackle a weather-inspired memory game on a giant touch-screen computer. The experience might look like playtime, but your

children will be gaining a whole new perspective on weather, climate, and the sun-Earth connection.

Allow your children time to make their own art at a station tucked behind the stairwell near the main entrance. Upstairs on the second floor, explore the Climate Exhibit to discover how we know our climate is changing, and what steps we can take to address climate change. While these hallways are a little more information-heavy, there's a can't-miss greenhouse gas game on level 2 and another art station for those who'd like to share their own climate story.

Free hour-long public tours are offered several days a week. After linking up in the lobby, tourgoers learn all about atmospheric science and current research as a guide offers an up-close look into the center's exhibits. There's no need to make a reservation, and if you miss the group tour, you can pick up tablets at the front desk, or download the NCAR Tour app on your phone for a self-guided audiovisual tour.

Why, you might be wondering, are there so many kid amenities in a working science lab? Mesa Laboratory's original director, Walter Orr Roberts, valued not only high-level science but connection with the public, too, and that has always driven the amount of effort and resources funneled into education and outreach.

Can't make it up to Boulder? Spark wonder and curiosity with a free 45-minute-long live virtual field trip with an experienced educator. All you need to participate is a computer, webcam, and internet access. A minimum group size of eight students is required for virtual tours. Call or email the lab for more information.

LEARN

If your kids are learning about weather and/or meteorology, a trip to Mesa Lab will definitely enhance in-class experiences with hands-on exploration. Level up with these additional ideas.

- **Nature Connection: On the west side of the building, discover the Walter Orr Roberts Weather Trail, a half-mile loop with informational signage. Craving more adventure? Take Mesa Trail until it links with Enchanted Mesa Trail. This 2-mile out-and-back hike weaves through a shady segment of Chautauqua Park before ending at Chautauqua Dining Hall.**
- **Experiments: Back home, go to NCAR's website, scied.ucar.edu, and click on "Explore" to access weather-themed science experiments created by NCAR scientists. Simple labs requiring minimal materials transform elementary school students into weather sleuths. To be really official, ask your junior scientist to record observations in a science journal when the experiment is complete.**

53 Philip S. Miller Park

Visit this destination park for a day of next-level adventure.

Cost: Free, but there's a charge for adventure activities
Hours: Open daily 5 a.m. to 11 p.m.
Location: 1375 West Plum Creek Parkway
Nearest Town: Castle Rock
Denver Drive Time: 30 minutes via I-25 South
Accessibility: ADA-compliant, stroller-friendly paved trail runs the full perimeter of the park, weaving around the notable activities
Bathrooms: Both indoor restrooms and portable toilets
Gear Suggestions: Sneakers, hats, sunscreen, swimsuits for splash pad, dry change of clothes, mountain bikes, clothes required for adventure activities
Insider Tip: There is so much to do outside at this park that you may not notice all there is to do inside the Miller Activity Complex (MAC). The MAC is the 64,000+-square-foot recreational facility on the north end of the park. If you run into a rainy (or particularly hot) day that calls for time indoors, dip into the MAC and, for a per person fee, play in the aquatics center equipped with a slide, climb on the three-story play structure, and jump around in the 5,000-square-foot trampoline zone (special socks available for purchase at the MAC required).

Explore

There are parks and then there are *destination* parks. This 300-acre park, just off West Plum Creek Parkway in Castle Rock, is worth the drive to explore its endless outdoor recreation options. With everything from trails to an epic adventure course, families can spend a morning or a day here, and go back again and again to try something new.

Named for a Castle Rock banker and philanthropist, Philip S. Miller Park first opened in 2014 and expanded in 2015. The park's many amenities are easily accessible via a 1-mile paved trail that winds throughout and past the plentiful parking areas.

To start the day, pick from one of the unpaved loop trails in the rolling hills around the park, ranging in length from a half mile to just over 2 miles. Along the trails you'll see native plants and views of the Front Range mountains, including Pikes Peak, as you traverse the hills and valleys. What you won't see much of is shade, so plan your hike time carefully and bring plenty of water and sunscreen. Use the small connector trails to create longer routes. These trails are all mixed use, so keep an eye out for bicyclists, hikers, and runners, and be sure to review the trail etiquette tips before you set out. Although the blue loop is the shortest, it is also attached to the 200-step Challenge Hill, which climbs 178 feet in elevation. The incline begins near the main paved trail and is open to all ages.

If you visit Philip S. Miller Park to wear out the kiddos, head to the 2.5-acre Adventure Playground designed for children 5 to 12 years old. Kids can climb, swing, dig, and fly down the 40-foot-long slide. A couple interpretive signs nearby introduce kids to the scrub montane habitat and wildlife around the park. After kids work up a sweat at

the playground, it's time to cool off. Backtrack around the turf field to the Core Plaza, where you'll find a splash pad near shaded picnic tables and full bathrooms.

The features that take this park to the next level are four adventure challenges managed by the Edge Zipline Tours. Adventure Tower is a climbing, rappelling, and free-falling structure for anyone 50 to 270 pounds. Ninja Course offers six levels and three wall climbs for ages 4 and up. Though the suggested starting age is 8 to 10 years old, if your 6-year-old is a ninja warrior fanatic, they are allowed to jump on. Sky Trek straps visitors in a double-clip harness system for climbing into a four-story aerial trekking course with 110 elements to navigate. Kids must have a reach of 5 feet above the ground to do the course, and anyone under 8 years old must have an adult accompany them on the course. Don't worry if you're not an adrenaline junkie, as you can choose from three levels: easy, moderate, or difficult. The last element is a series of ten zip lines soaring 110 feet above the ground. Participants must be at least 70 pounds to strap in for the zip lines. These features all require an additional fee, but there is so much to do in the park for free, you can always save the adventure challenges for a special occasion.

LEARN

Don't limit your study options to just plants and animals. Blend in a study of human biology and health as kids discover how the activities at this park affect their muscles.

- **Healthy Bodies:** Use this park to kick off a learning unit on exercise and health and wellness. Look at the many ways you can build muscle at the park: climbing the incline, hiking and riding bicycles on the trail, climbing on playground equipment, and scaling the ninja course. Learn the names of different muscles and where they are in the body.
- **Build a Simple Ninja Obstacle Course:** The key in a ninja course is to get your body moving up, down, and side to side, and to use a variety of muscles to lift, hang, balance, push, and climb. Brainstorm with the kids simple challenges using items around the house and yard like "lava trail," using pillows ninjas must jump between; "tunnel trip," requiring them to crawl under a table or line of chairs; or "incline," requiring ninjas to step up and down on a sturdy stool or step. Get creative and get active.

54 Plains Conservation Center

Glimpse historic life on the short grass prairie.

Cost: Free, fee for programs
Hours: Visitor center hours: Wed–Fri noon to 4:30 p.m., Sat–Sun 9 a.m. to 4:30 p.m. Hiking hours Mar 1 through Oct 31: Mon–Thurs 6:30 a.m. to 4:30 p.m., Fri 6:30 a.m. to 6 p.m., Sat–Sun 8 a.m. to 6 p.m. Check website for winter hours.
Location: 21901 East Hampden Avenue
Nearest Town: Aurora
Denver Drive Time: 35 minutes via 1-25 South to I-225 North
Accessibility: Visitor center is wheelchair accessible; trails are gravel. Use an assistive device to hear a reading of visitor center signage in English or Spanish.
Bathrooms: Full indoor bathrooms at the visitor center
Gear Suggestions: Sturdy closed-toed shoes for walking around the property, hats, sunscreen, bug repellent, binoculars to view animals
Insider Tip: One of the best ways to learn about this location is to combine a visit with one of the many programs or events hosted at Plains Conservation Center. Details and registration for the programs can be found on the Denver Botanic Gardens website, botanicgardens.org.

Explore

When most people think of Colorado, it's the majestic snowcapped Rockies that come to mind. While the towering mountains definitely inspire awe, there is a certain magic in open land where all you can see for miles is grass, especially in this era of newer, taller buildings popping up overnight. Just to the east of Denver, there was once a vast prairie that was home to rugged plants and animals, diverse Native American tribes, and, later, settlers homesteading and farming the land. Plains Conservation Center gives families a glimpse of what the once wide-open plains of eastern Colorado may have felt like. If not for the houses and city view on the west side of the property, you could almost feel as if you've been whisked to another place in time, walking amid 1,100 acres of graceful shortgrass prairie.

To tour Plains Conservation Center on your own, start in the visitor center. Check in and view the artifacts and hands-on displays featuring the many animals, humans, and plants that have called the prairie home. A small play area with toys and books engages little ones, and a porch on the back of the visitor center offers a shady spot to picnic or just enjoy a view of the mountains. This is also where you'll pick up trail maps and self-guided tour brochures that explain points of interest along the 1-mile Soddie Loop Trail. Just match the numbered posts along the trails to the descriptions in the brochures.

As you head out to explore, you will see a group of replica Native American tipis in the distance. This is your first stop. Plains Native American tribes like the Arapaho and Cheyenne relied heavily on the bison herds that once roamed these grasslands for their livelihood. The tipis were easy to pack up and move, which made them the

perfect home as the tribes moved around with the herd. Reference this tipi camp under #1 in the Prairie Culture self-guided tour brochure.

Now pick up the Soddie Loop Trail to visit the Sod Homestead Village. This area heralds the arrival of the settlers. In 1862 the Homestead Act allowed anyone at least 21 years old, or the head of a family, the opportunity to acquire up to 160 acres of land. Before the land became officially theirs, though, they had to file a claim, build a house, farm the land, and stay for five years. The MacLean Soddie shows what a typical homestead in Colorado looked like. The buildings are typically closed to visitors, so the best opportunity to see inside these unique structures is during special events or educational programs.

On a nice day, pick up one of the prairie trails for a longer hike through the shortgrass prairie. It may not look like much happens out on the plains, but use your senses and you'll experience fascinating plant and animal life along the 6.5 miles of trails to choose from. It is common to see pronghorn moving through the grass, especially in the morning and evening when the weather is cool. Plains Conservation Center is also home to prairie dogs, coyotes, red-tailed hawks, and bald eagles nesting in a protected zone of the prairie. Binoculars or a spotting scope will give you the best chance of seeing these majestic birds close up.

On a summer day, follow the lead of the pronghorn and explore early. There is minimal shade on the prairie and afternoons are hot. Another exciting way to see the

Plains Conservation Center is through one of their educational programs or events for kids and adults. The sunset wagon ride, offered through the Denver Botanic Gardens, is a particularly lovely way to spend a summer evening. Ride along with a guide from the Gardens to learn about the history and nature of the area. Then as the sun falls behind the Rockies, watch as the prairie grasses and the faces of your loved ones take on a warm glow.

LEARN

Nature and history overlap at the Plains Conservation Center. These activities help children understand how the lives of Native American tribes and settlers were intertwined with what nature provided on the plains.

- **Find Bison: The City of Denver maintains a herd of bison near Genesee Park off of I-70 West, at the Buffalo Herd Overlook (see chapter 4). These bison are direct descendants of the last wild herd of bison in the United States. Visit the herd to learn more about the animals that sustained Native American life on the plains.**
- **Play Prairie Games: Families on the prairie traveled light, whether Native Americans on the move with the bison or settlers heading west to homestead. They didn't have room to carry boxes full of toys and games. So how did they play? Research the ways that children on the prairie spent their playtime and then give it a try.**

55 Red Rock Canyon Open Space

Walk past 10,000 years of human history in Manitou Springs.

Cost: Free
Hours: Open daily from dawn to dusk
Location: 3550 West High Street
Nearest Towns: Manitou Springs and Colorado Springs
Denver Drive Time: 85 minutes via I-25
Accessibility: This rugged trail would be tough with a wheelchair or stroller.
Bathrooms: Portable toilets near Red Rock Canyon Trailhead
Gear Suggestions: Comfortable walking shoes, sunscreen, a hat, sunglasses, plenty of water, snacks, binoculars
Insider Tip: Are you and your kids familiar with Leave No Trace (lnt.org)? With its seven guiding principles, the organization is on a mission to ensure a sustainable future for our beloved Colorado wilderness by educating outdoors enthusiasts about how they can lessen their impact on the environment while recreating outside. LNT Principle 4 is "Leave What You Find," and it's an especially important ethic at Red Rock Canyon Open Space, where scientists are still turning up artifacts to this day. Sometimes it is permissible to travel off a beaten path when you're hiking or camping in areas where off-trail use is allowed. But going rogue is a big no-no at this fragile destination, where off-trail usage can cause major damage to the landscape. Here's your opportunity to help children learn about conservation by teaching curious kids to stay on designated trails and refrain from taking shortcuts.

Explore

There's so much more to Red Rock Canyon Open Space than pretty views. In addition to lessons in sedimentary geology, families will get a 10,000-year-old slice of human history told through ancient projectile points and ruins. There's a fabulous 2-mile "History Loop" hiking route that passes an old quarry, and it's easy to access.

From I-25, exit onto West Cimarron Street. The road becomes US 24 (Midland Expressway). After passing the stoplight at 31st Street, you'll turn left (south) onto Ridge Road. From here, simply drive to the end of the road, then take the second exit at the roundabout to reach the parking lot. If the first lot's full, keep driving to reach overflow parking.

Once parked, you'll combine three trails—Mesa, Quarry Pass, and Red Rock Canyon—to complete a loop. Starting from the Red Rock Canyon Trailhead, take an immediate right at the trail map to begin hiking on Mesa Trail. Grab a paper map from the bin to ensure you don't lose your bearings.

From the get-go, you'll notice the site's namesake rock formations. After passing the Lower Dog Loop off-leash area, keep straight at the next two trail junctions, then turn left onto Quarry Pass Trail at the four-way trail intersection. This short connector trail grants families access to a former sandstone quarry with some spectacular aerial views of the open space.

Stay on Quarry Pass for 0.5 mile until you come to a ledge. This is a great place to pause and tell your children about the area's unique history. According to an archaeological study from 2004, the earliest evidence of human life in the Red Rock Canyon area comes from projectile points such as arrowheads dating back to 7000 BCE. Given its proximity to Fountain Creek and the abundance of deer, the canyon has probably offered food and shelter to humans for a very long time.

Fast-forward to the late 1800s, when the same canyon generated building supplies for the Pikes Peak region's first settlement, Colorado City, a gold rush town founded in 1859. (Psst: You can still visit the small historic city today, located at the southern start of a 103-mile scenic byway retracing the early route of the area's explorers.)

The communities of Colorado Springs and Manitou Springs also used gypsum and sandstone mined at Red Rock Canyon. Significant quarrying occurred into the early 1900s, until building stone was replaced with concrete and steel. The quarry eventually closed due to declining demand, but that's not exactly the end of the story.

Opening in 1886, the Colorado-Philadelphia Company Mill used land inside Red Rock Canyon to refine the ore they shipped by rail from local gold mines in

the Cripple Creek area. The mill was the largest of its kind in the United States for decades.

John George Bock bought the land in the 1920s and later gifted it to his two sons. His older son, John S. Bock, lived on the land until his death in 2002. Ask your kids what they think it would be like having a home in a place like this. The Bock family initially planned to turn the area into a massive resort community, but that dream never materialized. In 2003 the City of Colorado Springs purchased the Red Rock Canyon property to be used as public open space.

After crossing the ledge and circling a rim, you'll turn right to follow the steps downhill, straight into the historic quarry. Watch the group's youngest hikers closely since this segment of trail is steep and rocky. Then, prepare to be wowed. Quarry work left behind enormous geometric cuts in the rock face, and you'll get an up-close view during your hike. The trail fades away for a moment, but don't worry, it picks back up shortly.

Exit the quarry, and walk toward the interpretive signs in the clearing, then take either Red Rock Canyon Path or Red Rock Canyon Trail downhill to reach an open-air pavilion overlooking a cute duck pond. It's the perfect spot for a picnic lunch or just lounging with snacks and drinks.

From the pavilion, it's only about 0.45 mile back to the parking lot. Bring Striders or bikes if your kids would like to spend some time at the free-ride stunt park after their history hike.

LEARN

Whether your child is learning about earth sciences or human history, Red Rock Canyon is a great destination for an active lesson extension.

- **Time Warp: If you're digging the site's rich human history, consider popping over to the Garden of the Gods Visitor & Nature Center (see chapter 32), which features a series of exhibits walking families through time. Back home, make a timeline specific to Colorado Springs history, starting with the Indigenous Peoples who first dwelled inside Red Rock Canyon Open Space.**
- **Mine Your Business: North of Colorado Springs, across from the Air Force Academy, the Western Museum of Mining and Industry, 225 North Gate Boulevard, wmmi.org, is a fun attraction for those who'd like to learn more about how science and industry intersect to create the technology that powers our modern lives. The Mining Museum has a variety of interactive exhibits exploring minerals mined right here in Colorado, and you'll also get to view some of the massive machinery that's used to pull minerals from the earth. Bonus: Your kids can try their hand at gold panning during your visit.**

56 Rock Ledge Ranch

Step back in time to learn what life was like for Colorado's settlers.

Cost: During Living History Program $$, Children ages 2 and under free. Outside of Living History hours, park is free.
Hours: Living History Program hours: Wed–Sat 10 a.m. to 5 p.m., Sun 1 to 5 p.m., closed Mon–Tues. Park visitation hours: dawn to dusk.
Location: 3105 Gateway Road
Nearest Town: Colorado Springs
Denver Drive Time: 1 hour 10 minutes via I-25 South
Accessibility: Accessible parking at the main entrance, some paved trail and some gravel trail throughout the property. Trail to the Galloway Homestead and Native American interpretive areas is not accessible. Platform lift to the first floor of the Orchard House when open. Narrated video tours available with captions, audio descriptions, American Sign Language interpretation, and an option for Spanish audio and captions.
Bathrooms: Standard and accessible restrooms in Carriage House
Gear Suggestions: Walking shoes, hats, sunscreen
Insider Tip: The Ranch grounds are part of the City of Colorado Springs Parks, Recreation, and Cultural Services Department, and are open daily from dawn until dusk. If you visit on a day when Rock Ledge Ranch is not hosting living history or a special event, walk around the property for free, but buildings will be closed.

Explore

In the shadows of the imposing red sandstone formations of Garden of the Gods sits a window into the life of early settlers in Colorado Springs. Rock Ledge Ranch is home to a collection of historic dwellings, from stately houses to a reproduction of a rugged settler's cabin of the late 1800s. Peppered in between the houses are a store, a barn alive with chickens and horses, and a blacksmith shop that often rings out with the clank, clank, clank of a hammer. The structures are all blended into a parklike setting made for strolling any time of year.

Roam the property as you like, but to start in the oldest settlement represented at the Ranch, find the trail out to the American Indian area, representing Ute tribal life in the area now called Rock Ledge Ranch. Next, weave past the Galloway Homestead cabin of the 1860s and 1870s, then make your way toward the farm, shops, and homes of the late nineteenth and early twentieth centuries. Along the way, the trail winds past a peaceful shaded pond and through grassy areas just perfect for a picnic.

From fall through spring, the ranch is quiet for visitors, with many of the buildings closed. But once school is out, the Summer Living History program (Wednesday–Sunday, June through mid-August) brings the historic site to life with costumed interpreters, live demonstrations, tours of the homes, and crafts. If you want to see the Rock Ledge Ranch alive with activity, this is the time to visit. Or you can attend one

of the seasonal special events like the fall harvest festival, Labor Day vintage baseball game, annual powwow, or Holiday Evening with St. Nick.

No matter what day you show up, there will be plentiful natural areas to explore along the trail. Camp Creek flows along the east side of the park, ducks wade in the pond with growing ducklings paddling behind, and a trail from the orchard, on the south of Rock Ledge House, leads into Garden of the Gods for a tour of the renowned rocks.

The sites and events at Rock Ledge Ranch will unravel the story of cultural and agricultural development in the Pikes Peak region. The Ranch also hosts educational programs outside of the Living History Program and special events for kids of all ages. Barnyard Buddies for preschoolers engages little ones with story time, a craft, and a snack. If you are a homeschool family, visit on Fall or Spring Homeschool Day (small per person fee) or register for School at the RANCH (Raising Awareness of Nature, Culture, and History), a 32-week hands-on enrichment program just for kids in homeschool.

LEARN

As kids walk through history at Rock Ledge Ranch, encourage them to observe the different styles of homes—tipis, cabins, and houses—and each occupant's way of life. Did they raise crops or buy their food at a store? Where did their household necessities come from? Apply their observations to these hands-on activities.

- **Create Your Own Exhibit: Use a shoebox, craft supplies, nature elements, and miniature plastic toys to build a historic scene inspired by the exhibits at Rock Ledge Ranch. Have older kids create labels to identify the various elements of the scene. Encourage kids to color or paint the unique backdrop of this valley with Garden of the Gods and Pikes Peak rising in the back of the diorama.**
- **Practice a Settler's Skill: Early settlers in Colorado did not have access to many household necessities like candles, soap, or butter, and often there wasn't a store around for miles. So, these resourceful folks learned how to make things for themselves. Try your hand at making simple candles or soap together with a kit or materials from a craft store. It's also fun for kids to make butter using a stand mixer or a mason jar and heavy cream. A quick Google search will arm you with instructions.**

57 Rock Park Loop Trail

Climb this short loop to the top of an iconic natural landmark.

Cost: Free
Hours: Open daily 5 a.m. to 11 p.m.
Location: 1470 Front Street
Nearest Town: Castle Rock
Denver Drive Time: 30 minutes via I-25 South
Accessibility: Not accessible
Bathrooms: Portable toilet at the trailhead
Gear Suggestions: Hiking shoes, water, hats, sunscreen, leash for the family dog if he/she is coming along
Insider Tip: Bring a pair of binoculars, if you have them, to glimpse birds and visible landmarks from the top.

Explore

This relatively short trail takes hikers around the iconic rock formation you see on the east side of Castle Rock as you drive through, or around, town. The hike is considered moderate to difficult, depending on who you ask, and while it is a short 1.5-mile loop to the top, it's the sloping climb that adds to the difficulty. However, we've seen parents with kids of all ages on the trail. One exception: You should wait until your toddlers are older and steadier on their feet to try this trail; otherwise you may end up balancing yourself as well as a wobbly tot on some of the steep spots.

As with any hike, pack plenty of water for each member of your group. One full water bottle for each member of your party should be plenty for this trail. Be sure to pack the water in a backpack or clip it in a secure side pocket. You don't want to learn the hard way that stepping up a couple of the steps might push your bottle out of an unsecured pocket and then, oops! Down it will tumble to an unretrievable spot.

There is some parking at the trailhead just off of Front Street, but if the lot is full, additional parking is available at Castle North Park (on-street parking is also allowed on Canyon and Sunset Drives). Start the hike at the trailhead near the portable toilet and picnic shelter. When you come to the fork, you will need to decide whether to go up the front or the back of the hill.

To the right, John Emerson Summit Trail, 0.5 mile up the front of the rock, is mostly dirt and rock path, with some uneven steps made of stone toward the top of the hike that could be challenging for little and big legs alike. To the left, the 0.5-mile Paul Hill Trail will take you up the back of the rock, with the same dirt and rock paths, but the last stretch to the top doesn't include steps, although it also gets a little steep—some consider this the easier side. You can go up the front and down the back to create a loop, or go up and down on the same trail, it's your choice. Both trails will lead to the base of the Castle Rock at the top (a 370-foot elevation gain) and take you back to the trailhead.

Once you reach the summit of the main trail, there is another 0.2-mile trail that circles the base of the iconic Castle Rock. Take a break on a bench or stop for a drink and a snack at a picnic table on the southeast corner. A split-rail fence or low wall goes around portions of the north, east, and south perimeter. It isn't continuous, so it's a good time to teach kids to stay back from the edge. This perimeter trail is as high as the trail goes. Climbing the Rock any higher is prohibited and dangerous. Though you may see folks ignoring the warnings, don't take the risk; some attempts have sadly had tragic results.

Continue to explore around the summit trail, looking below the rock overhang at birds' nests built into the cracks and crevices. Watch for birds soaring in the sky.

From the front of the Rock, you'll see Pikes Peak to the south, I-25 just below, and more hills and mountains to the west. See if you can identify buildings in the distance like the Outlet Mall or Downtown Castle Rock. Snap a photo of your accomplished hikers at the top before you head back down your chosen trail, surrounded by scrub oak, colorful wildflowers, and more rock formations.

The trail is short yet challenging and gives kids an opportunity to feel the accomplishment of climbing a "mountain," which makes this a worthwhile adventure.

LEARN

High above the town of Castle Rock, you'll see things from a different point of view. Turn this fresh perspective into creative ways to learn.

- **Nest of a Different Feather: Look at the migratory birds' nests on the underside of Castle Rock. Ask the kids how these differ from nests they see in the trees. Find a book on birds that explains the different materials and methods birds use to build nests.**
- **What Do You See in the Rocks?: Step to the northeast corner and look back at the edge of the Rock. Do you see the profile of a face? Maybe one of the rocks along the trail looks like a mushroom. Ask kids what shapes they see. Ask why they think it's called Castle Rock. Use this as a way to inspire a story kids could invent about how a mountain or location got its name.**

58 Rocky Mountain Arsenal National Wildlife Refuge

Commerce City claims one of the nation's largest urban wildlife refuges.

Cost: Free
Hours: Visitor center open Wed–Sun 9 a.m. to 4 p.m.; closed Mon–Tues and all federal holidays. Refuge open daily from sunrise to sunset, but shuts down for Thanksgiving, Christmas, and New Year's Day.
Location: 6550 Gateway Road
Nearest Town: Commerce City
Denver Drive Time: 25 minutes via I-25 to I-70, exiting at Quebec Street
Accessibility: A fully paved loop rings Lake Mary, and the visitor center is ADA compliant with additional paved loops in that area. Weekdays typically offer a quieter, low-sensory experience.
Bathrooms: Flush toilets inside the visitor center; pit toilets in the visitor center parking lot and on the north and south ends of Lake Ladora
Gear Suggestions: Binoculars, nature-journaling supplies, comfortable walking shoes, sunscreen, a hat, sunglasses, plenty of water, snacks
Insider Tip: The refuge is the perfect place for families to develop their fishing skills. Anglers of all ages are invited to try catch-and-release fishing at Lakes Mary and Ladora between April 1 and November 30. The daily fishing fee is currently $3 for anglers 16 and older; kids 15 and under and high school and college students with a current student ID fish for free. At "Fishing Basics" workshops, held at Lake Mary on select days throughout the season, staff provide fishing rods, bait, and instruction for newcomers.

Explore

Bison, deer, raptors, waterfowl, prairie dogs, coyotes—these are just a few of the many animals dwelling inside Rocky Mountain Arsenal's expansive, 15,000-acre borders. Given the abundance of fauna, your kids are pretty much guaranteed to spot wildlife on the peaceful stroll from the visitor center to Lake Mary, a 3.4-mile route passing a black-footed ferret exhibit, buffalo enclosure, and thriving prairie dog community.

The site is one of the largest urban national wildlife refuges in the country, and it comes with a rather sordid history. The refuge originally opened in 1942 as a chemical weapons manufacturing center that was operated by the US Army until 1992, shortly after bald eagles—formerly endangered—were discovered on the premises. That discovery was the impetus for designating the land as protected.

By 2004 a refuge was established by act, and site cleanup commenced. Up to eighty eagles still roost on the refuge annually in the winter. Raptors aren't the only ones flocking to this haven: More than 300,000 humans come each year, too, to observe some 330 species of wildlife. While the ecosystem is primarily shortgrass and mixed-grass prairie, there are also wetlands and wooded habitats, and families can access these distinct dwellings on an 11-mile self-guided auto tour that takes about

45 minutes to complete. Listen to the refuge podcast (available online in English and Spanish) while driving.

It's also fun to explore by foot. Across the refuge's 20-mile system of easy, linked, kid-friendly trails, observant explorers might spy white-tailed deer, bison, monarch butterflies, and burrowing owls nesting in abandoned prairie dog tunnels. Grab a trail map and activity backpack at the visitor center before beginning your adventure.

No need to rush outside: Children will love exploring the visitor center's exhibits on prairie wildlife and plants, and the full-sized bison mount offers a fun photo op. A special Discovery Room has seasonal displays, hands-on learning stations, microscopes, a puppet theater, and animal-themed arts and crafts that transform with the changing seasons.

Get with the program! All summer long, the refuge offers free nature programming for kids. Reservations aren't required; just check out the "Events" page on the refuge's website (www.fws.gov/refuge/rocky-mountain-arsenal) for specific details on classes covering topics such as "horns versus antlers" and nature art.

LEARN

From biology and animals to ecosystems, plants, habitats, and conservation, this site offers plenty of opportunities to sneak in off-the-clock learning. It's also a great place to learn about the Cold War era.

- Summer Reading: Sometimes I struggle to get my kids to read during our active summers. Located inside the visitor center, at the ferret enclosure, and along Legacy Trail, the refuge's interpretive panels make it easy to slip in a few minutes of reading. Look for a panel on plant roots on Legacy Trail. This fascinating slide explains why some plants thrive and others die in Colorado's arid climate.
- Photography Club: One of this refuge's most popular activities is wildlife photography. If you have a budding artist at home, bring along a good lens, and let your child hone their camera skills by capturing local wildlife against the backdrop of the majestic Rocky Mountains. Always stay on trails and follow posted signs. And remember, if you're close enough for a selfie, you are way too close! Give animals at least 25 yards of personal space; make it 100 yards for predators such as bears and wolves.

59 Rocky Mountain Botanic Gardens

Grow your family's horticultural knowledge in the outdoorsy town of Lyons.

Cost: Free
Hours: Open daily from dawn until dusk
Location: Near the intersection of 4th Avenue and Prospect Street. You can park on Prospect Street. Or park at the large lot servicing Bohn Park (199 2nd Avenue). Past the public restrooms and the Lyons Hidden Playground, follow a footpath alongside the St. Vrain River to reach a series of bridges. Use the bridges to carefully cross the water, then follow a few stone steps downhill to access Rocky Mountain Botanic Gardens via its main entrance gate. The walk from playground to garden is about 0.2 mile each way.
Nearest Town: Lyons
Denver Drive Time: 55 minutes via I-25 to US 36
Accessibility: The site's 5-foot-wide crushed-gravel paths accommodate wheelchairs and strollers. This peaceful destination generally delivers a low-sensory experience.
Bathrooms: Flush toilets adjacent to the playground at Bohn Park
Gear Suggestions: Comfortable walking shoes, sunscreen, a hat, sunglasses, plenty of water, snacks to enjoy at the nearby park, a notebook and pencil. If your children dig flowers, pack a field guide to Rocky Mountain flora such as *Southern Rocky Mountain Wildflowers* (FalconGuides, 2nd edition updated by Chris Kassar).
Insider Tip: Don't miss the library box near the garden's entrance gate. This "Little Nature Library" is stocked with all sorts of pamphlets, books, and free resources on topics in nature, including native gardening. If you have a local gardening or nature-themed book you can part with, bring something great to leave behind.

Explore

Boulder County's very first botanical garden has an unbelievable origin story. On September 11, 2013, the St. Vrain River's normal flow reached "biblical" proportions, as the National Weather Service put it, when water levels rose over twenty times the volume of a typical flood. The catastrophic event stranded residents for days until helicopters and high-water vehicles could evacuate the community. That was just the beginning.

The raging river didn't subside for weeks. Water damaged roads, sewer lines, and a significant number of homes, wiping out most of Lyons's affordable housing. The deluge destroyed the Foothills Mobile Home Park, which had been built adjacent to Bohn Park.

But out of the devastation, something positive grew. After purchasing the floodplain, the town of Lyons granted volunteers permission to build a garden that resident Garima Fairfax had dreamed about for twenty years. By 2020 a dedicated group was busy planting a wide variety of Colorado native plants with the goal of creating a beautiful outdoor space where visitors could learn about drought-tolerant gardening as well as plants that grow in local riparian areas and bogs and on peaks.

From the main entrance, a winding, looping, crushed-gravel path takes families through a series of enchanting "demonstration gardens" divided into Colorado's five key ecosystems. While wandering past foothills, prairie grassland, montane forest, and riparian and Southwest environments, enjoy the colors and smells of dwarf wild indigo, prairie verbena, golden smoke, fire wheel, and purple aster, to name just a few of the wonderful flora. The garden is also a fantastic place to spot butterflies, native birds, and other wildlife. Located in downtown Lyons, the Lyons Redstone Museum is a fantastic stop-off for history buffs who'd like to learn more about the town.

Fairfax thinks of Rocky Mountain Botanic Gardens as "nature with name tags." While hiking around, you and your kids will view all sorts of native plants that thrive

in local yards with little watering. Thanks to small signs listing both common and Latin names, families can walk away with a few ideas for their own gardens. Native plants tend to do well in Colorado gardens since they need less water and fertilizer than cultivated plants. Plus, they support wild animals, including native pollinators. Bring notetaking supplies in case you feel inspired.

Check the nonprofit organization's website, rmbg.org, for information on public classes, including native plant identification, gardening with native plants, xeriscape gardening, and tree and shrub pruning. And if you want to get more involved, consider helping in the beds with weeding, tidying, and planting during recurring volunteer hours, typically held a few mornings a week from April through December, weather permitting. More details are available online.

Rocky Mountain Botanic Gardens is not designed to be a playground but rather an educational site. Please make sure children are respectful of the native plants. If your kids need to burn off some energy before the car ride home, factor in time to enjoy Bohn Park, featuring a playground, dirt bike park, sports fields, and grills for serious picnickers. Gentle hiking trails branch off from either side of the garden, and who knows? You and your kids might discover something special if you take time to hike around the area.

LEARN

This native garden is the perfect place to learn about Colorado flora, of course, and a few supplemental activities can help budding botanists increase their passion and knowledge.

- **Seasonal Exploration: Since the garden's open year-round, why not try to visit once every season this year? Ask your children to pay attention to what's blooming when. Which plants are most colorful in autumn? Does anything flourish in the winter? Notice the fauna, too, especially birds. Are there different animals to view based on the weather?**
- **Tree-mendous Extension: The volunteers behind Rocky Mountain Botanic Gardens have also created the Lyons Walking Arboretum, a fun walking route through downtown Lyons that passes forty labeled trees, each a different species. This unique arboretum offers a great opportunity to spend time outside while learning even more about Colorado plants. Before visiting, print a PDF map and detailed illustrated guide, accessed through a link on the Rocky Mountain Botanic Gardens website (rmbg.org).**

60 Roxborough State Park

Human history and geology are oh-so pretty at this National Natural Landmark.

Cost: Daily vehicle pass required to enter Colorado state parks, or purchase a Colorado Parks & Wildlife annual parks pass.
Hours: Vary by season and are posted on the park's website at cpw.state.co.us/placestogo/parks/Roxborough. In the summer the park is generally open from 5 a.m. to 9 p.m.
Location: 4751 Roxborough Drive
Nearest Town: Littleton
Denver Drive Time: 50 minutes via Santa Fe Drive
Accessibility: The park's most popular loop, Fountain Valley Trail, is doable with a wheelchair or good jogging stroller, but the overlooks are inaccessible.
Bathrooms: Flush toilets inside the visitor center
Gear Suggestions: Comfortable walking shoes, sunscreen, sunglasses, a hat, sun-protective clothing, binoculars, plenty of water, snacks
Insider Tip: This is one of the few Colorado state parks where dogs aren't permitted. Be sure to leave Fido at home before venturing out to Roxy. Speaking from personal experience, it really stinks to drive all the way to this remote destination only to have to turn around and leave at the entrance gate.

Explore

Many Coloradans draw parallels between Roxborough State Park and the Garden of the Gods (see chapter 31). But really, Roxy is beyond comparison. This special destination is perfect for families who love nature, wildlife, and/or anthropology. In addition to its fascinating human history, the land inside Roxborough State Park is biologically, ecologically, and geologically significant—plus, it's just plain beautiful on a warm summer day.

Start this adventure at the visitor center, located at the end of North Roxborough Drive, just past the park's third and final parking lot. Here you'll find several interactive exhibits, and tucked away in a small room in the back, there's a short historical film.

Don't be shy about chatting up the ranger stationed at the front desk. Knowledgeable staff can enhance your experience by answering any questions your kids might have. If your children are 12 or under, borrow an activity backpack stuffed with trail essentials and a Fountain Valley Trail guide. You'll use the laminated guide to augment the twenty interpretive signs posted along Fountain Valley Trail—each corresponding to a page in the guide.

When you're ready to hike, exit the visitor center, and look right to spot two trails departing from Roxy's main trailhead. To your left, Willow Creek Trail is an easy 1.45-mile loop granting access to a handful of trails on the park's south side. But with kids, it's more fun to turn right and follow the wide dirt path tracking north to the first interpretive sign along Fountain Valley Trail.

Fountain Valley Trail is named for a large formation of red rocks jutting out of the meadow. Known as the Fountain Formation, the tilted sandstone formed more than 300 million years ago. For a bird's-eye view, take a detour to Fountain Valley Overlook, and look past the thickets of a tree called Gambel oak, a.k.a. "shrub oak," one of the most common plants inside Roxy.

If you enjoy this first overlook, you'll love the Lyon's Overlook, accessible via a narrow dirt path branching off from the main route about 0.55 mile into the hike. This large, scenic overlook is surrounded by quirky rocks and trees that might leave you feeling like you've wandered into a Dr. Seuss book.

Back on Fountain Valley Trail, continue following the numbered interpretive signs up a gradual hill as you pass through a grassland community that's home to nearly fifty species of grasses, ranging from narrow-leaved yucca to mountain mahogany. Diverse species of plants support a robust and stable ecosystem that draws in black-tailed prairie dogs, mule deer, cottontail rabbits, and red foxes, among many other animals. Keep an eye out for pocket gophers: These burrowing rodents tunnel along the park's trails.

About a mile into your hike, you'll stumble upon Persse Place, the former summer homestead of Henry S. Persse. Built in 1903 with locally quarried stone and red mud mortar, Persse's stone house quickly became a guesthouse. Persse envisioned a bustling resort, but then-mayor Robert W. Speer felt the place was too scenic for private ownership, so he nudged it into Denver's growing parks system instead. What do your kids think about the privatization of public lands?

Past Persse Place, the trail rounds a bend and winds through an unforgettable meadow offering close-up views of the Fountain Formation's red spires and awe-inspiring monoliths. If you're following along in the laminated activity guide, then everyone in your group can enjoy finding shapes in the red rocks—George Washington's profile, for example, and a howling wolf.

The sedge meadow you'll pass through can get mucky in the spring and early summer. In fact, sometimes it floods into a makeshift lake, welcoming ducks, herons, and western chorus frogs. Ask kids to listen for the frog's breeding call, which sort of sounds like a finger strumming the tooth of a comb. Spring and summer are also good times to look for the park's fifty-plus species of butterflies, moths, and skippers. (Don't know what a skipper is? Neither did we! Look it up with your kids; Britannica.com is a great online resource.)

Speaking of interesting animals, the trail's final interpretive sign describes the dinosaur freeway. It's worth a read before completing your loop and returning to the visitor center where you started.

LEARN

History, archaeology, geology, plant identification, ecology—the possibilities really are endless at Roxy, and these are just a few topics covered during a trip to this wonderful state park.

- **Wild Child: By May, wildflowers dominate Roxy's jagged landscape, thriving inside the park's varied environment. Bring along a field guide to Rocky Mountain wildflowers, and look for a variety of blooms in the sedge meadow community preceding the Fountain Formation. Identifying and recording wildflowers is a great science activity for kids of all ages. Younger children can simply draw their findings.**
- **Dig Deeper: In addition to being a National Natural Landmark, Roxborough State Park is also a National Archaeological Register District. Since the 1970s, archaeologists have discovered more than 200 artifacts inside the park, mostly of the Archaic and Woodland cultures. The Archaic time period ranged from 6,500 BCE to 200 CE, and Colorado was home to humans during this era. The Plains Woodland period followed, covering about a thousand years of Colorado prehistory. Wouldn't it be fun to start a family research project to learn more about the people who called Colorado home after the Paleo-Indians but before the Utes? FYI, new discoveries are possible inside Roxy. If you or your child uncovers an old-looking, man-made object while exploring, leave it where it is, and report the finding to a ranger.**

61 St. Elmo Ghost Town

This abandoned gold- and silver-mining settlement doubles as an outdoor history park.

Cost: Free
Hours: St. Elmo General Store is open 7 days a week, usually from Mother's Day weekend through Sept; check the store's website for specific hours. While the ghost town is always open to visitors, winter weather makes it difficult (sometimes impossible) to visit when the temperature drops. We don't recommend traversing remote High County roads after dark, so plan accordingly.
Location: 25865 County Road 162
Nearest Town: Nathrop
Denver Drive Time: At least 150 minutes via 6th Avenue to CO 470 to US 285
Accessibility: The dirt roads are rough with some ruts; you'll need an all-terrain wheelchair or jogging stroller for this destination.
Bathrooms: Flush toilets inside the St. Elmo General Store
Gear Suggestions: Sun protection, comfortable walking shoes, layers and a jacket, a camera, snacks, more water than you think you need
Insider Tip: There is no cell service in the area. We repeat, no cell service! Bring a map, printed directions, and this guidebook for reference, and consider downloading a free GPS app (Strava, for example) that uses GPS coordinates instead of cell towers.

Explore

The 11-mile drive from Mt. Princeton Hot Springs Resort across County Road 162 is flush with postcard-perfect views of the Sawatch Range, where strands of aspens dot the region's twenty highest peaks. Deep at the end of this sunny mountain drive sits the dusty ghost town of St. Elmo. Yes, it's a long haul for Front Range families, but don't let that dissuade you. It's worth the time and gas money to take a scenic stroll through Colorado history.

Despite its notoriety and spot on the National Register of Historic Places, this abandoned gold- and silver-mining settlement is so far off the beaten path that it's eerily quiet most days. Many ghost towns are just skeletal remains of buildings that once stood. But St. Elmo has all the characteristics of a full town.

Start with a quick visit to the Ghost Town Guest House, an authentic (and operational) three-story B&B at the top of Main Street. It's across from St. Elmo General Store, which is open seasonally in the summer, usually closing at the end of September. If you're lucky, the innkeepers might give your family a brief history lesson that starts in 1880, when St. Elmo was founded with a telegraph office, general store, town hall, and schoolhouse, plus a handful of saloons. The boomtown thrived, briefly, with completion of the Denver, South Park & Pacific Railroad, but after peaking at 2,000 residents, St. Elmo's population rode the last train out of town and never came back, as the story goes.

Children get a sense of what life was like in Colorado in the late 1800s while poking around St. Elmo, perusing a series of structures and storefronts preserved with classic Main Street finishes. Can't-miss buildings include an old courthouse, complete with jail cell, and the one-room schoolhouse, accessible via a bridge north of downtown. Step inside to view the interiors of these buildings, staged with 1880s furnishings, from a roped-off area. It's a bit like a trip to a living history museum, minus the interpreters. In 45 minutes to an hour, you can see the whole town.

LEARN

In addition to being a premium living history destination, the nearby town of Buena Vista offers up plenty of lessons in outdoor recreation.

- Walk On: You came all the way out here, so why not stretch your legs with a stroll to the Iron City Cemetery? To get there, backtrack on County Road 162 for a quarter mile, until reaching the turnoff for County Road 292. There's a pullout for parking where 162 and 292 meet. Ditch the car at the pullout, and walk onto 292, following the wide dirt road downhill, toward Iron City Campground. After crossing a bridge, you'll reach secluded tent sites. Go straight through the campground until arriving at the cemetery's enchanting white gate, located about 0.7 mile from County Road 162. Take time to read the headstones, which tell a story of courage and community in hard times.
- Paddle into Summer: From hiking and mountain biking to rock climbing, rafting, and hot-air ballooning, Buena Vista is a hub for outdoor recreation. The town's especially lively in May, when paddling season kicks off. One of the best ways for families to get in on the river action is at CKS Paddlefest, a free and educational festival held annually over Memorial Day weekend. During Paddlefest, whitewater aficionados converge for a weekend of entertainment, demonstrations, and discounted gears. If you're new to the sport, start on Main Street, where you'll find dozens of clinics and workshops covering a range of topics for all ages and skill levels. While you're in town, check out the Buena Vista Boulder Garden, a fun public bouldering park, as well as the Barbara Whipple trail system, with a series of well-marked trails offering entry-level hiking opportunities.

62 St. Vrain Greenway and City of Longmont Nature Areas

Fish and float along this 8-mile stretch of the St. Vrain Creek.

Cost: Free
Hours: Greenway trailheads and lands are open 1 hour before sunrise to 1 hour after sunset. The Greenway Trail itself is open 24 hours, 7 days a week. At night (one hour before sunset until one hour before sunrise) trail users must be in continuous motion.
Location: 8 miles through Longmont starting at Golden Ponds Nature Area and ending at Sandstone Ranch Community Park and Nature Area
Nearest Town: Longmont
Denver Drive Time: 45 minutes via I-25 North
Accessibility: ADA-compliant trails, parking lots, restrooms, and other facilities. Greenway Trail paved throughout the nature areas
Bathrooms: Portable toilets and clubhouse bathrooms at various nature area
Gear Suggestions: Walking shoes, sunscreen, hats, insect repellent, and binoculars; depending on the parks visited, bring swimsuits, float tubes, fishing gear, picnic blanket, and bikes.
Insider Tip: Weekly from April through November (8 a.m. to 1 p.m.), the Longmont Farmer's Market sets up at the Boulder County Fairgrounds just a 10-minute walk from Rogers Grove Park on the Greenway Trail. Plan a stop for fresh local produce and food for a picnic.

Explore

In September 2013, Longmont experienced catastrophic flooding along the St. Vrain Creek that damaged businesses, homes, city infrastructure, and the trail system. From that devastation grew an ongoing city initiative to revitalize and improve the affected areas called the Resilient St. Vrain Project. All along the revitalized stretch of St. Vrain Creek, water-loving families will find quiet ponds for casting a line or popular spots for wading or tubing. Starting at the west end of the trail and going east, here's a highlight of some places to play along the way:

Golden Ponds Nature Area: This 88-acre wildlife habitat and sanctuary, near the intersection of Hover Street and Third Avenue, is home to four ponds for catch-and-release fishing and some great opportunities for bird-watching. Fish from a shady spot along the shore of a pond or from the handicap-accessible fishing pier on pond one. But stay on the shore: Swimming and wading at this park are prohibited. You will, however, see interesting birds, like pelicans, swimming across the ponds. If you are there for the views of the Rockies reflected on the ponds, explore the 2.6 miles of trails (paved and crusher fines) winding through the park. This is also a trailhead for the St. Vrain Greenway, so when you are ready to move along, just hit the trail.

Izaak Walton Nature Area: The next stop for fishing is the 15.7-acre Izaak Walton pond, reserved just for kids 15 years old and younger. Each spring kids have an opportunity to participate in an educational Chick Clark Kids' Fishing Program here, to learn about fish biology, fishing equipment, and various techniques. Expect to see birds like tall, thin cranes standing on the railing of the pier and Canada geese hanging around the park.

Dickens Farm Nature Area: This spot along the Greenway is close to downtown Longmont. With large grassy spaces, a bathroom facility, and slower-moving water, families set up sunshades and spend the day tubing, paddleboarding, or wading in the water. There are no lifeguards on duty, so be mindful of the water level and movement, and watch children closely. If kids are bicycle enthusiasts, bring their bikes and safety gear along. A trail for kids with beginner bike skills offers a chance to ride on a variety of surfaces.

From here the Greenway continues on to its endpoint at Sandstone Ranch (see chapter 63). There are a number of other parks and nature areas along the trail, so plan to visit another day to discover something new. If you want to set up for a day of fishing but your family members have different outdoor interests, drop a line at St. Vrain State Park. Construction to connect the trail from Sandstone Ranch to St. Vrain State Park will begin in 2024. Although it's not currently on the greenway, it's not far off the trail (or the interstate), and the activities here range from hiking and watersports to birding and camping.

LEARN

The parks along the St. Vrain Greenway create a sort of wildlife-viewing superhighway. Birds, fish, turtles, rabbits . . . you never know what you will see. Tuck wildlife-viewing gear like binoculars and a magnifier bug box into your tackle box so you are prepared no matter whom you encounter. Here are two more ideas to slip in some secret brain boosters.

- Identify the Fish: An interpretive sign near the pier at Golden Ponds identifies the types of fish you may find in the ponds, with colorful illustrations and descriptions of their physical appearance. Check out a fish field guide from the library or search the internet to learn more about identifying fish. Make it fun by crafting your own game of Go Fish with free downloadable images of fish from the internet. Identify thirteen different fish photos, print four copies of each fish, then attach all of the images on the face sides of an old deck of cards. Include the fish name on the bottom. Then play with traditional Go Fish rules.
- Keep a Tally: Fishing can be a little slow for kids sometimes, so come prepared with fun side activities. Each of these nature areas is full of interesting wild things like waterfowl, insects, plants, and pond life. Bring a bucket, cup, and net to check out what you can find in a scoop of lake water—just be sure to let everyone go back to their watery home afterward. Take pictures and keep a tally of the very different birds and insects you find around the water.

63 Sandstone Ranch Community Park and Visitors & Learning Center

Play as you learn about this historic sandstone quarry and Longmont ranch.

Cost: Free
Hours: Park open daily 5 a.m. to 11 p.m. Nature area open from 1 hour before sunrise to 1 hour before sunset. Visitors & Learning Center hours vary seasonally: open May–Aug Mon 9 a.m. to noon, April–Oct second and fourth Sat 10 a.m. to 2 p.m.
Location: 3001 Sandstone Drive (Sandstone Ranch Visitors & Learning Center)
Nearest Town: Longmont
Denver Drive Time: 40 minutes via I-25 North
Accessibility: Paved trails, accessible picnic pavilions, ADA-compliant parking, first level of Visitors & Learning Center is accessible.
Bathrooms: Full bathrooms in the visitor center when open, and in the picnic pavilions
Gear Suggestions: Walking shoes, hat, sunscreen, insect repellent, swimsuit for play in splash pad, dry change of clothes, bikes
Insider Tip: A free "A Walk on the Ranch" coloring book is available to download at longmontcolorado.gov/sandstone-ranch. Be a good supporter of the park by leaving a couple dollars in the visitor center donation box, or if you don't have cash, donate through the center's page on the Longmont city website, longmontcolorado.gov.

Explore

One of the first white settlers to Longmont, Morse Coffin, came west, like many others, in the early days of the gold rush. In 1860 he settled on a piece of land along the St. Vrain Creek at the base of stunning sandstone bluffs near what is now Ken Pratt Boulevard/Highway 119. The house and ranch were in the Coffin family for one hundred years before being sold. Now the house and property, designated state and national landmarks, make up the Sandstone Ranch Community Park.

The western side of the 120-acre park includes a ballpark complex, but go 1 mile east of Weld County Road 1 and turn south onto Sandstone Drive to find the Nature Area and Visitors & Learning Center.

Once on Sandstone Drive, continue down the road past the sports fields, the picnic pavilions, and the pond. Follow the signs for Visitors & Learning Center parking; it will take you to a slight left turn onto a road sloping to the top of a hill. This is where you'll find the parking lot for the Visitors & Learning Center. (For handicapped parking, continue on the paved road directly to the Visitors & Learning Center.) From the parking lot, look for the entrance to a gravel trail near the bathrooms. This trail is part of a 0.7-mile loop that takes you to the Ranch House where the Visitors & Learning Center is located, around the property, and through the remains of an old sandstone quarry, then back to the parking lot.

Inside the Visitors & Learning Center, view displays about the habitat surrounding the center and the Coffin family's role in Colorado history. Knowledgeable volunteers are on hand to help answer questions. As you enter the house, the room to the right is filled with hands-on play opportunities.

The second floor is mostly event space, but turn left into the room at the top of the stairs, head to the big windows in the back corner, and you'll find binoculars and a viewing scope to look for birds and other critters around the property.

The property also has a barn, spring house, garden, and shaded picnic space. Pick up the trail again near the house (this portion will take you along part of the paved St. Vrain Greenway Trail, so watch for bicyclists, walkers, and hikers). As you head back to your car, look for a sign guiding you to a scenic overlook. The panoramic vista gives you an eyeful of the northern Colorado peaks of the Rockies. An interpretive sign helps identify which ones you see. Finally, head back to the parking lot through a field of grasses, sunflowers, and wildflowers.

On the way out, stop at the adventure playground to reward kids with some open play—just follow the signs for the sports fields and skate park. Choose from the Spring Gulch Play Corral for toddlers or the Tree House Play Area with a tall tree-house play structure, web climber, and climbing wall for older kids. A splash

pad (open daily 8 a.m. to 8 p.m. Memorial Day through Labor Day) and sand area give everyone a chance to cool down. Shady seating areas for parents and restroom structures with flush toilets make Sandstone Ranch a comfortable place to spend a morning.

LEARN

There are plenty of opportunities to play at this park. Engage kids in an exploration of the ways children used to play: making their own toys and venturing into nature.

- **Unplugged Toys: Ask kids to brainstorm how they can have fun without toys, as well as what they can find in nature to build a toy—children of the past made dolls from cornhusks. Get creative with the kids at home and see what toys or games you can create from items in nature. Maybe a checkerboard using rocks and twigs or pine-cone animals and dolls that can put on a play.**
- **Identify the Zone: The area around Sandstone Ranch is a riparian zone. Before your visit, create a list of characteristics that make up a riparian zone—the plants, animals, and fish—and seek out those elements as you explore the area.**

64 Staunton State Park

Learn to fish, then hike past historic cabins at this scenic park.

Cost: Daily vehicle pass required to enter Colorado state parks, or purchase a Colorado Parks & Wildlife annual parks pass.
Hours: Daily hours are 6 a.m. to 10 p.m.
Location: 12102 South Elk Creek Road
Nearest Towns: Pine and Conifer
Denver Drive Time: 50 minutes via 6th Avenue, CO 470, and US 285
Accessibility: Visitors with mobility differences can explore Staunton's rugged trail system through the park's Track-Chair program (more information below). Sign language hikes have been offered for guests with hearing impairments.
Bathrooms: Flush toilets inside the main visitor center; pit toilets at the Davis Ponds Loop Trailhead and near the Davis ponds
Gear Suggestions: KEEN sandals or similar shoes that work for walking and water play, sunscreen, sunglasses, a hat, windbreakers, binoculars, plenty of water, snacks to enjoy at one of the picnic areas. If you plan to cast a line, bring fishing gear and a valid Colorado fishing license (required for all anglers ages 16 and up).
Insider Tip: Fishing clinics are offered all year long, even in the winter, when families can learn how to ice-fish. (How cool is that?) No pole? No problem. If you show up for a fishing clinic, poles and bait will be available to use. You'll still need a fishing license, though, for anyone 16 and over. Fishing dollars pay for local hatcheries to fill area lakes, including Staunton's ponds, which are stocked with rainbow trout.

Explore

As one of Colorado's newer state parks, Staunton is a memorable place chock-full of natural beauty and western history. In fact, several nineteenth-century farms and ranches were combined to form the park, named for its largest parcel, Staunton Ranch, homesteaded by two East Coast doctors who were initially headed to California. When the Stauntons stopped to rest in Denver, they fell in love with Colorado.

Staunton State Park opened to the public in 2013 with nearly 30 miles of dirt trails crossing grassy meadows and forested hillsides framed by stunning granite cliffs. It doesn't really matter what you and your kids are into because Staunton has it all. There's archery, mountain biking, hiking, rock climbing, fishing, group picnicking, and geocaching. On top of that, you'll find entry-level hike-in camping at the park's 25 basic tent sites—a perfect opportunity for families who are ready for something more rugged than car camping without dipping into the backcountry.

The best way to familiarize yourself with the park is to hit the trails. For an excellent outing with kids, we'd recommend hiking on the park's David Ponds Loop, an easy 2.2-mile route with 143 feet of elevation gain. The loop is hikers-only, and it's great with strollers, passing two large, regularly stocked ponds. BYO poles and cast a line.

If you'd like to see a few of the site's original homestead cabins, including the house built by the Stauntons in 1916, take Davis Ponds Loop to Chase Meadow Trail. After 0.7 mile turn left onto Historic Cabin Trail, and walk until you reach the structures. Trail maps are available inside the visitor center near the park's main entrance. This is a great place to talk up the rangers and learn more about robust, year-round programming.

Meadow Parking Lot is just past the entrance gates, and it's where you'll go to get a track-chair, if you've reserved one in advance. Track-chairs are wheelchairs with tank tracks on them that allow users to hike rugged terrain that a typical wheelchair can't interface with. Staunton owns several track-chairs, all of which have attendant joysticks on the back, so somebody can drive the chair from behind it. Even if your child can't control the chair themselves, they can still use one. What's more, Staunton can accommodate the transfer of users into the track-chairs with a Hoyer lift with side rails. Two adaptive fishing poles are available at the visitor center, for those looking to hike Davis Ponds Loop and fish.

Staunton State Park launched its Track-Chair Program in 2017 to help hikers with mobility differences experience the site's incredible trails. Hiker Mark Madsen inspired the program. After a car accident left him paralyzed, Madsen and his friend Ted Hammond borrowed a track-chair so Madsen could experience the park's trail system.

When Madsen passed away in 2015, his family—with a little help from the Friends of Staunton State Park—established the Mark Madsen Accessibility Fund. The fundraising program morphed into Staunton's Track-Chair Program, and the rest is history. To make a track-chair reservation, visit Staunton's website, cpw.state.co.us/placestogo/parks/Staunton and click the "Track-Chair Program" link. All reservations are subject to inclement weather cancellations. For more information, email staunton.trackchair@state.co.us or call (303) 816-0912.

LEARN

In addition to seeing relics from Colorado's bygone mining days, parkgoers can also develop other skills, including geography, navigation, and wildlife identification.

- Hunt for Treasure: Geocaching (JEE-oh-cash-ing) can turn an otherwise lackluster hike into a bona fide adventure, and it's a great way to develop a child's map-reading skills. The term is a mash-up for two words: "geography" and "cache." Instead of searching for treasure with a paper map, geocachers use a mobile device and observations to find trinkets hidden above ground, at sites marked by GPS coordinates. What's really special about Staunton's geocache collection is that park managers oversee the addition of new caches, making them great for first-time hunters. To play, you'll need a smartphone and app, such as Geocaching or Cachly. Every cache has its own page where participants will find useful tips and hints. Good luck!
- Track It: Visit Staunton after a summer storm, and you might encounter a little mud. That's not so bad because a slightly muddy trail is a great place to find animal tracks. The park's varied terrain and vegetation create a fantastic habitat for many local mammals, including red foxes, coyotes, deer, and the rare Abert's squirrel, distinguished by its dark-gray back, white belly, and tufted ears. An elk herd also lives inside the park, coexisting with resident predators such as bobcats and black bears. You aren't likely to spy many of these animals during a daytime hike with noisy kids, but you could definitely see evidence of them if you're keeping an eye out for tracks and scat. Up the educational element by bringing along prints of animal tracks to compare to any paw prints you and your kids find. Teach your kids to walk through mud, not around it, and if a trail's closed due to mud, always respect the signs.

65 Sunflower Farm

This rural haven is one of the Front Range's best agricultural destinations.

Cost: $$$
Hours: The farm's open to the public year-round, on weekends only. On select summer evenings, the farm opens for music. Reservations are required.
Location: 11150 Prospect Road
Nearest Town: Longmont
Denver Drive Time: 55 minutes via US 36 and US 287
Accessibility: The site is stroller accessible. Bathrooms are ADA compliant. While concrete has been poured on some areas inside the farm, a standard wheelchair might be tricky on the site's woodchip walking paths. Sunflower Farm hosts some private events for Colorado's special needs community. Call the farm's main line for more information: (303) 774-8001.
Bathrooms: Flush toilets in the center of the farm, near the bonfire area
Gear Suggestions: Comfortable walking shoes, sunscreen, a hat, sunglasses, plenty of water, snacks and/or a picnic lunch, a windbreaker if joining for evening music. Pack a rain jacket, too, because the farm will remain open in light rain.
Insider Tip: Held weekly from late May into early October, Summer Music Evenings are an unforgettable way to experience Sunflower Farm. The nighttime gatherings feature a local band and food truck. Kids can mingle with the farm animals and participate in all the usual Farmfest activities, while parents and older siblings listen to live music. Talk about a win-win situation.

Explore

At Sunflower Farm, guests are welcomed to a simpler, smartphone-free life that's shaded by century-old shade trees with tire swings overlooking alfalfa fields and an intricate system of interconnected tree houses, all nestled among goats, baby sheep, free-roaming chickens, and peacocks. It's every bit as wonderful as it sounds, and tickets to the 55-acre working farm are one of my family's favorite splurges.

The project launched in 2001 as a way of tailoring farm life to children's interests. Over the decades, Sunflower Farm has grown into a one-of-a-kind local treasure fostering self-guided exploration and farm-based education that's sure to inspire passion in kids while promoting serious brain development.

The farm's main offering for the general public is called Farmfest. Held on weekends only in the summer and early fall, this is a time for families of all ages to hang out on the farm, interacting with animals and exploring the property. Due to the site's limited capacity, you'll have to reserve tickets to Farmfest in advance online at sunflowerfarminfo.com. We're big fans of the reservation system because it ensures all guests get a serene morning away from city life.

Everywhere you go there's a nook with something different. Excitement builds as kids discover the farm's various offerings: John Deere tractors, a sandbox inside a silo, an airplane, haystacks ripe for the jumping, tree houses, and slides. Near the back of

the property, look for Mulch Hill, a giant pile of woodchips where kids can "sled" all summer long. (In the winter the area turns into a real sledding hill and staff usually get a bonfire going.)

Keep exploring. Acres of land allow kids the opportunity to play creatively in the outdoors. If you brought the recommended picnic lunch, you can enjoy it at one of the picnic benches near the stage. Be advised, Sunflower Farm doesn't sell food, but you can purchase water, juice, and Popsicles during your visit; bring cash. (Psst: Marshmallows are available for toasting in the winter months.) After you eat, encourage kids to participate in farm activities such as feeding hay to the site's various animals.

If your kids love the farm, look into summer day camps, which give campers ages 5 to 10 a real sense of the farm lifestyle. Camp activities include animal care and education, planting and harvesting, recycled and nature-based art projects, lawn games, talent shows, animal races, and good old-fashioned outdoor play. There are also school-year programs available for preschoolers and lower-elementary students (ages 5 to 8).

LEARN

This educational site's all about animals, agriculture, entrepreneurship . . . basically everything it takes to make a working farm work.

- **Get Involved: Teen Volunteer Days are a great opportunity for older kids who are looking for a unique way to give back. Starting in April, teens can sign up to volunteer on the farm during 3-hour-long sessions held once or twice a month (depending on seasonal needs). Volunteers try all types of farm work, from weeding and raking to painting, planting, harvesting, and animal care, including feeding. For more details, email the program administrators at sunflowerfarmmail@gmail.com.**
- **Dig In: Have you or your kids ever been curious about urban farming? You don't have to live in a rural setting to run a farm. (Case in point: The Urban Farm; see chapter 67). In fact, the urban farm movement has been gaining ground in cities across the United States, and it's especially popular in Colorado, where some dedicated city dwellers grow vegetables in their backyards and keep chickens or other livestock (local ordinances permitting). There's no shortage of books on urban farming, so the public library is a great place to read up. Denver Urban Gardens, dug.org, is a fantastic resource for Front Range families, offering classes and events, including special youth programming. And if you really want to dig in, check out WWOOF USA, wwoofusa.org/en, a very cool organization pairing volunteers with local farmers for some intensive hands-on learning.**

66 University of Colorado Museum of Natural History

Dinosaurs, fossils, and apples tell a story about Colorado's past.

Cost: Free, but a small donation appreciated. Fee for parking.
Hours: Mon–Fri 9 a.m. to 5 p.m., Sat 9 a.m. to 4 p.m., Sun 10 a.m. to 4 p.m., closed on all University of Colorado officially observed holidays
Location: 1030 Broadway St., in the Henderson Building on the University of Colorado Boulder's main campus
Nearest Town: Boulder
Denver Drive Time: 35 minutes via US-36 West
Accessibility: ADA and stroller accessible entrance on the north side of the museum and an elevator inside for moving between floors. Exhibit and directional signage in both English and Spanish.
Bathrooms: Full restrooms with changing stations in both the men's and women's bathrooms
Gear Suggestions: Walking shoes, exploration journal
Insider Tip: Look down as you tour this museum. Little doors along the baseboards open to reveal Peri the Pinyon Mouse, the museum's curiosity guide, in his mouse house. Peri shares activities to engage kids in each gallery. See if you can figure out Peri's full name and the meaning behind it. Hint: You may need to visit the entrance desk.

Explore

Heading to Boulder and have a little extra time? This gem of a museum on the University of Colorado Boulder campus features a collection of artifacts, specimens, and hands-on activities to keep big and little guests engaged.

The museum's original collection of a few fossils, rocks and minerals, and several mounted birds and mammals was first organized into a museum at the beginning of the twentieth century. Today the museum's collection includes more than 4 million objects—it's the largest natural history collection in the Rocky Mountain region. You won't see all 4 million objects on display, but you will be treated to five exhibition galleries featuring items curated from Colorado, North America, and around the world.

As you enter the Henderson Building—named for the first curator of the museum and home to the museum since 1937—take a moment to look at the exterior. The red sandstone walls and clay-tiled roof reflect CU Boulder's distinct "Tuscan vernacular" style of architecture. Kids may be interested to know that the sandstone on the historic CU buildings is from Colorado.

As you step inside the historic building, head up the grand staircase to the front desk. A helpful Visitor Services staffer, a student or volunteer will be on hand to answer any questions. There is also a small gift shop with a selection of children's toys and books.

On this floor, start in the Paleo Hall to discover a captivating collection of prehistoric fossils. Kids will learn that Colorado was once part of the Dinosaur Freeway, an ancient coastline traveled by dinosaurs, crocodiles, and birds, evident by the more than twenty fossilized track sites found around the state. Seek out the display of tracks

among other prehistoric treasures in this gallery like the collection of teeth and jaws. Scan the room for the Family Corner. Chances are, your kids have already spotted it. These activity spaces with kid-size tables are stocked with activities and toys related to the artifacts and displays around them. Pull out baskets for coloring pages, plastic dinosaurs, and books. There is a Family Corner in each of the three main galleries, and a supersized activity space for children on the lower level.

Now step across the hall to the Tree Space gallery, which currently highlights an ongoing CU project studying Boulder's history of growing apples in orchards. Here, kids will find out how researchers, CU students, and citizen scientists are working together to preserve the story of Boulder's dwindling historic apple trees.

On the lower level, the Anthropology Hall features ancient pots and baskets, as well as a collection of more than eighty stone tools from the ice age found in a Boulder backyard in 2008. Now, cross the hall to the BioLounge area, which features a comfy spot to have a seat and see rotating exhibitions like a display of Trash the Runway garments made by local teens using, you guessed it, trash. Remember that mention of a supersized kids corner? This is where you'll find it. The Discovery

Corner is a large hands-on play zone just for kids. Little ones can color, dig, and play with puppets or games to learn more about natural and cultural history.

If you are looking for things to do at home, visit the Museum From Home area of the museum's website (colorado.edu/cumuseum) for a collection of family activities, with instructions in both English and Spanish.

LEARN

This mini museum is a great springboard for an afternoon of inspired art. Make the morning lessons stick with these tactile craft projects.

- **Make Tracks: Take inspiration from the dinosaur tracks in the Fossil Hall and set your child's footprint or handprint in clay or plaster of Paris. If you'd rather forgo the mess, play with different ways you can leave footprints or handprints behind—permanently or temporarily. Step in wet sand or dirt together, then observe which holds the prints longer, or experiment with what makes them dissolve. Use washable paint to make simple handprint designs on paper.**
- **Apple Art: As you explore the Tree Space, look at the apple art displays together. Some apples were sketched, some were sculpted. Get creative at home and have the kids make their own apple art from clay, with paints, papier-mâché, or whatever inspires them.**

67 The Urban Farm

This city farm delivers experiential learning opportunities and practical work experiences.

Cost: $
Hours: They vary by season; always check TUF's website, theurbanfarm.org, before visiting.
Location: 10200 Smith Road
Nearest Town: Central Park
Denver Drive Time: 25 minutes via Brighton Boulevard to I-70
Accessibility: The farm is wheelchair and stroller accessible, but some of the trails circling the animals might be tricky with a standard wheelchair.
Bathrooms: Flush toilets inside the main entrance building
Gear Suggestions: Good walking shoes, clothes that can get a little dirty, sunscreen, a sun hat, plenty of water, snacks
Insider Tip: The equestrian program is one of TUF's best-kept secrets. The Urban Farm has an impressive year-round English riding program suitable for ages 5 to 18. And don't miss the farm's weeklong summer horse camps, which include basic riding and trail riding classes.

Explore

Nicknamed TUF, The Urban Farm is exactly what it sounds like—an urban farm, sitting on a 23-acre campus in the heart of a major city. The space was developed for growing food and also bolstering community and supporting local wildlife. The concept has been drawing families of all ages to this one-of-a-kind destination since the nonprofit organization's inception in the early 1990s.

After being founded in Firestone, the farm was relocated to Central Park in 1998 and rebuilt around an old weather station from the Stapleton Airport, which has been repurposed into an industrial barn. TUF delivers a wide range of experiential learning opportunities and practical work experiences to its young visitors. That's because the organization's overarching mission is to instill a love of learning in youth. Doing farmwork can also help kids pick up a host of great attributes—confidence, resilience, teamwork, and problem-solving skills, for starters.

Basically, non-members can come out to the farm on a day it is open to the public and explore the premises. Guided tours, including field trips for schools and groups, are an option, but we think most families will enjoy self-guided excursions.

Walk around and view the community gardens, then meander over to the animals—they're what makes TUF stand apart from other urban farms. In addition to dozens of horses and miniature horses, kids can see a couple of cows plus flocks of goats, sheep, and chickens. If children are quiet and calm, most animals will come right up to the fences to say hello. There are also two play structures for the farm's youngest guests.

TUF uses its farm as a tool to work with youth. In fact, the organization has one of the largest, most robust 4-H programs in Colorado. But you don't have to be part of the national youth program to get up close with the livestock.

Families are invited to sign up to volunteer alongside TUF staff members on designated volunteer days (check the organization's website for age restrictions). Volunteers get a chance to perform basic farm maintenance chores, along with weeding and planting in the gardens. There's plenty of sowing to do in the spring and summer, in raised beds and state-of-the-art aeroponics towers. On weekends, volunteers have an opportunity to help with larger projects—fence building, for example, or modifying the on-site hoop house. All volunteers tend to animals, which is a big hit with most kids. If you're interested in learning more, fill out the online form, available at theurbanfarm.org/individual-volunteer.

Let's wrap up this chapter with a few safety notes. Do not let children climb on the fences surrounding TUF: Some are electric and will deliver a small shock to those who touch them. Also, guests should watch their step while visiting the farm because prairie dogs occasionally leave holes on walking paths. There's no chewing gum allowed on the farm, and last but not least, be sure to leave Fido at home. Because of the animals, pets are not permitted on the farm.

LEARN

This destination covers all sorts of farm-themed topics, from animals and wildlife to plants, gardening, biodiversity, conservation, and urban planning. Here are a few ideas for enhancing these educational components.

- **Learn through Play: There's nothing young children love more than a make-believe game. Gather up a handful of barnyard stuffed animals, and put together a pretend farm of your own. If available, use cardboard boxes to create outbuildings and stables for your livestock, then have kids tend to their animals. It might even be fun to get out a doctor playset or veterinarian kit and give some of the "sick" animals checkups. Large-animal veterinarians work with horses and other large animals, often specializing in livestock or farm animals. If this interests your children, encourage them to research this special area of veterinary sciences.**
- **Take Root: Read Kate Messner's wonderful picture book *Up in the Garden and Down in the Dirt*. When you're finished, show your children a few root vegetables such as carrots, beets, turnips, radishes, and potatoes. Next, grab some white paper, pencils, markers, and crayons. Draw a horizontal line across the paper to symbolize the ground. Ask kids to draw the vegetables they saw in the garden, using both their knowledge and imagination to determine what goes above and below the dirt. If you're up for it, grow a root vegetable from seed in a transparent container, and observe what happens above and below the soil. With older children, you may want to spend time learning more about root vegetables and "true roots," which are botanically distinguishable.**

68 Walden Ponds Wildlife Habitat

Wander through a wetlands habitat while enjoying scenic views.

Cost: Free
Hours: Open daily from sunrise to sunset
Location: 4729 Twin Rocks Road
Nearest Town: Boulder
Denver Drive Time: 40 minutes via I-25 and US 36
Accessibility: Many trails inside the open space are wheelchair and stroller accessible. Look for ADA-compliant fishing piers at Wally Toevs Pond.
Bathrooms: Outhouses at Wally Toevs Pond and near the Cottonwood Marsh trailhead
Gear Suggestions: Binoculars, nature-journaling materials, comfortable walking shoes, sunscreen and/or sun-protective clothing, plenty of water, a picnic lunch, books to read pondside
Insider Tip: There are a couple of parking options inside this Boulder County refuge. Bypass the first lot at Wally Toevs Pond and park at Cottonwood Marsh instead, located near the site's large welcome sign and outhouse. This gets you to the prettiest features fastest.

Explore

Walden Ponds Wildlife Habitat is the locational equivalent of sipping chai lattes in your favorite pair of cotton joggers on a lazy Saturday morning. It's hard to believe the refuge was a gravel pit in the 1950s. Open pits and puddles of groundwater were pretty much all that remained in the area after the property had been stripped down to bedrock.

In 1974, when locals voiced their interest in creating a wildlife habitat, the county began cleaning things up, compacting piles of rock into dikes to create three main ponds, planting trees and shrubs, and reseeding dry areas to support natural revegetation. Staff stocked the water with fish, and in the 1990s, two additional ponds were added.

Today, families are greeted with 2.9 miles of flat and serene trails weaving through a pristine marsh. In addition to the five ponds, there are interpretive signs and plenty of nooks where curious kids can get up close with their surroundings. Heed the one-way traffic flow by crossing a series of wooden bridges first (you'll see the signs), then explore at your child's pace. My kids loved the shallow bank at Duck Pond, and we also stumbled upon a secret shelter near Bass Pond.

Bring binoculars! This biologically diverse site attracts large numbers of migrating birds. During our first visit to Walden Ponds, my kids and I spotted two bald eagles hanging out on a utility pole near Wally Toevs Pond. Like all wildlife viewing, birding requires patience and a certain level of silence. Challenge your kids to listen for birdcalls.

Right past the Walden Ponds entrance, equipped with an ADA-compliant fishing pier, Wally Toevs Pond is a fabulous fishing destination reserved exclusively for people with disabilities and guests 65 and older (youth companions welcome). The pond is stocked seasonally, in the spring and fall. A valid Colorado fishing license is required for all persons 16 and up, and fishing is not allowed at Cottonwood Marsh.

Contrary to popular belief, Walden Ponds Wildlife Habitat is *not* a reference to Thoreau's iconic pond. It is named instead for Walden "Wally" Toevs, the Boulder County commissioner who oversaw the plan to convert the site's gravel pits into a wildlife habitat.

Speaking of Boulder, Walden Ponds is only 7 miles east of Boulder's Pearl Street Mall, so if all that nature exploration revs up your appetite, head into town for a snack. Or better yet, turn left onto 75th Street, and drive north to the town of Niwot. The cute-as-a-button shopping district on 2nd Avenue is only a block away from Whistle Stop Park and Niwot Children's Park, with its crowd-pleasing, nature-based playground.

LEARN

Whether your children are studying birds, wildlife, habitats, or conservation, Walden Ponds is a natural destination for hands-on learning. The following activities will add an educational boost to your adventure.

- **Be a Nature Detective: Before heading out for your day trip, print a *Mystery Guide*, available on the Walden Ponds Wildlife Habitat homepage (start at bouldercounty.org and follow the links). An innovative Nature Detectives Club program keeps grade-school kids entertained while exploring select areas in Boulder County, including Walden Ponds. In addition to a kid-friendly trail map, the Walden Ponds guide contains several activities for children to tackle on-site. Don't forget to pack a pencil so your children can complete their guide while hiking.**
- **Write On: Even though this Walden Ponds isn't tied to the beloved author and naturalist Henry David Thoreau, it's still fun to while away the time Thoreau-style, immersed in nature, journaling about the experience. Bring notebooks and writing supplies, and ask your children to take notes on their surroundings, focusing on what they experience through each of their five senses. Younger children who can't yet write can still participate by dictating notes to their caregiver and/or drawing pictures.**

69 Waterton Canyon and the Strontia Springs Dam

Bike up a scenic canyon past a herd of bighorn sheep.

Cost: Free
Hours: Open year-round, 30 minutes before sunrise to 30 minutes after sunset
Location: Waterton Road, between Denver Audubon Kingery Nature Center and the South Platte River. To reach Waterton Canyon Trailhead from Denver, follow Wadsworth Boulevard south of CO 470, past Chatfield Reservoir. Turn left onto Waterton Road, then take your second left, into a dirt parking lot. This large, bumpy lot is directly across the street from the trailhead. Cars go fast down Waterton Road; always cross the street carefully at the designated crosswalk.
Nearest Towns: Roxborough and Highlands Ranch
Denver Drive Time: 35 minutes via Santa Fe Drive and CO 470
Accessibility: The first 6.2 miles of the trail are well-packed crushed gravel. It's doable with a wheelchair or jogging stroller, and you'll find accessible fishing piers 1.25 miles up the canyon. Waterton Canyon gets crowded, especially on summer weekends. If your child requires a low-sensory experience, visit on a weekday morning.
Bathrooms: Outhouses on the far end of the parking lot servicing Waterton Canyon, and at the rest areas located approximately every mile up the canyon, until reaching the Colorado Trail Trailhead
Gear Suggestions: Comfortable athletic shoes, binoculars, a camera, sunscreen, sunglasses, a windbreaker or light jacket, extra layers, plenty of water, snacks to enjoy when you reach the dam. If you're planning to bike, mountain, gravel, or hybrid bikes will work best.
Insider Tip: Before visiting, you should always—always!—check to see if the trail is open. This is true for any trail you're visiting, but especially Waterton Canyon. You'll find up-to-date information on Denver Water's website, at denverwater.org/recreation/waterton-canyon-strontia-springs-resevoir. The Colorado Trail Foundation posts information about trail closures (coloradotrail.org), and don't underestimate social media sites—they're invaluable resources for learning about current trail conditions and closures. While we're talking nuts and bolts, dogs and other pets are not allowed on canyon trails. This important rule is in place to protect the bighorn sheep who live inside Waterton Canyon.

Explore

Waterton Canyon's name isn't just for kicks: The river running through this incredible recreation area is an important water source for Denverites. In fact, Denver Water manages the first segment of Waterton Canyon.

As you cross Waterton Road and head into the canyon, look left. See that block of fenced-off buildings? You're looking at the remnants of a historic water-treatment plant, Kassler, which opened in 1902 at the base of Waterton Canyon.

An entire town cropped up around the water plant, and Kassler employees lived on-site with their families while operating and maintaining the facility. There was

even a one-room schoolhouse for the children of Kassler's few hundred residents. At its peak, using the English slow-sand filter process, Kassler delivered more than 50 million gallons per day of treated drinking water to Denver residents, but that wasn't enough for the growing city. Unable to keep up with demand, Kassler closed in 1985. Now, the ghost town is a National Water Landmark. You can't hop the fence, but Denver Water does offer tours to school groups throughout the year.

Stream fishing is a popular activity at Waterton Canyon, and you'll see people fly-fishing from the South Platte River as you trek up the canyon. In case you're curious, Colorado Parks & Wildlife manages the stream fishery, and the US Forest Service oversees the portions of Waterton Canyon within Pike National Forest.

Waterton Canyon is an incredible wildlife-viewing destination. For birders, the recreation area hosts more than forty species of birds. In addition to mule deer, elk, black bears, and mountain lions, Waterton Canyon is renowned for its herd of Rocky Mountain bighorn sheep. The majestic and agile animals can be seen on the canyon's steep and jagged walls.

There are no guarantees with wildlife viewing, but with that disclaimer out of the way, I'll tell you what, I've never *not* seen bighorn sheep while recreating inside Waterton Canyon. The trick is to go far enough up the canyon. Bighorn sheep are most common between mile marker 2 and Strontia Springs Dam. As you hike or bike, keep your eyes peeled, and have your binoculars ready. Sometimes bighorn sheep will

come down to the trail to snack on shrubs, but more often you'll spot them in the distance, on rocky ledges.

The full route to Strontia Springs Dam is 12.4 miles out and back. It's a steady, 6.2-mile climb in, which would be a lot of hiking for most of the kids I know. If you have mountain, gravel, or hybrid bikes available, I'd recommend making this a bike adventure. (For the first 6.2 miles of trail, road bikes will work in a pinch. Beyond the dam, mountain bikes are a must.) If bikes aren't available, walk for as long as your family is having fun, then turn around and hike back. It's a straight shot, you can't get lost, and there are shelters and restrooms about every mile.

Strontia Springs Dam is worth seeing if you've got the time and energy. It's not the Hoover Dam, but it's still an incredible landmark. Water rushing into the river, driving through the canyon walls—it's one of those remarkable things you've got to experience for yourself.

The shaded picnic table at the Bighorn Sheep Rest Area, the one preceding the dam, is an ideal place to sit down and enjoy whatever snacks you packed. You'll find bathrooms just up the trail, and past those, the path becomes significantly more rugged as it narrows into the treasured Colorado Trail, a mixed-use route that'll take thru-hikers and riders all the way to Durango. Waterton also connects to the Roxborough State Park system and Indian Creek Trail, but those are feats for another day.

With kids, 12.4 miles is a lot. The best part about Waterton Canyon is it's all downhill back to the car. Just coast to the lot, keeping your eyes peeled for any bighorn sheep you might have missed on the way up.

LEARN

Whether your child is studying water use or wildlife, a trip to Waterton Canyon is overflowing (pun intended) with tangible lessons in a variety of subjects. Here are a few ways to expand your child's knowledge.

- **Clean Energy: Water is a powerful force of nature that sustains all life on Earth. It is also capable of producing energy, and there's no better place to learn about hydropower than at Cabin Creek, Xcel Energy's hydroelectric generating facility, at 600 Griffith Street in Georgetown. Nearly every day since opening in 1967, Cabin Creek has provided power to Georgetown, Silver Plume, and beyond. Xcel owns and operates the high-altitude pumped storage plant. On the premises, there's the charming Georgetown Energy Museum, offering seasonal, family-friendly tours. For more information, visit georgetownenergymuseum.com/tour. Schedule a tour by emailing info@georgetownenergymuseum.com.**
- **Go Wild: Bighorn sheep neared extinction at the turn of the century, after unregulated hunting and livestock diseases decimated western populations. But thanks to the North American Model of Wildlife Conservation, Colorado's herds have returned and are doing great. In the heart of downtown Denver, the Denver Museum of Nature & Science, 2001 Colorado Boulevard, is a great place to learn more about bighorn sheep and other local wildlife. The site's extensive wildlife halls showcase a variety of fauna in their natural habitats. Nearby, the Denver Zoo, 2300 Steele Street, also houses a variety of Rocky Mountain animals, including bighorn sheep. Learn all about these agile mammals at denverzoo.org/animals/rocky-mountain-bighorn-sheep.**

70 Western Museum of Mining and Industry

Dig into Colorado's mining story.

Cost: $$
Hours: Mon–Sat 9 a.m. to 4 p.m., guided tours at 10 a.m. and 1 p.m.
Location: 225 North Gate Boulevard
Nearest Town: Colorado Springs
Denver Drive Time: 1 hour via I-25 South
Accessibility: Wheelchair-accessible museum and parking
Bathrooms: Restrooms in the museum
Gear Suggestions: Walking shoes
Insider Tip: Visitors who go to the museum on Summer Family Days are treated to a demonstration of the machines around the WMMI campus, including the Stamp Mill, the Blacksmith Shop, and the Osgood Steam Shovel. Visit wmmi.org for upcoming events.

Explore

Turn onto Mining Museum Road toward the Western Museum of Mining and Industry and the first thing you will see is the historic Reynolds Ranch House. Lazard Cahn, an internationally recognized mineralogist and founder of the Colorado Springs Mineralogical Society, owned the house from 1909 to 1930. In 1927, while living here, he had a small white crystal he discovered named after him—Cahnite. The well-preserved ranch has stood in this location for more than one hundred years and is on the Colorado State Register of Historic Properties. The 28-acre site is a peaceful spot to walk, hike, and picnic under mature shade trees, after a visit to the Western Museum of Mining and Industry (during normal business hours).

Drive past the farm buildings to a row of historic mining machines and vehicles that will leave any machine-loving kid slack-jawed. The Osgood Steam Shovel sitting near the museum is one that fans of the book *Mike Mulligan and His Steam Shovel* by Virginia Lee Burton will surely recognize. The book's main character, Mary Anne, is based on a similar model. Bring a copy of the book to read at one of the picnic tables nearby.

As you look up the hill behind WMMI, you'll see historic mining headframes and the reconstructed Stamp Mill from the Yellow Jacket mill near Montezuma, Colorado. Visitors are welcome to explore the equipment and buildings, but you will need to come back during a special event to see them in use.

The museum itself is stocked with exhibits and artifacts that tell the story of mining in the west from the discovery of gold in California in 1848 to the present. A number of mining machines on display, like the mine hoist and enormous air compressor, are impressive to look at, but sign up for one of the guided tours (included in admission price) and the machines will roar to life with the help of your tour guide. Speaking of the tour guides, they do a good job of engaging kids as they tell the stories of young boys who often worked dangerous jobs in the early days of mining.

Follow the exhibits back to the Model Mine Drift to walk through a replica nineteenth-century gold and silver mine. Kids will experience the miners' working conditions deep within the mine, without actually descending below the earth's surface. As you leave the model mine, a darkened room filled with fluorescent minerals is on your right. This is currently the state's largest public exhibit of such minerals that glow green, red, and blue in the dark.

If you are on a guided tour, it will end back in the lobby with an impressive power-up of the machine collection representing the dawn of the Industrial Revolution. The centerpiece, an 1895 Corliss steam engine, came to Colorado from a paper plant in Massachusetts and was installed in its current location when there was still just an open field. The museum was built around it.

Gold panning is also included in the cost of a museum ticket. Although the panning zone is just beyond the entrance to the exhibits, resist the urge to dip into the troughs "seeded" with small flecks until after you've toured the museum. When you're ready, grab one of the pans located near the troughs. A video on loop shows young prospectors correct panning technique, and the promise of "keep what you find" may occupy them for a while. Ask at the front desk for a small plastic bag to hold what you find.

LEARN

There is a saying, "If it's not grown, it's mined," meaning that everything we use in our daily lives comes from either a growing thing or something extracted, or mined, from the earth. Try these activities to get kids thinking about our planet's natural resources.

- **Make the Mining Connection: Look for the "What's Mined Is Yours" exhibit. This display tells the story of the connection between mined rocks, minerals, and metals, and many things we have or use in our homes. Back at home, see if your child can find five things around the house that have a connection to something that has been mined.**
- **Research Recycling: Once kids start to identify items around the house with a mining connection, encourage them to think about each item's life cycle. What happens to these items when we are done with them? Do they go in a landfill? Can you recycle these precious resources? Can they be reused? Children are enthusiastic about preserving the planet, so let them set up a recycling area in the house or garage for items no longer being used—old cell phones, aluminum foil pans, batteries, your old CD collection, even the kitchen sink. Make it a project to find out if the items can be recycled or reused and where.**

71 Wild Animal Sanctuary

Learn about efforts to protect rescued large carnivores.

Cost: $$$
Hours: Open daily (except New Year's Day, Independence Day, Thanksgiving, and Christmas Day) 9 a.m. to sunset. Visit the website (wildanimalsanctuary.org) for a list of specific sunset times.
Location: 2999 County Road 53
Nearest Town: Keenesburg
Denver Drive Time: 45 minutes via I-76 East
Accessibility: Facility, ramps, elevators, and walkway accessible and ADA compliant. Wagons and wheelchairs available for rent at the Welcome Center and Education Center on a first-come, first-served basis.
Bathrooms: Restrooms available at Welcome Center, Resource Center at the end of the walkway, and at two spots along the walkway
Gear Suggestions: Dress for the weather; sunscreen, hats, wagon or stroller; bring binoculars for the best animal viewing.
Insider Tip: Hot summer days send animals in search of shade, so they may be difficult to see. On these days the best time to see the animals active is in the evening. Plan for a visit that starts 2 or 3 hours before sunset.

Explore

The more than 750 resident large carnivores at this 1,214-acre sanctuary east of Denver have been rescued from abusive situations or were abandoned or kept illegally as pets. This is not a zoo but rather a space where animals who were once held in captivity in disreputable circuses, attractions, and even private homes have been given refuge. They get to live out their lives in a healthy, caring environment. For visitors, this means that instead of the up-close interaction you may be used to at a zoo, the animals at the Wild Animal Sanctuary are given acres to roam, run, laze, and hunker down.

Before you get to the animals, purchase tickets (or check in if you purchased tickets online) in the Welcome Center. This is where you will find full restrooms, a gift shop, the Lion's Den Cafe, and an ice cream shop. Don't miss the 15-minute introductory film. It's a chance to learn about the sanctuary itself as well as any guidelines to follow for a safe and rewarding visit.

After the film, head up to the 1.5-mile-long elevated walkway to stroll above the habitats. Why elevated? It's for the well-being of the resident animals. Most carnivores are territorial and any threats to their space on the ground level, or feeling of being trapped in an enclosure, can create stress. The sanctuary discovered that the large carnivores don't consider the area above them to be territory, so folks moving high above are not seen as a threat.

As you step onto the walkway, look at the habitats around and below you. The sanctuary map will help you identify what lives in each area. It may be difficult for kids to find the animals at first, so make it a game. Take time to use your senses, scan

the area for signs of movement, listen for rustling grass or interesting sounds, look in the shaded areas and by the water. Helpful and informative volunteers along the walkway can point out which animals might be out and where to see them. Another sure sign that an animal has been spotted is groups of visitors pointing into the habitats. The search for the elusive residents creates a camaraderie among visitors. Be sure to point out any animals you see.

Audio kiosks are located along the walkway. Push the button to hear an interpretive audio description or scan the QR code with your phone to open a web page where you can read a transcript of the recordings.

The walkway itself is out in the open. Look for shady spots at two stops along the way: the Bear Deck, which has tables and benches, and portable bathrooms nearby, and the Lion House. There are tables in the Lion House for a cool, shaded place to picnic—and, yes, food is allowed in this area.

At the end of the walkway is the Education Center, where videos introduce various stories about the sanctuary and its residents. Just below is the tiger and mountain

lion rehabilitation compound, where new residents begin their life at the sanctuary while adapting to the environment. The building nearby houses tables, a snack bar where you can pick up cold drinks, a hot dog, or ice cream treats, and another set of restrooms. This is where you turn around to retrace the walkway back to the Welcome Center.

LEARN

Animals are great teachers. Incorporate them into learning whenever you can.

- **Put on Your Animal Face: Create your own animal face masks and use them to "put on" different animal personalities. Roar and nap like a lion, then switch to a bear and growl.**
- **Learn about Animal Rescue: Use this visit to inspire the family to learn more about conservation and the rescue of wild animals. Books like *Tarra & Bella* by Carol Buckley, *Senna Helps the Sea Lions (And You Can Too!)* by Megan Pincus Kajitani, and *The Story of Jane Goodall* by Susan B. Katz introduce kids to the role they can play in protecting wildlife.**

THE TEN ESSENTIALS OF HIKING

American Hiking Society recommends you pack the "Ten Essentials" every time you head out for a hike. Whether you plan to be gone for a couple of hours or several months, make sure to pack these items. Become familiar with these items and know how to use them.

1. Appropriate Footwear

Happy feet make for pleasant hiking. Think about traction, support, and protection when selecting well-fitting shoes or boots.

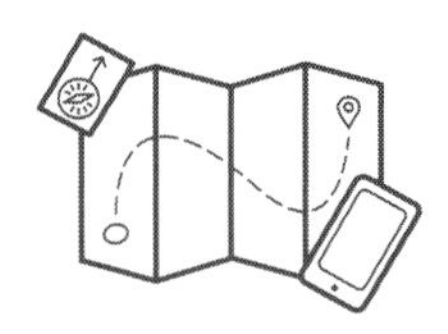

2. Navigation

While phones and GPS units are handy, they aren't always reliable in the backcountry; consider carrying a paper map and compass as a backup and know how to use them.

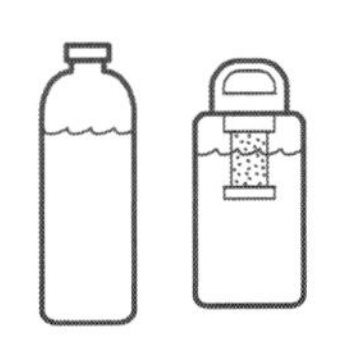

3. Water (and a way to purify it)

As a guideline, plan for half a liter of water per hour in moderate temperatures/terrain. Carry enough water for your trip and know where and how to treat water while you're out on the trail.

4. Food

Pack calorie-dense foods to help fuel your hike, and carry an extra portion in case you are out longer than expected.

5. Rain Gear & Dry-Fast Layers

The weatherman is not always right. Dress in layers to adjust to changing weather and activity levels. Wear moisture-wicking clothes and carry a warm hat.

6. Safety Items (light, fire, and a whistle)

Have means to start an emergency fire, signal for help, and see the trail and your map in the dark.

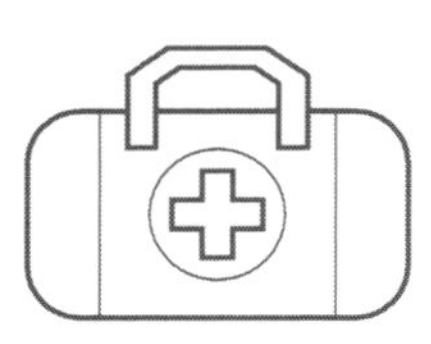

7. First Aid Kit

Supplies to treat illness or injury are only as helpful as your knowledge of how to use them. Take a class to gain the skills needed to administer first aid and CPR.

8. Knife or Multi-Tool

With countless uses, a multi-tool can help with gear repair and first aid.

9. Sun Protection

Sunscreen, sunglasses, and sun-protective clothing should be used in every season regardless of temperature or cloud cover.

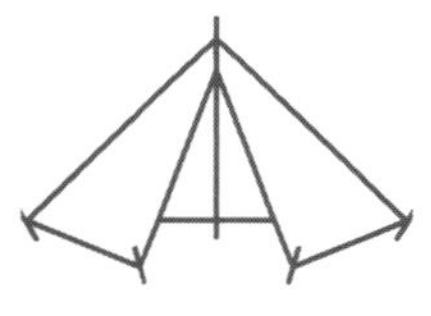

10. Shelter

Protection from the elements in the event you are injured or stranded is necessary. A lightweight, inexpensive space blanket is a great option.

Find other helpful resources at AmericanHiking.org/hiking-resources